CRUISERS

CRUISERS

BERNARD IRELAND

HAMLYN
London · New York · Sydney · Toronto

Published by the Hamlyn Publishing Group Limited
London . New York . Sydney . Toronto
Astronaut House, Feltham, Middlesex, England

ISBN 600 32127 4
Phototypeset by Filmtype Services Limited, Scarborough
Printed in Singapore

Colour drawings by John Batchelor

Acknowledgements
Front and back cover illustrations, the Imperial War Museum.
Other photographs by: Aldo Fraccoroli, Bibliothek Für Zeitgeschichte, British Aerospace, Canadian Forces, Hamlyn Group Picture Library, the Imperial War Museum, John Batchelor, John W. R. Taylor, Kowinklijke Marine, Marius Bar, Ministry of Defence (Crown Copyright Reserved), Musée de la Marine, National Maritime Museum, Novosti Press Agency (APN), Royal Swedish Navy, Science Museum, London (Crown Copyright), Ufficio Storico, US Bureau of Ships, US Official (Navy Departement), Vickers Shipbuilding Group Ltd.

CONTENTS

FOREWORD

When, in 1798, the French fleet under de Brueys succeeded in eluding Nelson's blockading squadron off Toulon, it sailed for Alexandria with some 36,000 of Napoleon's finest troops. They were to secure Egypt and then prepare for India. Had the British caught this enterprise at sea, history might have been written differently, but in spite of a double voyage in record time, Nelson was frustrated in his attempts, though at one time he was so close to his quarry in poor visibility that his signal guns were heard by the French. Deeply disappointed, the Admiral was to write 'To this day I am without the smallest information on the French . . . I have again to deeply regret my want of Frigates.'

The frigates, the lack of which he so bitterly lamented, were the forerunners of cruisers – ships of such versatility and invariably in such great demand, that many a commander since has ruefully echoed Nelson's words. Not only in reconnaissance, but also in the protection and destruction of commerce, in escort and shore support, independent operation and 'showing the flag', cruisers, following the frigates have been involved in so diverse a range of historical incident that it is surprising that they have not attracted the attention of the historian far more than they have.

Cruisers do, in fact, pose a problem in that, unlike the majority of warship types, they were not introduced at a specific point in time to meet a new and well-defined threat. Rather, they emerged over a long period and then, when their day appeared to be done, they did not disappear so much as enter a phase of metamorphosis that is still in progress today. If this book can give some recognition to a class of ship that has previously received less than its share, then it will have fulfilled its purpose.

The author would like to thank those, too numerous to mention by name, who have helped along the way with material or with advice, but particularly he would like to thank his wife, without whose assistance and forbearance none of his books would ever be written.

Bernard Ireland

THE WOODEN NAVY – the birth of a breed

During the long years of Victoria's reign, the size and influence of her country and its empire reached dimensions unique in the world's history. Supported by a million toiling backs, the whole edifice was buttressed by the Royal Navy, honed to a fine edge by years of combat. Subsequent to the peace agreements of 1815, however, this magnificent fighting force embarked on what was to be nearly a century of freedom from major involvement and, from being the nation's primary weapon, it became concerned with the servicing, advancement and protection of the empire. With the main battle fleet now assuming a deterrent role, it was the turn of the smaller ships to become noticed. Their long years of achievement, working singly, or in small squadrons, harassing the enemy or strangling him by slow blockade, had largely been hidden from public gaze by the greater glories of the battle fleet but, with the coming of the Pax Britannica, Great Britain became the world's policeman and her cruising ships were often the instruments of her policies. They applied discipline where none existed, they brought succour in time of need, their 'presence' impressed her subjects with the influence of their far-distant Sovereign, and they smote the wrong-doer in true Biblical fashion. Radio did not exist and London was as remote as the moon, so ship captains were truly Captains under God, men of resource whose decision was absolute.

In these days, when we assume – often wrongly – that all is orderly and categorised, the labelling of HM ships has an attractive randomness which has changed but little over the years. Elizabethans, with their fine turn of phrase, took pride in a fleet consisting of Ships Royal, Great Ships, Middling Ships (a nice term), Small Ships and Pinnaces, terminology geared to their 'tons burthen', a figure often estimated rather than calculated.

During the early Stuart period ships were reclassed in 'rates', based on payroll strength but, as this also affected the number of guncrews and thus armament, it became more realistic to rate by number of guns. But, until precise establishment of number and weight of guns were prescribed during the reign of George I, the weight of broadside as a yardstick led to some overlapping of rates. With the adoption of well-defined allocation of armament, ships could be compared more directly, and the new orderliness was reflected in modified fighting instructions which slightly relaxed the rigid 'line-of-battle' ideas.

Initially, rates had round numbers of weapons; the 1st Rate mounted more than 100, the 2nd Rate 90–100, the 3rd Rate 60–80, the 4th Rate 50–60, the 5th Rate 30–40, and the lowest, the 6th Rate between 10 and 20. In addition, the composition of these batteries was also laid down. For instance a 50-gun 4th Rate would be a two-decker carrying 22 eighteen-pounders on the lower deck, 22 lighter nine-pounders on the upper deck and a half-dozen six-pounders shared between forecastle and quarterdeck.

To lie in a line-of-battle, a ship needed firepower, sailing qualities and an ability to absorb punishment; only 4th Rates and above were deemed so qualified, and the general descriptive term 'line-of-battle ship' eventually gave rise to the word 'battleship'. For the remainder it was customary to refer to 'cruising ships', a term that persisted for about two centuries to denote ships of independent command, or 'private ships'. Some were, of course, attached to the fleet, but their duties were ancillary and their place strictly on the 'disengaged side' in the event of battle.

Largest among the cruising ships was the 40-gun 5th Rate with two gun decks, resulting in a lofty hull which, in spite of a length-to-beam ratio of only about 3½, tended to be crank, making the lower tier of guns useless in a blow. As it was customary to seek the weather gauge, this was a decided disadvantage and the type died in favour of single-deckers of near equal arma-

Cochrane, one of the Royal Navy's finest frigate captains, is shown in action during 1806. In close proximity to a powerful French Squadron, anchored under the guns of shore batteries on the Ile d'Aix, he took the *Pallas* 36 well inshore and endeavoured to take the 44-gun French *Minerve*, but was checked by squally winds and shoal water.

ment, inspired by ships captured from the French in the 1740's. With notable exceptions, such as the 'seventy-four', warships tended to be referred to in general terms by their rate or, more specifically, by name and firepower, such as the 'Torbay 90' or 'Brilliant 36'. Lesser ships such as brigs or schooners were known by their rig.

Another term that crept in was 'frigate', a word of doubtful origin but probably Italian, passing to the French and then the Dutch by the early sixteenth century. Adopted by the English, it was very loosely used, being applied even to 3rd Rates, but foreign usage was generally quite precise, referring only to a full-rigged warship with one major gun deck. This was not universal, however, the great Swedish designer Henrik af Chapman producing in the early eighteenth century some beautiful armed merchantment with flat counters also described as 'frigates'. Nevertheless, the single-decked 5th Rate rapidly grew in popularity as a general-purpose workhorse which, though at first carrying only 24 guns, mounted them high enough to work them in any weather. She was handy in size and with a good turn of speed, enabling her to seek or decline action as required. Ideal for operations against enemy commerce, she was also the obvious choice for the marshalling and control of friendly convoys which, at that time, could number some hundreds of sail. Scouting ahead of a main fleet was refreshing to those aspiring junior captains with a dash of independence, and the chance to be detached, away from the Admiral's eye, was seized upon and many a fine reputation was founded upon a frigate's deck.

Inspired by their ex-French acquisitions, the Royal Navy commenced construction of a class of 32-gunners, led by the *Southampton*, launched at Rotherhithe in 1757. Tiny by today's standards, she was some 124½ feet on the gundeck (the usual quoted length) and was of 671 tons 'builders measurement', based on capacity rather than on displacement, and analogous with our gross tonnage. She had two complete decks, the lower of which was used for accommodation and confusingly referred to as the gun deck; in this small compass some 220 men had their existence. Twenty-six twelve-

A British frigate of about 1810. Hove-to with all inmast canvas aback, she has lowered a boat. In the background is a French cutter.

The early years of the 19th century saw the small US navy engaged in a campaign against the depredations of the piratical seamen of the Barbary Coast. During the course of this war, Bainbridge's *Philadelphia* was captured in the port of Tripoli. Decatur earned a promotion to captain by taking the *Intrepid* in to destroy the prize by fire.

pounders were mounted one level higher, with six six-pounders on the raised quarterdeck. High, protective bulwarks ran in a smooth profile from break of quarterdeck to forecastle, enclosing a waist that was spanned by spare spars, the supports of which also acted as boat stowage. With the fore and aft gangways running the length of the top of the waist bulwark becoming ever wider on later ships for fighting and access purposes, the waist tended gradually to total enclosure. By the end of the century the frigate had been scaled-up in size by about one sixth and, though still rated for the same number of guns, these were often 18-pounders below, with 9-pounders on the quarterdeck and two 12-pounders right forward for chase fire.

Gun construction had advanced little since the introduction of the cast cannon, with lack of precision in both bore and ball making gunnery an art rather than a science. Rigid fighting instructions still dictated the conduct of major engagements in a formalised and increasingly sterile manner, and it was the 'cruisers' on their independent missions that developed the art of single-ship action. Spurred by the promise of prize money or 'pewter', it paid them to take an enemy rather than sink him, and the silent advance of a British ship to within a pistol shot before the delivery of the inevitable crashing broadside demoralised the majority of opponents before action was joined. Besides personal gain to both officers and crew, the Admiralty thus acquired useful ships, though all too often it was the slow sailer at the end of an enemy column that was taken.

The great variety of naval guns that persisted to the time of the Restoration had been rationalised to only seven, namely 42, 32, 24, 18, 12, 9 and 6-pounders. Only some 1st Rates carried the enormous and unwieldly 42-pounders, each weighing about 67 hundredweight, and the 32-pounder was the standard heavy weapon for ships down to 70-gunners at the time of the Seven Years' War. Range was short, with a 32-pounder hefting a 6-inch diameter solid shot about 2,100 yards and a 9-pounder a 4-inch shot over 1,600 yards. Another good reason for close-range action lay in the lack of destructive power of a frigate's guns for, while an 18-pounder ball could pierce two feet of oak and wreak havoc with its splinters on penetrating through to a gun deck, it took many such 'hulling' shots to disable even a small ship. Guns were often double- or even triple-shotted; spectacular and dangerous, it increased point-blank effectiveness but greatly reduced muzzle velocity.

It was, therefore, hailed as a breakthrough when the Falkirk-based Carron foundry began production of a new Army-inspired gun, designed to throw a maximum size of shot over a short distance. Known as a Carronade, it needed only a short barrel, a 32-pounder, for instance, being only four feet in length compared with the usual size, so that it could be carried by smaller ships, and higher up. Fine casting technique reduced 'windage' in the barrel, so that a 2½ lb charge of powder could take a 32-pound ball about 1100 yards. The real innovation was the 68-pounder which, double-shotted with grape or 'langridge', could reduce a crowded upper deck to a bloody shambles. Its lightness and simple sliding carriage (another Chapman idea) meant that it could be laid and operated rapidly by a smaller guncrew. The excellence of its bore gave rise to proposals for fluting to spin the shot, and the use of filled explosive spherical 'shells' of the type fired by the mortars of bombketches since the early 17th century. Unfortunately technology had not yet advanced sufficiently to guarantee that the shot's centre of gravity lay at its geometric centre and marvellously wayward trajectories resulted. Inevitably, some commanders were so smitten with the possibilities of the new weapon that they shipped them to the exclusion of all else, and a few paid dearly at the hands of cool adversaries with the weather gauge and long-ranged cannon.

Dominated by endless wars with France, the last years of the eighteenth century saw a rapid expansion of the Royal Navy with 30- to 36-gunned frigates alone increasing from 31 in 1778 to 99 at the turn of the century. This period had opened with the American War of Independence where the revolutionary fervour of the colonial soldiers was matched by the seamen of an infant navy. The 'Continental Navy' had been established in 1775 for the protection of what were still the United Colonies and though lacking a regular fleet, sought to hit Great Britain where it hurt most – her trade. With the difference between privateering and regular naval operations hard to distinguish, they discovered rich pickings from Nova Scotia to the West Indies.

Several of the new commanders made names that were later to be part of the traditions of the US navy, and first among them was John Paul Jones, English by birth, who, based on France, made two highly successful cruises in British waters. With a small squadron led by his elderly 40-gun *Bonhomme Richard*, he attacked a convoy off Flamborough Head in 1779, during the course of which action he grappled the British frigate *Serapis*. The latter injured the American so gravely that she foundered but, in an extraordinary reversal of fortune, *Serapis* was boarded and taken by Jones' men.

Continental fleets had always sought to exploit the vulnerability of British trade but here was a new foe who could really fight. Convoys properly escorted were rarely molested, but once dispersed in the chops of the Channel, independent ships became easy meat for the bold corsair prepared to hover around a popular landfall. Though the Royal Navy stationed 'cruisers' at likely points, usually these could only react to an actual incident, and the fleet had to bow before a storm of public abuse. No fleet, however powerful, can be omnipresent and the problem remains to this day.

Having reached the respectable size of over fifty ships, the Continental Navy was nevertheless ground down by the sheer power of the British fleet. However, before its disbandment in 1785, it had played its part in bringing a grand design to a successful conclusion, for the Treaty of Paris of 1783 meant that Britain recognised the sovereignty of the infant United States of America.

Within the decade Britain was again locked in war with France and the superbly offensive qualities of her fleet were once more typified by its frigates. Such was Pellew's 44-gun *Indefatigable* which,

Top
An extremely fine impression of the 1812 duel between HMS *Java* and the USS *Constitution*. In spite of great dash, *Java*'s gunnery had been neglected, and the big American had the advantage in both weight and broadside accuracy.

Above
The *Constitution* 44 of 1797 was among the largest of the American frigates. Under the able captaincy of Isaac Hull, she took both the *Java* and the *Guerrière* in 1812. Though a replica, the vessel shown is an exact copy and gives an excellent idea of the frigate of the time.

supported by the *Amazon* 36, encountered the French 74 *Droits de l'Homme*. Separated by a gale from a force making an unsuccessful attempt at a landing in Ireland, she was sighted some 150 miles upwind of her destination of Brest and subjected to an afternoon and night of unremitting harassment by Pellew's smaller ships. Though her guns were of larger calibre than those of the British, her axial fire was too weak to prevent one or other of her nimble tormentors from raking her almost at will. The big Frenchman was driven into Audierne Bay, an inhospitable place when a lee shore, and grounded. Taking his example from Hawke at Quiberon in 1759, Pellew followed her in to ensure her destruction. In doing so the *Amazon* also grounded and was lost but Pellew clawed out and returned safely.

Nelson's trio of great victories so dominate accounts of the sea war of the period that the layman might be forgiven for assuming that it ended with Trafalgar in 1805. It did not, for Napoleon was a land animal and it was to be another decade before the chief instrument of his policies, the Grande Armée, was to be defeated at Waterloo. At sea, though unadorned by major victories, the period was one of almost total ascendancy for the Royal Navy in European waters, where their responsibilities were extended by the spread of the war to the Peninsular in 1808. With the army needing flank support, new opportunities arose for the bold commander to vary his activities from the task of blockade. Cochrane, in the *Imperieuse* 38, supported by *Spartan* and *Cambrian*, was particularly active in harassing coastal waters and sending away raiding parties. Hoste meanwhile reduced Adriatic trade almost to nil single-handed in the *Amphion*, taking near 200 sail in about six months, capping the achievement in 1811 when, with a squadron of four frigates, he soundly defeated a Franco-Venetian force of nearly double his strength near the island of Lissa. Larger frigates of 40 to 44 guns were now coming into service, some even more powerful than this figure implies, for it was not usual to count carronades, of which up to a dozen could be mounted topsides.

As the period had commenced with a war against America, so it ended with another, an unnecessary affair coming about in 1812 through a blend of contempt and high-handedness. The Yankee fleet made up for its lack of numbers with a series of large frigates, powerfully constructed and armed, and captained by picked men. Britain, deeply engrossed with European problems, had few ships to spare for what was regarded as a backwater, and the few available frigates that sought to establish sea control on the eastern seaboard met with a series of demoralising reverses in single ship actions. These duels were never shunned, even with obviously superior adversaries, for the Royal Navy was not used to defeat, but during 1812 within five months the *Guerriere*, *Macedonian* and *Java* were all lost. They fought bravely but failed through over-confidence and inferior gundrill, the latter something that would not have been tolerated in European waters where its high quality had been the cause of so many French losses. Broke's magnificent capture of the *Chesapeake* restored confidence in 1813, and underlined the values of gunnery discipline.

In 1814 another US frigate, the *Essex*, rounded the Horn and created mayhem amongst the vulnerable British Pacific whaling fleet. Promptly, the Admiralty despatched the 38-gunned *Phoebe* and the sloop-of-war *Frolic* to deal with her, an action that may well have inspired Fisher's after Coronel exactly one century later. Run to ground outside Valparaiso, the *Essex* paid the penalty of an addiction to the carronade, her few remaining 12-pounders being no match for *Phoebe*'s long 18's, used French-style firstly to wreck the American's rigging. This kind of action caused the carronade to lose some of its popularity, even though Perry had proved triumphant on the Great Lakes the year before when he took the weather gauge and closed the British rapidly to use his carronades to the best advantage.

'Sloops-of-war', as mentioned, were generally ships of twenty guns or less, ranking below 6th Rates and providing useful auxiliary support, though lacking the endurance and fighting potential that came to be associated with the term 'cruiser'. Large British frigates of 50-guns also existed, but were never to be matched against a similar-sized American; so much, however, did the latter impress the Admiralty that several 74s were cut down by one deck as a rapid substitute. They were known as 'razees'.

Brave and persistent men were still persevering with the 'shell' idea, particularly in France where it was seen as a means of off-setting British superiority in ships. Its possibilities against an inflammable wooden warship were very obvious, but unfortunately fuses still needed to be lit before firing, a simple matter in a short barrelled weapon but hazardous in a cannon! A Colonel Paixhans gave the French a safer version in 1824, capitalising on the 'windage' in the barrel to light the fuse at the moment of firing by means of the firing charge itself. Known as the 'canon-orbusier', it was introduced rapidly, causing the British to develop a similar flat-trajectory shell-gun of 8-inch bore and firing a 56-pound spherical projectile, but it was to be the middle of the century before the new weapons were to be proved in earnest.

An obscure conflict of 1827 was to provide an event of some significance when a combined Egyptian and Turkish fleet were, not surprisingly, routed at Navarino by an allied British, French and Russian force. It was to be the Royal Navy's last major action for 87 years and it was also the last to be fought by sailing ships alone.

Steam power had been around for some time; it had propelled small craft before the end of the eighteenth century and, in 1818, the American-built paddler *Savannah* had crossed the Atlantic. However, though the Royal Navy had introduced many steam tugs and auxiliaries in the 1820s, the idea of a steam warship did not appeal due to the size and vulnerability of the paddle-boxes and the space taken by machinery and bunkers, which cut down the broadside armament. Ericsson's screw propeller was installed in the merchant ship *Archimedes* in 1840, influencing Brunel to add one to his *Great Britain* soon after. The Admiralty showed interest, and had cut the *Penelope* 46 in two for the insertion of 650 ihp paddle machinery. However, though her length was increased by nearly 65 feet to 215, her armament had to be reduced to only sixteen guns, demonstrating that the broadside armament was not likely to suit a powered ship. This was the age of quirky inventions and the frigates *Active* and *Galatea* had been fitted with hand-powered paddle systems, the former working hers from her capstan, the latter from a system of winches. It is recorded the two-thirds of *Galatea*'s crew could move her at 3 knots in a calm!

That wooden ships could be lengthened at all was due to a new system of diagonal framing that put longitudinal stiffness into hulls that had previously tended to 'hog' if constructed beyond a certain point, the limit with a frigate being about 150 feet. Proposals for this method had been made by af Chapman but it was to be forty years before Seppings introduced it to the Royal Navy.

Two issues now had to be resolved, whether propellers were superior to paddles and whether the iron hull should replace wood. The celebrated 1843 tug-of-war between the equally-powered paddle sloop *Alecto* and the propeller-driven *Rattler* was won by the latter to everybody's satisfaction, resulting in two purpose-designed screw frigates, *Arrogant* and *Dauntless*,

A builder's model of a 50-gun frigate built in 1813-1814 of pitch pine because of the growing shortage of suitable oak. The main gundeck is pierced for twenty-eight 24-pounders; sixteen 32-pounder cannonades (now reckonable for classification) are carried on the quarter deck, and four more, with a brace of 9-pounders are behind the heavy, French-style bulwarks forward.

An iron-clad model of a proposed heavy frigate of about 1813 shows the extremely heavy framing and the 'Cod's head and mackerel tail' of the hull form. She is pierced for 52 guns, and would have been of nearly 1,700 tons burden and 152 feet long at the gundeck.

being laid down in 1844, no doubt hastened by the news of the French building the screw-propelled *Pomone* 40. Both British ships were built at Portsmouth, *Arrogant* a 200-footer with steam only for occasional use, and *Dauntless* slightly larger to accommodate full-power engines of 580 ihp. In spite of this, *Dauntless*' performance was disappointing as her full lines prevented a proper water flow over her propeller. And steam was still regarded as very much an auxiliary to sail; unreliable, inefficient and greedy of fuel, it could be used for only limited periods.

With its resistance to combustion and penetration by shell guns, the iron hull had come to stay even though its beginnings were full of uncertainties. Iron merchantmen were in service, but Laird's suggestion in 1836 for a similar warship had been rejected, and the speculative construction of an iron frigate in 1842 met a similar fate and she was sold to Mexico. The following year the Navy ordered the 850-ton iron sloop *Trident* from Blackwall, but they were still plagued with doubts, for rather questionable results had been obtained on firing trials against the small iron steamer *Ruby* in 1840, followed by unfavourable reports based on the very inconsistent qualities of plate then available. Finally, in 1850 their misgivings got the better of them and no less than seventeen iron warships then under construction were completed, but for non-combatant duties only.

By mid-century, the Royal Navy was in a ferment of transition. In 1845 there were on the Navy list 48 sailing 5th Rates of between 36 and 46 guns, together with a hundred lesser 'cruising ships', such as brigs and sloops. Seven paddlers were termed 'frigates', though with armaments ranging from 21 down to only 6 guns they were often weaker than the steam sloops and granted their status only by virtue of being the command of a full captain.

In 1853 the shell gun came into its own in the virtual annihilation of a wooden Turkish squadron by the Russians off Sinope in the Black Sea, and need for armour to keep projectiles out became as obvious as the obsolescence of the wooden ship. Guns were improving fast with the introduction of a barrel built-up from concentric tubes and less liable to bursting than cast weapons. However, steels were not yet fully reliable and problems with screwbreeches meant that the muzzle-loader was to persist for a while. Rifling was satisfactorily combined with elongated projectiles which, by spinning, followed a more predictable trajectory. With no windage, smaller firing charges were required and the percussion fuse continued the transformation.

The old type carriage developed into a slide mounting capable of pivoting (with the energetic use of levers), and the actual moment of firing could be controlled with the percussion cap, replacing the flintlock mechanism. With increasing ranges came the need for improved gunsights but, until optics could be made to withstand the shock of a gun firing, the slow method of triangulation by double sextant angles persisted.

Still mutually suspicious, Britain and France became allies in the Crimean War, during which the latter, probably inspired by the American Stevens Battery of 1841, constructed a group of floating batteries carrying eighteen 50-pounders protected by slabs of 100 mm wrought iron. They were able to approach and destroy Russian fortifications, whose return fire did them little damage. Though these craft were of metal-clad wood construction, designers were having to consider all-metal ships if for no other reason than that timber components were getting in very short supply. On the Baltic front, meanwhile, a Captain Cowper Coles was experimenting with a single 68-pounder mounted on a raft. In its ability to train

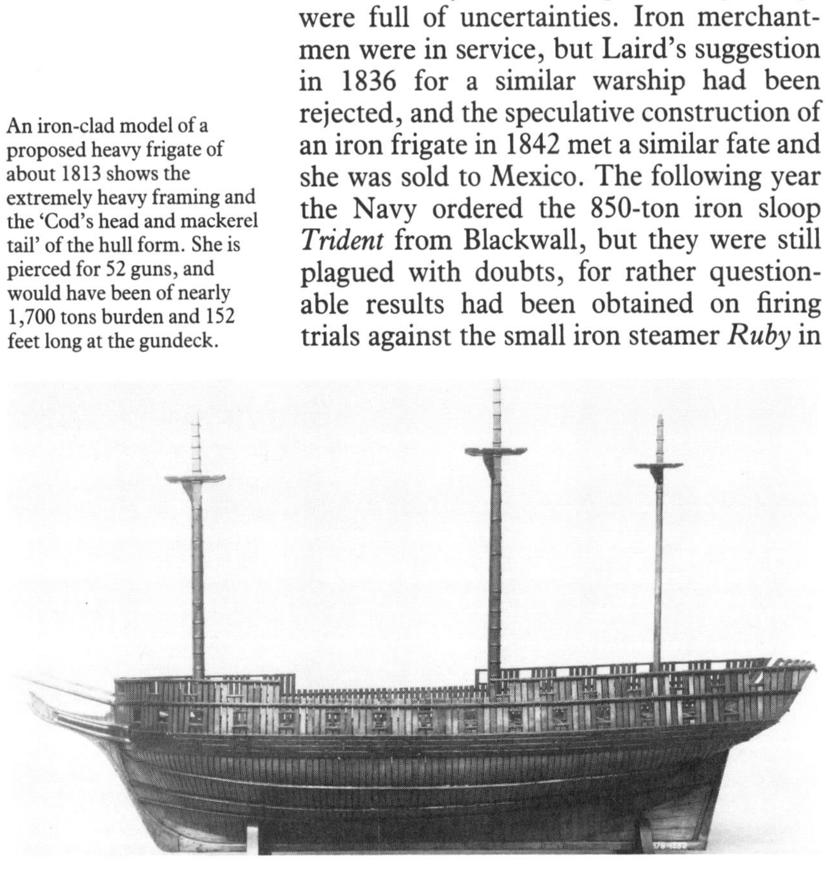

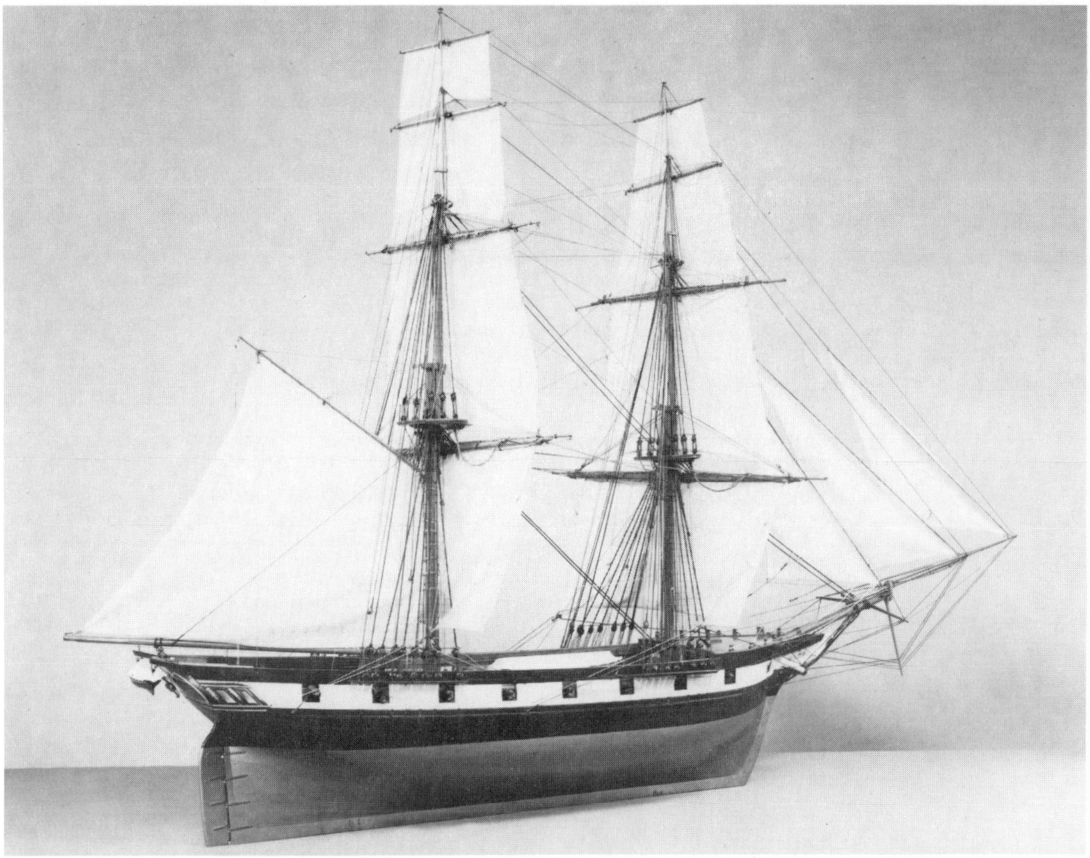

Among the Royal Navy's smaller 'cruising ships' were the brigs, and this model of the 16-gun *Fantôme* of 1839 shows what pretty ships they were. Chatham-built, she was one of the so-called 'Symonds' Brigs', and introduced a finer hull form and a boomed gaff mainsail.

This superb model of the French *Gloire* of 1859 shows clearly the extent of the external iron cladding, with the coppered wooden hull exposed below belt level. The layout of the armament was still that of a sailing frigate, though the line of the stern had been drastically altered to decrease its vulnerability.

rapidly lay the genesis of the turret and the beginning of the end for the broadside battery.

From the completion of the first screw frigate in 1847 their numbers proliferated, largely because screw propulsion did not interfere to any great degree with the layout of the gun deck. The screw itself, which exerted a drag when the ship was under sail, was made to retract into the counter when not in use. About 45 were built for the Royal Navy but, with numbers of guns ranging from 13 to 51, they were increasingly difficult to categorise and, in 1856, the rating system was revised yet again on a basis of crew strength.

But the growing popularity of the screw corvette complicated matters. Where the frigate retained only a vestigial well between forecastle and poop and was developing into a two-decker, the corvette (often of equal size) carried her main battery on the uncovered upper deck, though by the time that the type was abandoned in the 'seventies, it, too, was developing end houses.

The French navy had, at this time, a brilliant Director-General of Construction in Dupuy de Lôme, dedicated to the development of the armoured ship as a counter to the shell gun. He instituted the building programme of the so-called 'frégates blindées' which, when first seen by the British in 1858, prompted the immediate response of the large iron frigate. A new age had dawned for the warship.

THE METAL AGE – enthusiasm and experiment

Dupuy de Lôme's great trump card, the *Gloire*, was not, in fact, particularly revolutionary. Together with two sisters, she was an incomplete two-decker, razed to one and clad in wrought iron plate of about 100 mm thickness and continuing the 'Crimea Battery' theme. *Couronne*, the fourth ship, was of all-iron construction, lined internally with an iron-and-teak sandwich up to 21 inches thick. Such was the weight of the new protection that only one gun deck could be tolerated on grounds of stability but the ships could steam at about 12 knots and thus pick their range and bearing on a sailing warship in most conditions.

Faced with this sort of threat, the British Admiralty reacted early by calling for ideas from no less than fourteen separate builders. Compared with *Gloire*'s 5,600 tons and 256-foot hull, proposals were made for ships between 6,500 and 11,200 tons and between 336 and 430 feet in length. All were turned down and the Admiralty designed its own.

Thus, in 1859, *Warrior* and *Black Prince* were laid down, 380 feet long between perpendiculars and displacing over 9,200 tons. *Couronne* had, in fact, been laid down some three months before, but *Warrior* was put into the water more quickly, to be proclaimed the world's first iron-hulled ironclad. Over machinery and the greater part of the gundeck she had 4½ inches of iron, backed with 18 inches of teak, both ends being 'soft'. Fine-lined and elegant, she made 14 knots on 5,300 ihp developed by a low-profile Penn trunk engine. Completed in 1861, she carried fourteen of the new Armstrong breech-loaders, ten of 110 pounds and four of 70 pounds, together with standard 68-pound muzzle loaders. The breech-loaders proved unreliable and were changed for the older type of gun in a great Admiralty about-turn.

Wood construction was abandoned for British warships from 1863 and, except for the unsuccessful two-decked French Magenta type, the new breed was single decked. Full-rigged and with 40 guns they came to be termed 'frigates' (though built to defeat a 1st Rate), and the latest wooden frigates, the Merseys of 1859, were actually only forty feet shorter than *Warrior* and carried twenty 10-inch shell-guns and twelve 68-pounder smooth bores. In them the 'great iron frigate' passed beyond what could possibly be interpreted by the word 'cruiser', but for the moment the earlier true frigates and what was generally termed the 'cruising fleet' were adequate to their tasks. Near the end of its long career, the wooden ship had changed its form, the bluff-ended tub of a hull exchanging beakhead for a 'clipper' stem, and the after end given a fine run to improve propeller performance. Some, inspired by the non-event at Second Lissa, were saddled with a ram bow, useless in wood, and with a long, overhanging bowsprit.

Stimulus for development came from across the Atlantic for, in 1861, the 'United' States were again at war, this time with themselves. With their taste for big frigates undiminished, they had five 275-footers with a typical armament of two 10-inch, twenty-four 9-inch and fourteen 8-inch guns. These, in turn, were eclipsed by the corvette (i.e. open gundeck) *Niagara*, 328 feet in length and armed with fourteen 11-inch Dahlgrens, cast iron, smooth-bore monsters, muzzle-loaded with spherical shot, whose short range battering effect (racking) was considered to make them superior to shaped shot against a metal hull.

In home waters the largely Union navy had virtually its own way, but the Confederates wreaked havoc on Northern commerce with a series of fast raiders. Some of these were built covertly in Britain, the best-known being the *Alabama*. Only moderately armed, she survived by virtue of her speed and, in a two-year career, took 69 prizes before being sunk in European waters by the USS *Kearsarge*.

The principal object of the Confederate raiders was to draw Union warships from

HMS *Warrior* of 1860, the great iron frigate that rendered obsolete the finest line-of-battle ships afloat. Though of all-iron construction, her size permitted armour over the battery area only. Note the two-bladed propeller in its lifting frame.

With the General-Admirals of the early 1870's, the Russians introduced what came to be the armoured cruiser, provoking a British reply in the Shannons. *Minin*, shown here off Toulon, was a later refinement, having a complete armour belt and a 13½-knot speed.

their choking blockade of Southern ports; though there were too few of them to succeed in this policy, their depredations did not pass unnoticed by those abroad who had responsibility for protecting the trade routes.

Seven Wampanoag-class ships were completed by the US Navy too late to take part in the war. Carrying few but heavy guns, they were capable of 18 knots through having a high speed engine geared to a single shaft. Designed to catch commerce raiders they were, of course, ideal for the role of raiders themselves.

Britain rapidly produced an answer in the *Inconstant*, launched in 1868 as the first so-called 'masted cruiser'. Designed big to accommodate machinery for 16½ knots, she displaced 5,780 tons, but her fine lines gave her weak chase fire. So as to be a stable gun platform, she was designed with a low metacentric height, a drawback matched by a poor bunker capacity. Like many a cruiser to follow, her iron hull was wood-sheathed and coppered over to reduce fouling, and an interesting fitting was a pair of launchers for the new Whitehead locomotive torpedoes. Some 337-feet in length, *Inconstant* was longer than the contemporary central-battery line ships and of comparable armament. Indeed, for the next quarter-century the difference between a large cruiser and what came to be termed a 'second-class battleship' lay mainly in protection and speed. The smaller 'cruising ships' would develop, as will be seen, along a separate path.

Roughly similar to the *Inconstant*, the *Shah* and *Raleigh* were beamier in order to be less tender, but all three proved expensive ships to operate with machinery rated at 6,500 ihp, and they were followed by a trio of the more modest 3,950-ton Bacchantes, together with a clutch built as 'corvettes' to save topweight.

A ship such as a hunting cruiser needed strong end-on fire for pursuit purposes but, as we have seen, fine hulls precluded this. In an effort to solve the problem, the first class of French ships to be referred to as 'cruisers', the two 5,500-ton Tourvilles, mounted chase guns on prominent sponsons, an idea which led to the adoption of the exaggerated tumble-home so much a

During the period of the transitional fleets there was little to choose between what was coming to be called a 'battleship' and an armoured cruiser. This picture of the French battleship *Turenne* of 1867, shows her to be little superior to the Russian *Minin*.

HMS *Naiad*, of the ubiquitous Apollo class and a second-class protected cruiser, seen in the original Victorian livery and wearing the flag of the Admiral of the Fleet at the fore. Where the two 6-inch guns are obvious, the 4.7-inch and 6-pounder secondary weapons are unobtrusive behind folding bulwarks in the waist.

feature of their ships for several decades.

In 1877, the *Shah* was to be tested in action – a rare event in the Victorian navy – when sent, with the wooden corvette *Amethyst*, to apprehend the renegade Peruvian turret ship *Huascar*. The operation proved a stalemate, with the rebels running into shallow water to avoid capture. In a long distance (1,000 yards!) bombardment, the *Shah*'s guns scored nearly 70 hits but succeeded in piercing their target's 3½-inch armour only once. The untrained Peruvians did not score once, but their two 10-inch muzzle-loading rifles were mounted in the newly-introduced turret, giving all-round fire that commanded respect. Though *Shah* launched a torpedo, the first ever used in action that, too, missed. An insignificant action, but one which nevertheless pointed to the need for perhaps fewer, perhaps larger, but certainly better guns, together with protection that would enable a cruiser to close an opponent with confidence.

Early failures with breech mechanisms had caused the British to revert to muzzle loading guns for a period but new, slower-burning propellents and tests by the Germans proved the superiority of longer-barrelled weapons and began the movement back again.

Two exceptional British ships, *Iris* and *Mercury* were built in the late 1870s deliberately fine and with the greater part of the hull given over to the machinery. Their two 4-cylinder compound engines developed 6,000 ihp and had to be placed in tandem, driving shafts of unequal length and giving 17½ knots. Nothing but their bunkers protected their vitals and armament was very light. Though carrying the still-obligatory sailing rig, their narrow-gutted form (*Iris*: 331½ feet overall, 46 feet beam) made them nervous sailers and it was later removed. With them the fast scouting cruiser had arrived, though their being labelled 'Despatch Ships' rather inhibited their use. Their value was recognised, however, in the construction of the four broadly similar Amphions in the early 'eighties.

The Royal Navy's first all-steel cruisers, *Iris* and *Mercury* of 1877–8 were for a while, at 18½ knots, the fastest ships afloat. Unarmoured, they were designed for scouting and despatch duties, coupled with commerce protection.

The three French Charner class armoured cruisers of 1895–6 were notable for their wildly eccentric bow profiles. Though obsolete at the outbreak of war, they were kept active in low hazard zones. Note here the armoured tower masts of the *Latouche-Treville*, and how the muzzle of the forward 194 mm gun nearly reaches the stem-head.

Charged with the defence of four coastlines, the Imperial Russian Navy of the time was large and innovative. Always-fragile relations with Turkey across the Black Sea exploded into another war, prompting the Russians to produce the General-Admiral class, cruisers more lightly armed than British contemporaries but of great range. They were notable in having a waterline belt and protective decks of especially-imported hardened steel; they can claim fairly to be the first armoured cruisers.

The Royal Navy, of course, had to respond and produced the *Shannon* of 1875, followed by *Nelson* and *Northampton*. The last to be full-rigged, they carried their mixed armament of 9- and 10-inch guns virtually unprotected, but featured a waterline belt 9 inches thick terminated in two transverse bulkheads of equal thickness. In conjunction with a 1½-inch protective deck against the threat of plunging fire from longer-ranged guns, the arrangement was termed the 'central citadel' and was designed for end-on action. Being of nearly 7,500 tons the Nelsons were of a size with second-class battleships, but were not powerful enough to lie in a line of battle, yet not fast enough to be effective cruisers. They were not considered a success.

Eleven derivatives followed in the 2,400-ton Comus-class corvettes, built to replace wooden cruising ships now reaching the end of their time. Having only a 1½-inch protective deck, they were also the Royal Navy's first protected cruisers, iron-plated on steel frames, wood-sheathed and coppered externally. Later units had breech-loading 6-inch guns on sponsons to improve end-on fire, and were larger in order to incorporate machinery of 4,000 ihp. This latter feature was to stand the *Calliope* in good stead when she fought her way out of the harbour of Apia in Samoa in a hurricane that wrecked every other ship present.

As long as cruisers retained full rig, all-round fire from an optimum number of guns was impossible. On the other hand, such ships such as the Comus class needed a six-month endurance for colonial duties and, with coal bunkers limited to only 500 tons, sail was essential. For fleet duties, however, fighting ability took priority and when, in 1880, the French laid down the four Magenta's, their layout influenced the British reply, the *Imperieuse* and *Warspite*.

Completed unrigged, the Frenchmen carried four large guns in barbettes, disposed one at either end and one either side amidships, giving a three-gun concentration on any bearing. The British pair were 8,500 tonners and the first to mount the excellent new 9·2-inch BL gun, which was to last a long time with the Royal Navy. Their barbettes, lighter than turrets, were placed high and had excellent firing arcs, but were unpopular with the conservative 'broadside' school. They followed the Shannons in protection but the vertical armour was so narrow that they were termed 'belted cruisers' (confusing, but better than the original classification of 'armour-plated steel barbette ships') but exceeded their legend displacement by so much that their speed was limited to about 16 knots.

The Hermione class cruiser *Cambrian* of 1892. As protected cruisers of 4,360 tons, they relied on a light 2-inch protective deck, with small patches of thick armour over machinery, conning tower, etc.

The two Cramp-built Columbias of 1892–3 were designed as 21-knot commerce destroyers. *Minneapolis*, otherwise known as Cruiser 13, had two funnels to her sister's four. Armament was on a light scale and very mixed. Both ships lasted until the 1920s.

The wreckage of the *Maine* rusts in Havana harbour in February 1898. Though almost certainly a victim of unstable explosives, her sinking aroused American public fervour against the Spanish, a contributory reason to the war that broke out only two months later.

Though again failing in their designed functions, they did provide the basis for the seven-strong Orlando design. These useful little ships displaced about 5,600 tons and had a belt so narrow that it was usually submerged with full bunkers. They also introduced the modern cruiser silhouette. Never designed with the trappings of the sailing era, they could carry a single 9·2 at either end and five 5-inch on either side, high on the superstructure. They also adopted the newly-introduced triple-expansion engine.

Though armoured cruisers were still, in essence, cut-down battleships, they had not yet inherited the gun turret. In spite of Cowper Coles' early experiment, the Admiralty did not introduce the turret ship until the wooden-hulled coast defence ship *Royal Sovereign* of 1864, two years after the famous duel between *Monitor* and *Merrimack* in the American Civil War. Development then proceeded through the sea-going turret ships (of which the ill-fated *Captain* capsized and sank in 1870) to the breastwork monitors that set the pattern for future battleships. The faster cruiser line kept to smaller calibre weapons in open mountings.

America, however, was turret-minded, following a series of low-freeboard coast-defence monitors with the 6,600-ton *Maine* of 1888. Inspired by a cruiser designed in

Britain for Brazilian account, she had two twin 10-inch turrets placed en echelon, but capable of being trained on either beam through gaps in the superstructure. She was a 17-knot armoured cruiser and was to sail into history about ten years later when she was sent to Havana, Cuba to safeguard American interests during a civil war there. She erupted in an immense explosion which destroyed her, killing three-quarters of her crew. Almost certainly due to spontaneous combustion of her own ammunition, the incident, nevertheless, inflamed US public opinion to the extent it became a major cause of the Spanish-American war.

The large Comus group was followed in Britain by another class of slender 17½-knotters, the four Leanders of 1882–3. Their sole protection was a 1½-inch deck, and though they were of only 4,300 tons, they carried a homogeneous armament of ten 6-inch guns, partially sponsoned. Their design was obviously excellent in an anti-commerce role and they inspired the American *Chicago* of 1885, a 5,000 tonner which, with the smaller *Atlanta* and *Boston*, was the only bridge between the wooden Trentons (of which the name ship had been wrecked in the Apia hurricane), and the technically advanced *Maine*. They proved too over-armed and underpowered for their designed role.

Cruisers of this type and period were commonly unable to meet the speeds required for their duties, and in Britain Lord Armstrong argued for a fresh approach. 'Great speed and nimbleness of movement, combined with great offensive power . . . little or no side armour but otherwise constructed to minimise the effects of projectiles', was how he put it. If armour slowed a ship to the point of uselessness, why not seek protection in speed? Delete the vertical armour – which could not, in any case, stop a large-calibre shell – and substitute a full-length protective deck, overlaid by water-

Atlanta, one of the American 'ABC' trio of protected cruisers of 1884–5, airs her sails while laying to a buoy. The raised central battery section was a feature of US cruisers of this period. Note the size of the 8-inch gun forward.

USS *Olympia* (Cruiser 6) was completed in 1895 and had her 8-inch main battery turret-mounted. She was the flagship of Admiral Dewey during his defeat of the Spanish at Manila Bay, and was later preserved.

The ultimate in French armoured cruiser construction were the two 13,900-ton Waldeck Rousseau class ships, completed in 1899. The main armament of fourteen 194 mm guns was shared between twin and single turrets and casemates. Seen here is the *Edgar Quinet*.

SMS *Victoria Luise*, one of the five-ship Freya class of 1898, seen in an Italian port. Protected cruisers of about 5,700 tons, all of them survived until after the First World War. Note the stern walk, 8·4-inch gun, and partial funnel casings.

tight cellular construction and coal-bunkers. Lacking official enthusiasm behind him, his first ship built to the new format in 1884 was the 3,000-ton *Esmeralda*, destined for Chile. She was to be the forerunner of a long series from Armstrong's Elswick yard, noted for their elegance, efficiency and longevity. Her protective deck, a mere inch in thickness, curved sharply in the transverse plane, but she was stoutly armed with two 10-inch BL guns and three 6-inch on either beam. Guns 6-inch and smaller were now supplied on centre-pivot mountings and were termed 'quick-firers' (QF) by virtue of having shell and cartridge case in one. Loading was thus speeded dramatically, the case forming a perfect seal during combustion, and the barrel not needing to be sponged out after each round. In Admiralty trials at Shoeburyness in 1888, an Armstrong 4·7-inch QF fired ten aimed rounds in 47·5 seconds, compared with no less than 5 minutes 7 seconds for the current 'issue' weapon. Accuracy was also improved dramatically by propellants with predictable combustion characteristics.

This sudden surge of interest in the QF gun was due to the emergence of the torpedo as an effective weapon. Admirals were haunted by the bogey of a swarm of small torpedo craft swamping their line of battle, and the light cruiser with a rapid rate of fire seemed an admirable antidote.

Though the French immediately replied to the Armstrong design with the 4,500-ton *Sfax*, the British Admiralty was more cautious in producing the four transitional Rivers of 1885/6 with a complete 3-inch deck and a pronounced ram bow. One of the most ancient of marine weapons, the ram was enjoying a revival since the battle of Lissa in 1866, when the disabled Italian *Re d'Italia* was rammed and sunk by the Austrian *Ferdinand Max*. The fact that the victim was disabled and near stationary, and that other forays by purpose-built ships had consistently failed on moving targets was given scant attention. Every action, however minor, was seized upon by naval luminaries of the time in a search for 'lessons', and warships for decades afterward were to be saddled with these useless appendages that were to prove more a menace to friend than to foe.

Armstrongs built the *Piemonte* in 1888 to

Design of the American armoured cruiser *Brooklyn* (CA3), completed in 1896, shows a strong French influence in masts and armament distribution. Note how four of the eight 8-inch guns are in wing turrets, prominently sponsoned.

a design modified from the revolutionary *Esmeralda*. An Italian-flag ship, her armament was a mix of six 6-inch and six 4·7-inch guns, a wise choice in the days of hand working, when a 6-inch projectile of about 100 lb weight was the largest that could be handled by the average loading number. *Piemonte*'s very limited displacement of about 2,500 tons precluded the working-in of a double bottom – a useful defence against damage from grounding or possibly from a mine – yet allowed the inclusion of 3-inch thick sloping faces to the protective deck. This area was usually overlaid by coal bunkers, coal being able to absorb the explosion of a medium calibre shell without being seriously displaced, so keeping flooding to a minimum. On the *Piemonte*, Armstrongs packed briquettes of compressed coal-dust in this space and claimed that it would stop a 6-inch shell; as these could now pierce 15 inches of wrought iron or 10½ inches of compound armour, it may be as well that the claim was never to be tested in earnest, particularly after a long passage without bunkering! Two triple expansion engines, developing 11,000 ihp when utilizing the newly-introduced forced draught, gave a speed of 21 knots.

About this time the various types of cruiser were rationalised by the British into 'Armoured' or 'First, Second or Third class Protected'. Full clarification was still impossible, however, as many examples fell into more than one group. In general, an armoured cruiser was still looked upon as a diminutive battleship which, at a pinch, could take its place in a line of battle – an idea which was to prove fallacious. First class cruisers tended to be of better than 5,000 tons displacement, with vertical and horizontal protection which was on a scale lighter than that of the armoured cruiser. Faster in addition, they were regarded as a match for hostile commerce destroyers if they used their speed to keep the range open, their shallow belts being then little embarrassment.

Second class cruisers tended to lie in the 3,000–5,500-ton band and had only a protective deck with sloping sides to offer greater resistance to penetration. This system became far more effective with the introduction of the four-cylinder triple-expansion engine and the water-tube boiler, both of which had profiles low enough to be contained below the deck, which previously had been pierced by machinery tops, which meant the addition of glacis plates. They were viewed as valuable for the protection or destruction of trade, but in practice the emergence of the submarine invalidated the first intention, and the almost total disappearance of enemy commerce in the event of war virtually negated the second. This was to leave the type free for a wider variety of purely naval tasks.

Third class cruisers, whilst envisaged as

French cruisers of about the turn of the century had oddly-proportioned features. On the *Gloire* of 1904, the mainmast appears exceptionally lofty and close to the stern.

scouts were, almost invariably, too slow for the purpose and most spent their lives backing-up and replacing the many smaller 'cruising vessels' in the manifold duties of empire.

Naval thinking of the 1880s was greatly coloured by the torpedo, developing rapidly under the commercial impetus of its demand for smaller navies, which saw in it a means of offsetting their numerical inferiority in ship strength. As it had an effective range of barely half a mile at the time (the submarine being still an inventor's plaything) the problem of delivering it in the teeth of QF guns needed to be resolved. Thornycroft had produced in 1876 the *Lightning*, the first of a long line of torpedo boats, yet they were still fragile and of short endurance. To carry the war to an enemy the 'torpedo-gunboat' was developed, typified by the elegant little Alarm class and looking like miniature cruisers, but of only 810 tons. Limited by a lack of speed commensurate with their size, they were complemented by the 'torpedo cruiser' of which the *Fearless* and *Scout* were built in 1885/6. Only three 18-inch torpedo tubes were carried, with a defensive 5-inch gun armament on a 220-foot high freeboard hull that would have made a magnificent target whilst disengaging at a top speed of about 17 knots.

The idea was not developed further and thinking went off at a tangent with the lone 6,630-ton *Vulcan*, which could make 20 knots and which, superficially, could have passed for an orthodox cruiser. Again, however, only a defensive armament was fitted and her profile was dominated by a pair of enormous gooseneck cranes which, with derricks, could handle the six small torpedo craft carried aboard. *Vulcan* had six tubes and, presumably was supposed to support a mass attack by her brood; a brave idea, hailed as revolutionary, it went no further at the time, though cruisers devoted to the use of the torpedo were to reappear at odd intervals later, right up to the Japanese Kitikamis of the Second World War.

The convolutions of cruiser nomenclature were not exclusively the province of the Royal Navy. The French, for instance, cheerfully confused the issue perhaps by changing the rating of a ship or group on its being rearmed, or again by the status changing in relation to a class built at a later date. Prior to 1860 the Marine Nationale had, like the British, frigates and corvettes, rated First or Second Class. Less significant vessels were termed Avisos, again rated by class. The first two categories were replaced in 1874 by the term 'Croiseur' with three classes, but there were to be other variations before 1892, when 'Croiseur' covered the complete band. In the Royal Navy it was to be 1913 before the final simplification to 'Cruiser' and 'Light Cruiser' came about, but that is to anticipate.

At the end of the 1880s the fleets of Britain and France were still the world's most powerful but, beyond a cutlass-rattle from time to time, looked less and less likely to engage in any major conflict. It was unfortunate, therefore, when a new complication arose and a grandson of the ageing Queen Victoria took the throne of a newly-unified Germany as Kaiser. His nation, largely land-locked and with a military tradition, the young Wilhelm II put in motion the creation of a fleet in a belated attempt to acquire wider influence and colonial possessions. It was a move to which the British were to take exception.

INTO THE 20th CENTURY– towards war

At the beginning of the last decade of the 19th Century, there was nothing of any import to disturb the international naval scene. Just a quarter of century earlier, the Royal Navy had commissioned its last wooden first rate but had since accomplished its greatest transition with a minimum of trauma. Gone were the straining acres of canvas, gone were serried ranks of gleaming black guns. This was the age of the engineer – smoke, oily steam and the clang of the stokehold shovel. Cathedral-like spaces were dedicated to capricious machinery and, topsides, a few heavy guns were dependent upon the whims of the laws of hydraulics.

Many had predicted that this enormous, technologically-induced change would cost the fleet its pre-eminence, but they were proved wrong. Instead, there were to exist rivalries in developments by which various fleets sought to outstrip each other. To make these developments, as they affected the cruiser more coherent, it is appropriate to take each main type in turn and follow its progress over the quarter century to the outbreak of the First World War.

It has already been related how early armoured cruisers failed in their designed objectives. The price of their protection and heavy guns was paid in speed, to the extent that lighter cruisers and much commerce could elude them, whilst their margin was insufficient to escape the attentions of a battleship bent on their destruction. Though belted and protected cruisers had therefore proved popular there did still exist other schools of thought. One such in France was the so-called *Jeune Ecole*, which believed firmly that any future war with Britain could best be won by the destruction of her trade. As any cruiser bent on this course of action would need first to despatch a convoy's escort, vertical armour would be necessary for decisive close-range action.

In keeping with this line of thought, the French cruiser *Dupuy de Lôme* was completed in 1891. Of some 6,500 tons, her complete hull down to one metre below the waterline was given 100 mm protection, backed by 40 mm horizontal armour. Her armament was disposed in odd fashion, with a single 190 mm (7·6-inch) gun on either side amidships, and three smaller weapons of 160 mm (6·4-inch) at either end. The extreme tumblehome of the hull enabled five guns to bear in any direction but produced a grotesque appearance, rendered the stranger by a ram bow of Homeric proportion. She was the first major triple-screwed warship and capable of 20 knots.

Together with the *Pothuau* and the four Charners that followed, she created much interest, but Britain did not immediately reply. A conservatively-minded Admiralty was not impressed with a series of French mechanical mishaps, and the fine lines of the newcomers (L/B about 7¼ compared with about 6 for the contemporary British Edgars) suggested speed at the expense of stability and bunker capacity. Not until the end of the decade did the Royal Navy re-introduce the deep armour belt, no lon-

One of ten armoured cruisers built for various flags, the Italian *Varese* is seen after her launching in 1899. Note the size of the ram popular at this time, and the sponsons in the hull to give near-axial fire to some of the secondary armament.

ger such a burden by virtue of the availability of higher quality steels used in thinner plates, and of the greater size of the ships themselves. It should be remembered that the British, unlike the French, viewed the armoured cruiser as a fast wing of the battle fleet, gaining intelligence, acting as close support, and, if necessary, tackling the smaller enemy battleships.

During the early 1890s, before the German challenge really began to become serious, the Royal Navy's main rivals in size were the navies of France and Russia. In order, their 1893 strengths were as follows: Battleships (1st and 2nd class) 48, 30, 15; Armoured cruisers 18, 13, 9 and Protected Cruisers (1st, 2nd and 3rd classes) 54, 19, 2. It can be seen that the Two Power Standard, by which the British fleet should have been capable of matching the combination of the two next most powerful, had already lapsed in armoured cruisers and the relationship was deteriorating.

Three large armoured cruisers were completed about this time for the Czarist fleet, the *Rurik*, *Rossia* and *Gromoboi*. They were impressive ships, and their great freeboard included a two-metre-deep belt of armour of between 100 and 200 mm thickness, backed internally by an upper deck of 65 mm and a lower patch of 150 mm steel over the vitals. Triple-screw machinery of 18,000 ihp drove them at 20 knots, and an armament of four 8-inch, sixteen 6-inch and six 4·7-inch guns gave a fort-like appearance. They created a great impression but the obvious threat that they posed as commerce raiders was never to be realised because they were fated to encounter a squadron of Japanese armoured cruisers during the Russo-Japanese War. The Elswick-built Asamas were a quartette also disposing four 8-inch weapons as a main battery and, at what came to be called the Battle of Ulsan, sank the *Rurik* and heavily damaged the other two. *Gromoboi* escaped through her higher speed, but only her thick hide had prevented destruction from about twenty-five hits of 8 and 6-inch calibre.

France, keen on the armoured cruiser, continued with ever-larger examples, starting with the *Jeanne d'Arc* of 1899 displacing 11,100 tons and progressing by stages to the 13,900-ton *Edgar Quinet*, completed at the late date of 1908. The large number of water-tube boilers required to develop their designed 28,500 shp were split into two compartments flanking the machinery spaces, so as to reduce the risk of total loss of power in the event of damage. This arrangement led to a multitude of funnels – the *Jeanne d'Arc* had six – spaced in two groups. A weakness still existed in the adjacent engine rooms, ruthlessly exposed by submarine torpedo when the *Leon Gambetta* was sunk in 1915 off the Italian coast.

French protection favoured a comparitively shallow belt, enclosed top and bottom by armoured decks. American designers preferred a fairly thin belt of the new Harvey steel, with a tough core and a hardened surface, and a single substantial deck. The ill-fated USS *Maine* was followed by the *New York* (later *Saratoga*) in 1891, four of whose six 8-inch guns were twinned in centreline turrents. Her 8,200 tons were increased to 9,200 in the following *Brooklyn* of 1895, which carried four such turrets, two of which were sponsoned amidships in the shadow of the three lofty funnels. Both

The small, 2,700-ton German protected cruiser *Frauenlob* sails under the Grünenthal Bridge in the Kiel canal, built primarily to allow warships to be passed from the Baltic to the North sea.

Sister of the better-known *Scharnhorst* was the *Gneisenau*, both built in 1907. The common feature of a rounded deckedge, for the rapid clearance of loose water, can be seen.

were interesting mechanically in having four triple-expansion engines coupled to two shafts, either of which could be driven by only one prime mover. *Brooklyn* was involved in the crushing, but hollow, victory over the Spaniards (dismissed by Mahan as 'inept') at Santiago de Cuba in the war of 1898. Little was taught by the action except that warships were still highly inflammable, encouraging US designers to reduce combustibles from then on. Like the Japanese, when they defeated the Chinese at the Yalu four years earlier, the Americans pressed in close but, even at below 3,000 yards, their accuracy was appalling and hidden only by great superiority in strength. The combinations of 12- and 13-inch, and 6- and 8-inch splashes made gun-laying a nightmare, and difficulties such as these paved the way for director control and the end of mixed-calibre armaments.

Elswick's record on production runs was rivalled at this time by the Italians with a series of armoured cruisers, stemming from the *Giuseppe Garibaldi* of 1893. Ten were built averaging 7,350 tons, four for Argentina, three for Italy, two for Japan and one for Spain. They, too, were long-lived, the Argentinian *Puerreydon* lasting until the 1950s. Very distinctive in profile, their two large and widely spaced funnels were separated by a single heavy mast with fidded topmast. A full-length belt of 80 to 150 mm thickness was complemented by a 30 to 50 mm protective deck but, by the end of the series, this was considered insufficient to keep pace with gunnery developments. Their own armament was of 8- or 10-inch weapons mixed with 4·7- or 6-inch.

France's impressive *Jeanne d'Arc* followed, in 1897, hard on the heels of Germany's first armoured cruiser, the 10,550-ton *Furst Bismarck* and prompted the British Cressys of 1899–1901. These were really uprated versions of the Diadem class of protected cruiser, dignified four-funnellers with a homogeneous armament of no less than sixteen 6-inch. Unfortunately, half of these were placed in casemates set too low to be of any use in a sea and the Diadems' twin 6-inch mountings were replaced by single 9·2s in the Cressys, which thus effectively became six-gun ships. They were, however, good for 21 knots, had a belt up to 6 inches thick and a 3-inch deck. They were also the last class to be painted in the elegant red, white, black and buff Victorian livery; with the Edwardian era came the universal grey, known to the fleet as 'crabfat'. Obsolescent by 1914, they were used in supposedly 'low-risk' areas but three, *Cressey*, *Aboukir* and *Hogue*, became something of a *cause célèbre* when sunk together in short order by a German submarine.

The interim Cresseys were followed by the four Drakes, which represented an increase in tonnage from 12,000 to 14,100, with great 530-foot hulls that housed machinery for developing 30,000 shp. In parallel were built ten smaller Monmouths, aimed at commerce protection rather than fleet roles. Following the American pattern, four of their sixteen 6-inch guns were paired in turrets, but again their weakness was in their casemated armament, a weakness highlighted at the battle of Coronel in 1914 when one of each group was to be outclassed and sunk by the German armoured cruisers *Scharnhorst* and *Gneisenau*.

Germany had built few examples but had early abandoned the 240 mm gun, roughly equivalent to the 9·2-inch favoured by the

British, for the 210 mm, or 8·2-inch, which was to prove an excellent weapon. The 11,400-ton Scharnhorsts represented an enlarged and improved version of the Roons of 1903–4 and mounted eight 8·2s. Four of these were in twinned turrets and the remainder, together with the 150 mm (5·9-inch) secondaires were close-grouped high-up amidships to allow the thickest possible protection over the small area that they occupied.

British armoured cruiser design now entered its final phase with a series of related classes. At 450 feet, the six Devonshires were near-identical in length with the Monmouths but had a lower and more business-like profile with four funnels, due to a rearrangement of the 30 boilers necessary to produce their designed 21,000 shp. About 3,000 tons smaller than the Drakes, they also adopted a new-pattern gun in the 7·5-inch. Four of these were shipped in single turrets, one on the centre-line forward and aft, and two flanking the bridge to give forward fire of three guns. *Hampshire*, of this class, is remembered for taking with her Lord Kitchener when she sank after mining near the Orkneys, the month after Jutland.

Where the Devonshires combined a 6-inch belt with a 2-inch deck, the two Duke of Edinburghs that followed increased the latter to a total of 3½ inches. *Black Prince*, of this type was to be sunk at Jutland by close-ranged (i.e. low trajectory) fire from calibres up to 11-inch, where even a 6-inch belt was inadequate. Capable of 23½ knots, this pair had an uprated main battery with three 9·2s at either end. Their ten casemated 6-inch guns were recognised later as being of limited value and were replaced by six singles on the upper deck. That it was 1916 before this was done, points to the lack of realistic gun practice at that time. *Black Prince* was interesting also in being one of the first ships in the Royal Navy fitted for burning oil fuel; this was, in fact, sprayed into the furnaces on coal burning there already and producing, reportedly, a prodigious capacity for making smoke!

The four Warriors of 1905 were near-identical but had no casemates, their secondary armament consisting of four 7·5s, two on each side on the upper deck amidships. They would seem an odd calibre to combine with the 9·2s of the main battery, having also too slow a rate of fire to repel the feared destroyer attack. By comparison, however, German battleships up to the Wittelsbachs of 1901–2 were armed with four 230 mm (9·4-inch) and eighteen 150 mm (5·9-inch) guns, with a speed of 18 knots on an 11,150 ton displacement though, of course, far more powerfully protected. Though an armoured cruiser was, theoretically, in with a chance, the inability of their guns to pierce a small battleship's hide was to be highlighted by the experiences of the Japanese at Tsushima in 1905 and, later, by the British at Jutland. From the Braunschweigs of 1902–4 the Germans compounded the problem by introducing the 280 mm (11-inch) gun to their battleships.

This factor in itself would have stimulated a re-think on the design and role of the armoured cruiser but a change of thought was, in fact, already in hand. Before it was to be translated into actual steel, however,

The British armoured cruiser *Black Prince* off Rapallo in about 1908. Note how the forecastle deck is cut away to allow the 9·2 wing turrets axial fire in the forward direction. The 6-inch guns are mounted in low casemates.

The hybrid *Blücher* in 1910, built to counter a faulty assessment of the first British battlecruisers. Her twelve 8·2s were mounted in twin turrets, and the layout of the wing mountings and the secondary 5·9s compare interestingly with those of the *Scharnhorst*.

the ultimate trio of armoured cruisers were produced in the incredible Minotaurs. On a 14,600 ton displacement, these carried a twin 9·2-turret at either end and no less than five 7·5s down either side, an increase in topweight that was compensated by a thinner protective deck and shallower belt. Built in 1906–7, they were rendered obsolete on completion through the emergence of the 'Dreadnought cruiser' or battlecruiser, whose unique combination of speed and offensive power spelt the end of the armoured cruiser upon which she was designed to prey as well as to usurp her major functions.

An interesting by-product of the speed and secrecy of Britain's Dreadnought plans was in the immediate German reaction. Acquiring faulty intelligence (possibly by British design) they assumed the new buildings to be no more than 'cruiser destroyers' armed with nothing larger than 9·2s. As a result the *Blücher* of 1908 was a 15,550-ton one-off with twelve 8·2s and a 26-knot speed, incorporating protection on the British scale. Realising their error, the Germans thereafter switched to the design and production of a series of excellent battlecruisers but, instead of using *Blücher* as an orthodox large armoured cruiser – of which she was a fine example – they persisted in employing her as a runt to the battlecruiser squadron. Inevitably placed as 'tail-end Charlie', she was exposed to long-range fire from persuing British battlecruisers at the Dogger Bank action. Her 50 mm deck was little better than paper in keeping out the plunging 13·5-inch projectiles, but her sacrifice preoccupied the British to the extent that the remaining Germans escaped.

Though adopting the armoured cruiser late, the Americans had some excellent examples. The six Pennsylvannias (later known as the Pittsburghs when State names were reserved for battleships) were really 13,700-ton equivalents to the British Drakes, but with two twin 8-inch turrets and with their fourteen 6-inch guns in what amounted to a box battery rather than casemates. Protected from gunfire by a 6-inch belt, they nevertheless had a weakness in the shape of a centreline bulkhead in the machinery spaces, a controversial feature that was instrumental in the rapid capsize of *San Diego* after being mined in 1918. Diminutives of this design were the three Charlestons of 1904 which, at 9,700 tons and with an all-6-inch armament, countered the British Monmouths. Finally, the four Tennessees (later Memphis) were contemporary with the *Black Prince* but certainly equal to the later Minotaurs. With two twin 10-inch turrets and sixteen 6-inch guns they were among the best of their kind, but with the *Montana*, launched in late 1906, the Americans, too, had finished with the armoured cruiser.

Britain's unique dependence upon her fleet resulted occasionally in a neurotic overreaction to developments abroad or a 'war

Painted in the colours of Victoria's navy, the Highflyers were completed in 1900–1. *Highflyer*, the class nameship shown here, was notable for destroying the German NDL express liner-turned-raider *Kaiser Wilhelm der Grosse*.

scare'. Public opinion, that nebulous and unquantifiable force, could produce surprising results when fanned by an interested Press, carefully tuned to 'patriotism'. The late 1880s saw such a campaign, coinciding with Wilhelm II's accession. Suitably alarmed, Parliament (which included representatives of those lobbies involved in the campaigning) passed the Naval Defence Act of 1889, a grand plan for some 70 fighting ships, including ten armoured and no less than 42 protected cruisers of various classes.

Britain's answers to the French *Dupuy de Lôme* and her kind were not armoured cruisers but the First Class protected ships *Blake* and *Blenheim*. Stemming from the successful Orlandos, they traded protection for machinery, their 20,000 shp being good for 22 knots. Their two 9·2 and ten 6-inch guns were an advance on the French armament, and the 'box batteries' of earlier classes were abandoned, six 6-inch being placed on the upper deck and the remaining four in the newly-introduced casemates. With fewer, but quick firing, guns now being carried, the casemate was seen as a safe way of spreading the armament around a ship's periphery to achieve an optimum

Among the earliest of the few German armoured cruisers were the two Prinz Adelberts of 1903, both 9,050-tonners. The nameship is shown here in 1911. Layout is uncluttered, with twin 8·2s at either end and four 5·9s grouped on either side amidships.

coverage of firing arcs.

Though the British Blakes never made their contract speeds, they spawned two diminutive classes during 1890–2. The six Edgars had a similar armament to the Blakes but, with only half their installed power, had a displacement reduced from 9,150 to 7,350 tons; the Crescents had a similar hull and exchanged the forward 9·2 for a twinned 6-inch whilst, oddly, retaining the after 9·2. For a modest increase in displacement they also incorporated 20 per cent more power but, in spite of their lack of speed, the Edgars were fully employed

The ill-starred *Monmouth* was leadship of a class of ten Counties of 1901–3. Though armoured cruisers, their belts and protective decks were of only 2-inch steel over the greater part of their area. She was sunk at Coronel. Note the new-style twin 6-inch turret.

during the earlier part of the war in the vital contraband control activities of the Northern Patrol.

Continuing foreign developments led to the monstrous pair of 'answers', *Powerful* and *Terrible* (the latter universally known as ''orrible'), 14,200-tonners that needed 48 of the new Belleville water-tube boilers to develop the necessary 25,000 shp to drive them at the same speed as that of the Edgars. 538 feet in length they carried six more 6-inch guns and, at 900, about 350 more crew. Extremely imposing ships, they would have been ideal on foreign stations but for the inordinate expense of keeping them running, a factor that put them out of the active fleet before the war, in which they took no part.

Only two more ships aimed specifically at commerce-raiding were to be built by the French before the common threat of the expansionist German Naval Act of 1898 drove them more into line with the British. These were 23-knot *Chateaurenault* of 1898 and the *Guichen*, the former with a strangely mercantile profile, obviously designed to confuse her prey. Another pair had been built by the Americans, who also had solid experience of Britain's mercantile vulnerability. These were the 7,475-ton Colombias, whose 23 knots demanded three triple expansion engines of high profile, requiring the 4-inch armoured decks to be sloped as far as the glacis. With these two, the Americans abandoned the type and Germany, with no maritime background, built only one class of larger protected cruisers, the five-ship Freya group of 1898. Though of only 5,650-tons and lightly protected, they carried a respectable armament of two 8·2 and six 5·9-inch guns.

Britain's last First Class cruisers were the eight Diadems of 1896, 11,000-tonners designed to be more economical alternatives to the Powerfuls. Some 462 feet in length, they looked underarmed with only a paired 6-inch fore and aft and the remaining twelve in casemates. In addition the first four were incredibly underpowered, being capable of only 16 knots. Nevertheless the design was sound and, with the revival of interest in the armoured cruiser, it was easily modified with a belt and more powerful armament to provide the basis of the 'Cressy' class, which retained a near-identical profile. From 1913, both Armoured and First Class protected cruisers in the Royal Navy were re-rated, simply, as 'Cruisers', the remainder becoming 'Light Cruisers'.

Of the latter, the largest were the Second Class protected cruisers, which stemmed from the rather odd River type of 1885, increasing in displacement with each succeeding group but usually armed with a mix of 6- and 4·7-inch guns and powered for about 20 knots. Economical and versatile, the type was built in large numbers, the Naval Defence Act resulting in 1890–91, in 21 Apollos alone. These were of 3,400 tons, only 300 feet in length and, classed as obsolete by 1914, they served largely as minelayers, though four were gloriously expended as blockships. With a 2-inch protective deck, they were able to ship a 6-inch gun at either end and had six 4·7s in the waist, which took the form of a well-deck. This reduced topweight but tended to fill with water in a seaway, so the following eight Astraeas were increased to 4,350 tons with a flush weather deck.

These, in turn, were succeeded by the Eclipse class ships which, at 5,600 tons, were larger than some First Class cruisers. For better seakeeping they featured a raised forecastle and – eventually – adopted a homogeneous armament of eleven 6-inch guns. The French were not keen on the type and limited themselves to the three Friants of 1896–6, which rivalled an Elswick in having a main battery of six 165 mm guns on a displacement of under 4,000 tons, and the larger *Jurien de la Graviere*, an eight-gunned version that never realised her designed 23 knots.

Two Elswicks were, in fact, acquired by the USA at the time of its war with Spain. These were 3,440-tonners actually building for Brazil and had six 6-inch apiece. They joined the home-built *Olympia* which, although of only 5,500 tons, carried four 8·9-inch and ten 5-inch guns as well as a 2-inch deck that had 4½-inch slopes. Another pair of Elswicks went to Japan, which already operated a trio of French-built oddities, the Matsushimas, which featured a single, barbette-mounted 12·6-inch (320 mm) gun forward. Low rates of fire and lack of salvo spread made the chances of a hit from a single large weapon infinitesimal, but the idea was to return from time to time, culminating in the ultimate folly of Fisher's 'tinclads' of which the *Furious* was supposed to fight with two 18-inch.

Russia also built protected cruisers and, though her confrontation with Japan in 1904–5 resulted in maritime disaster, it gave good practical insights into the ability of modern examples to withstand punishment. Protective decks did, in fact, work well but the effect of high explosive shells was to reduce topsides to sieves, with guncrews suffering from the hails of splinters. Riven funnels reduced draught to boilers but the ships survived, their conning positions, casemates, armament hoists, etc, being separately protected. With ranges still

tending to be short and trajectories thus flat, a measure of vertical protection could pay dividends.

The Royal Navy's Eclipse class were followed by the four Arrogants of 1896–7. Of the same displacement, they were, at 320 feet, some 45 feet shorter but 3½ feet beamier. This resulted in their being very handy, a factor that influenced the choice of *Vindictive*, of the class, for the Zeebrugge raid (Chapter 4). The Arrogants also reverted to a three-funnelled layout, followed by the very similar Highflyers, which carried eleven 6-inch guns on a hull of only 350 feet in length. They were built in two groups, in 1898 and 1902, four making 20 knots on 10,000 shp and the later Challengers being stretched to accommodate 25 per cent more power – which gave them a speed advantage of barely one knot! With their completion, came a swing back to belted ships to keep enemy fire out at closer ranges, a concept which, as shall be seen, resulted in the true 'light cruiser'.

Smaller, Third Class protected cruisers were originally conceived as scouts but, having insufficient size for the necessary boiler capacity, failed again in speed. They proved invaluable, however, in taking over the Imperial duties of the earlier 'cruising ships' of the sailing navy. Their basic form was established by the five Medeas of 1888, with raised forecastle and poop, two funnels and a vestigal sailing rig. With a 2-inch protective deck, their displacement was still only 2,950 tons and they carried a useful six 6-inch armament.

Calibres then diminished through the 4·7s of the Barham and Pallas classes to only eight 4-inch in the eleven-strong Pelorus class of 1896–9. Where the Pelorus class may be held to epitomise the Third Class cruiser, the type terminated, like the Second Class, in a three-funnelled group, the Gems, important because they represented a transition to a new line of cruiser evolution. Though of only 3,000 tons they were, at 360 feet, longer than the Highflyers, with about the same power for 22 knots. One of them, the *Amethyst*, was the first major warship with a steam turbine plant, which was not only more compact and vibration free, but also developed 13,000 shp from the same boiler installation from which her sisters derived only 10,500. This represented a difference of 1½ knots and the reciprocating engine had nearly run its course.

At the turn of the century with aircraft and radio yet to make their impact, vitally required intelligence for a fleet commander still required the use of specialised ships. 'Reconnaissance in force', knowledge acquired and brought back against opposition, was the province of the armoured cruiser, but there was still a need for a

Laid down in 1906, but not completed until 1910–11, the Italian *San Giorgio*, and her sister *San Marco*, were just about the last 'classic' armoured cruisers to be built. Of less than 10,000 tons standard displacement, they mounted four 10-inch guns and eight 7·5s, all twinned.

A milestone was passed when, in January 1911, Eugene Ely successfully landed a Curtiss biplane on a temporary platform at the after end of the American armoured cruiser *Pennsylvania*. He took off again later.

small, fast vessel (analogous to the unarmed, high-flying reconnaissance aircraft of our own time) that would seek to avoid action in its quest for intelligence. Mahan saw her in terms of the old sailing frigate: '. . . rapidity in action is their primary object. Defensive strength does not conduce to rapidity of movement' was the way he put it. Such a ship would also be capable of running down and destroying torpedo boats, whose growing size and seaworthiness posed an increasing threat.

Germany, which had completed a number of attractive, but conventional, Third Class cruisers during the 1890s, produced the *Novik*, a 3,000-ton 'ocean scout' to Russian account in 1900. Capable of about 26 knots, she created a great impression and inspired an alternative Elswick design. This 3,800-tonner looked like a stretched 'Gem' and carried only six 4-inch guns, but the argument advanced for her construction, that she could observe enemy ports closely but safely, was ironically made in the very year that the British Admiralty acquired Holland's design for a submersible. These craft led the way to the practical submarine, the very instrument that finally destroyed the traditional weapon of close blockade.

Though the Elswick proposition was not taken up, the 1902 and 1903 Estimates provided for a pair of 'Scouts' from each of four builders. Their specification was broad, in that the ships should be capable of maintaining 25 knots for 8 hours and have a 3,000-mile endurance at 10 knots. They were to carry two torpedo tubes but guns no larger than 12-pounders, whilst protection, interestingly, was to be a sloping protective deck at least 1½ inches in thickness *or its equivalent in a vertical belt*, indicating that there was still no firm commitment to the virtues of either. The resulting interpretations of these requirements were interesting to compare. Lengths varied from 360 to 374 feet and displacements from 2,640 to 2,900 tons. All looked like 'super destroyers' with a short raised forecastle, only the Fairfields pair also having the raised poop typical of a Third Class cruiser. Three pairs had three funnels apiece, the Armstrongs (Elswick) four. Where all incorporated protective decks, Laird and Fairfield managed in addition to work in a 2-inch vertical patch along the machinery spaces. All had triple expansion machinery but achieved contract speeds, though the fastest were the Elswick pair, longer and narrower than the rest and developing lower power. One result of this hull form was a draught of only 12 feet, some two feet less than the remainder and considered an asset as the Japanese scouting forces – mainly destroyers – were then showing the advantages of being able to work in very shallow water against the Russians.

Many remained unconvinced of their uses, however, and pointed out that, at £284,000 apiece they cost some £57,000 more than a Gem, offered inferior armament and range, and only a two-knot advantage over the turbine-driven *Amethyst*. They did prove to be superb seaboats and their potential against destroyers was quickly appreciated, though they lacked sufficient punch. A role with which they rapidly became identified was as leader to one of the large destroyer flotillas then common. Even the Admiralty remained unsure of their value and were to wait a further five years before developing the idea. One reason for this was, undoubtedly, the completion in 1904 of the German 'light cruiser' *Bremen*. She was rapidly followed by a further four which, though of a length with the British Scouts, had a two-deck freeboard over their full length. This resulted in a 3,260-ton displacement and a lower speed of 23 knots but permitted an armament of ten 105 mm (4·1-inch) guns. They were a re-affirmation of the Gem design, one of their number, *Lübeck*, even having steam turbines (and an interesting arrangement of eight propellers on two shafts, which were direct-driven). Their obvious versatility resulted in the next British class moving away from the 'Scout' idea, the three Boadiceas being of 3,300 tons and carrying a more respectable six 4-inch guns. All were turbine-driven and could maintain 25 knots easily on 18,000 shp. Four Actives followed in 1911–2, similarly powered but stretched to 385 feet to mount ten 4-inch.

This design provided the basis of the eight Arethusas, completed as the world teetered on the very brink of war, and from which sprang the long line of C, D and E classes, to be dealt with later. Though of only 3,520 tons, they carried six 4-inch guns, sided in the waist and a single 6-inch at either end. Further punch was vested in eight torpedo tubes, the new 21-inch variety whose projectile could stop a large target that would not have been unduly embarrassed by the earlier 18-inch weapons. Machinery was also improving apace, turbines being powered by boilers fired by oil only and developing 40,000 shp for 29 knots. Oil had tremendous advantages in being transferred by pump without the back-breaking toil associated with coal. It could be stowed almost anywhere aboard and the earlier squads of stokers were no longer required, though one drawback was that it lacked the protective qualities of earlier bunkers, a deficiency met in the Arethusas by a 3-inch belt.

German construction kept pace, their first operational turbine ship being *Dresden* of 1909. Because of the 105 mm gun's excel-

The German light cruiser *Stralsund* in the Kiel Canal at Rendsburg in 1913, with her original armament of twelve 4·1s, later to become seven 5·9s. She became the French *Mulhouse* after the war. The arrow on the stem-head is on a 'wappen' or escutcheon, with which every German ship of any size was emblazoned.

lent range and reliability it was retained after the British had adopted the 6-inch. With the Kolberg and Breslau classes of 1909–12, however, displacement began to increase rapidly, for the Royal Navy had gone off on a new tack in 1909 with the quartette of Bristols, the first of a long line of Towns. These, essentially, were Boadiceas enlarged to about 4,800 tons and featuring a mixed 4- and 6-inch armament, but the type developed rapidly like their German equivalents, through smaller successive groups to remarkably similar ships, lean of line, hard hitting and with an all 6-inch armament and a 25-knot speed. Subsequent to the Breslaus, the Germans favoured a 65 mm belt and a nominal protective deck; the British preferred a 2-inch deck and a double skin over the machinery but, from the Birminghams of 1913, fell into line with the Germans.

With their 'light cruisers' both fleets, so soon to be locked in battle, had evolved a basic form that would see no drastic change until the guided missile era. In spite of this, the concept was as yet far from universally accepted; America, for instance, had tried the water with the three 3,750-ton Birminghams of 1907 but, finding them rather limited for ocean warfare, did not try again for nearly a decade until the much larger Omahas at 7,100 tons. Italy had tried with the three 3,500-ton Quartos carrying a mix of 120 mm and 76 mm guns and having a very high speed of 29 knots, but their performance at sea was mediocre. Elsewhere in Europe, both Russia and Austria-Hungary had produced a few useful examples but neither fleet was to play a significant part in the conflict ahead.

In the course of their war with Spain, the Americans had used fast ocean liners for the purpose of scouting, and proposed to repeat the practice in a major war. In Britain, too, the same proposal was made, the Government paying owners a subsidy for strengthening certain ships and installing extra power, so they could act as auxiliaries and enable Royal Naval allocations to be dedicated to purely offensive ships. In the event, the proposal was not taken up on the grounds that such ships would be urgently needed for other purposes in the event of hostilities, and that their fuel consumption was prodigious. A certain amount of prejudice also showed in one summing up: '(You cannot) turn a wheelbarrow into a perambulator, nor an omnibus into a hansom cab; if you attempt it you will not make a good one out of either'. Nevertheless, subsidies were paid for modification to certain 'second division' liners, which served with varying degrees of success as auxiliary, or armed-merchant cruisers (AMCs) in both world wars.

The German *Graudenz* storing at Kiel soon after completion. With the *Regensburg*, she was a three-funneled version of the Karlsrühes. Note the disposition of the 4·1s, later replaced by 5·9s, and the armoured conning tower. After the war she became the Italian *Ancona*.

THE CRUISER IN THE FIRST WORLD WAR

With vastly differing aims in waging war, Britain and Germany, as might be expected, used their fleets, both naval and mercantile, in very different ways. The Germans were particularly strong in light cruisers, having developed them in succeeding groups from the five Bremens of 1904/5 for use primarily with the inappropriately-named High Seas Fleet. As this force rapidly established itself as a fleet-in-being, greater significance attached to those units already in foreign waters which, as they were generally used imaginatively, were to tie down disproportionately large British forces until they were brought to account. The odyssey of von Spee's East Asiatic Squadron will be related later but the battle cruiser *Goeben*, along with the light cruiser *Breslau*, also became something of a cause célèbre before joining the Turks. Then there were the lone cruisers *Karlsruhe* and *Konigsberg* and a handful of armed merchantmen but, although they enjoyed a few isolated successes, they succumbed rapidly to the forces deployed against them or to mechanical problems caused by want of dockyard attention. Remorselessly whittled away, their activities ceased by July 1915 with the inglorious end of the *Konigsberg* far up a remote East African river. After that, German cruiser activity remained closer to home.

Until it was rendered largely obsolete by the introduction of the battle cruiser, the armoured cruiser had been popular in the Royal Navy, which possessed many more than its opponents, together with a large force of smaller protected cruisers. A score of light cruisers (although not yet officially called such) were available in the Town-class, although others were to join the fleet in large numbers from 1914 onwards. With both 4- and 6-inch armaments, the 5,000-ton British Towns tended to be larger than their German counterparts and, although their 6-inch gun scarcely outranged the enemy's 4·1, it threw a heavier projectile. Finally, there were about fifteen Scouts of about 3,000 tons, with 4-inch weapons.

To the Royal Navy, the cruiser was a many-sided ship and there were never enough of them, a situation aggravated by the discovery that many of the older units were of very limited practical use in action, developed as they were from generations of Victorian classes that had never seen hostilities. Protected cruisers proved too small and slow while the formidable-looking armoured cruisers suffered from mixed armaments, some of which were mounted low in side casemates and were therefore unworkable in any sea.

There was, therefore, a progressive shift during the war years from squadrons of large and nominally powerful units, geared to working closely with the battle fleet, to homogeneous groups of light cruisers of more flexible capability. Employment was anything but rigid, with ships being detached for a variety of duties.

Designed to operate as a fast wing of the fleet, five squadrons – the 1st, 2nd, 3rd, 4th, and 6th, each composed of four armoured cruisers – were attached to Jellicoe's Grand Fleet at the outbreak of war in August 1914, although the 6th was always on detached duties and the 4th was in the West Indies. Apart from their main function, which was to prove disastrously outdated, they had the task of what today would be termed 'sea denial', with aggressive patrols of all near waters up to neutral limits.

With four more armoured cruisers, the 5th Cruiser Squadron (CS) had as its patch the 'Narrows' between North and South Atlantic. The 7th, with five elderly Cressys, supported flotilla operations in the southern North Sea. There was no 8th, but the 9th and 11th, each with six smaller protected cruisers, worked (largely out of Gibraltar) over the greater part of the eastern North Atlantic. Four more protected cruisers of the 12th CS joined French units in patrolling the English Channel's western approaches while the bulk of the Crescents and Edgars formed the 10th CS, which was allocated to the Northern Patrol, controlling mercantile traffic in the Shetland-Norway gap with the aim of denying the enemy all seaborne materials. Although this blockade was vitally important, the little cruisers were found wanting in the unremittingly vile northern weather and they were soon replaced by Armed Merchant Cruisers (AMCs).

In spite of the lessons of history, prewar planners considered that a convoy system would not be necessary; arguments invariably centred on the invulnerability of powered ships to attack, disruption to trade, defensive thinking and so on, and this rhetoric led to the official belief that it would be sufficient for fast cruisers to patrol the trade routes, with particular attention to focal points. A handful of German raiders exposed the weakness of this thinking and the previously unconsidered submarine eventually caused its tardy abandonment in 1917.

Operating from a coastline plagued with shallow approaches, most German cruisers had a minelaying capacity. Minelaying in the Royal Navy on the other hand was a minor pastime and, one suspects, was

Damage to the funnel casings of the *Frauenlob* during the battle in the Heligoland Bight was more picturesque than serious, but could slow the ship through loss of draught to the boilers. *Rostock* is in the background.

HMS *Birmingham* with one of the earlier Southamptons. She has spread canvas baffles between the funnels to break up their sharp profiles, useful to enemy range-finders. Note the disposition of the 6-inch guns and the pronounced curve of the stem.

considered slightly underhand. Only one minelaying squadron existed in the form of seven converted Apollo-class veterans. Their life span was short as it was found that destroyers and converted merchantmen were superior.

Attached to the Grand Fleet was one light cruiser squadron of six Towns, which formed an efficient scouting force under the highly able Commodore Goodenough, together with a Boadicea-class scout seconded to each of the four battleship squadrons. The remainder of the scouts acted as leaders to destroyer flotillas (DFs) which, at this time, could consist of over twenty boats, taking a deal of controlling. They were to be superseded in this duty by the emergence of the destroyer-leader, built basically to the same design but with extended accommodation for a Captain (D) and staff.

On 5th August 1914, the second day of hostilities, sixteen Is of the 1st DF, led by *Fearless*, followed by the 3rd DF of fifteen Ls and the *Amphion*, swept up the Dutch coast, supported by three Bacchantes of the 7th CS. In the sea war's first incident, the enemy auxiliary minelayer *Konigin Luise* was sunk beyond the Outer Gabbard. Unwisely returning along the same track the following morning the British force ran into the minefield laid by their erstwhile victim, losing *Amphion*, together with most of the enemy survivors aboard. With their lighter draught, the destroyers escaped without damage.

Meanwhile, in the Mediterranean, the *Goeben* and *Breslau* made their erratic way eastward toward Turkish waters, dogged by a British squadron with a singular lack of purpose. An exception was the light cruiser *Gloucester* whose captain, Kelly, knew his duty and pursued it to the letter, worrying at the heels of his infinitely superior opponents in a classic track-and-report operation until he sadly observed them enter safe neutral waters, unscathed.

The Mediterranean was regarded very much as a French lake, this ally's aims being to maintain defensive forces on her north and west coasts and to establish domination in the south. Cooperation was to prove lukewarm, the French seemingly as concerned with rivalries with their Italian allies as with containing and defeating the not-inconsiderable Austro-Hungarian fleet in the Adriatic. Always keen on the armoured cruiser, with its possibilities in war against commerce, France had no less than eighteen (together with fourteen protected cruisers) at the outbreak of war.

Most modern were the pair of 14,000-ton Edgar Quinets, whose construction was to be paralleled by the first British battle cruisers in 1906. Correctly recognising the latter as the utimate antidote, the French built no more Quinets, although they were themselves formidable ships with fourteen 194 mm (7·64-inch) and eighteen 65 mm (2·56-inch) guns. Paradoxically these ships, designed for commerce destruction, found themselves devoted to an unexciting war of commerce protection. Indeed, French naval direction lacked flair throughout the war and the British contingent, urgently needed elsewhere, found itself with such major tasks as the bulk of the Otranto blockade.

The first major encounter of the sea war was on 28th August in the Heligoland Bight. British submarines had rapidly

HMS *Arethusa* accompanies the Harwich boats to sea in 1914. She was to be mined in 1916. Notice the rakish lines and mixed armament. Adjacent to the single 6-inch guns fore and aft are pill-box-like armoured conns.

established that this sensitive area was regularly patrolled by enemy destroyers, supported by light cruisers, covering minesweeping forces. Superficially secure with the heavy ship anchorages within easy reach, the German position was weakened by bars across the estuaries which inhibited forays by major units except when the tide was right. Thirty-one destroyers of the 1st and 3rd flotillas (the latter now led by *Arethusa*) appeared at first light off Heligoland and swept westward, supported further out by two battle cruisers from the Humber force. Jellicoe, the C-in-C, concerned lest the High Seas Fleet appear in force, ordered Goodenough's six Towns and three of Beatty's battle cruisers to rendezvous with them. Unfortunately, in an early instance of poor Royal Navy communications, the light forces were not informed and Goodenough was lucky not to be summarily mauled by his own compatriots as he appeared out of the dawn. In addition, poor radio discipline warned the enemy of the impending operation and the Germans withdrew all except a few decoy ships whose task was to fall back, luring the British into ambush.

Thus, just before 07.00 on a fine but misty August morning, the whole pack romped joyfully in full cry after a few scattered Germans under the very guns of Heligoland until they were called off to the west. In the uncertain visibility, it soon became apparent that a larger-than-usual number of hostile light cruisers were afield. They were soon pressing *Arethusa* hard; damaged, she was saved only by Goodenough's timely arrival but had already sent a call for Beatty's help. *Fearless* and her group arrived first at the scene but a torpedo attack on the *Mainz* was broken up in disorder by the latter's rapid and accurate fire. With two further enemy cruisers arriving, the British position looked critical when, *deus ex machina*, Beatty's battle cruisers loomed out of the mists. *Köln* was shattered by only two salvoes and *Ariadne* suffered a like fate. *Mainz*, damaged, was finished off by the Towns and the first real trial of strength went to the British, with the heavy enemy support still firmly locked in the Jade by lack of water.

It could easily have gone the other way. *Arethusa* was probably saved by the extra weight of her 6-inch projectiles and by her consorts' spirited defence. British communications were poor and tactical control of the mêlee non-existent. Beatty and his battle cruisers emerged national heroes; his decision to go in was correct, but courageous in view of the many torpedoes running almost indiscriminately. That the enemy light cruisers were overwhelmed by major calibre gunfire at close range was not surprising, but the action also showed the toughness of the British cruiser: *Arethusa* was hit by over thirty enemy shells of 4·1-inch calibre. Her 3-inch high-tensile side armour was hit nine times but penetrated only three, and then only by the caps of shells which had exploded in the belt.

Another early British success was the sinking of the 14,349 grt. liner *Kaiser Wilhelm der Grosse*. This old NDL flyer had gained the Atlantic Blue Riband as far back as 1897 and together with several running mates, was converted into one of the most unlikely auxiliary cruisers ever. Prodigious in her demands for coal, she had accounted for only four merchantmen when she was tracked down by the little *Highflyer* of the 9th CS. Caught refuelling in neutral waters off Spanish Rio de Oro, her commander chose to fight but was summarily sent to the bottom in shallow water. For want of supplies the slightly larger *Kronprinz Wilhelm* sought internment in April 1915.

A distinction should perhaps be drawn between the German commerce raider and the British AMC. Although both were drawn from the ranks of newly-superfluous liners, the German ships largely retained their regular crews, stiffened by a mixture of naval personnel. British units, on the other hand, were usually commissioned into the Royal Navy, manned by reservists and used either for blockade purposes or long range patrol duties. Occasionally they met, as when (in September 1914) the ex-Cunarder *Carmania* was supporting Stoddart's regular cruisers in the South Atlantic in search of the enemy light cruisers *Dresden* and *Leipzig*, known to be heading south to join von Spee's squadron, then crossing the Pacific. In a routine check of the lonely island of Trinidada, some 750 miles off the Brazilian coast, *Carmania* surprised the raider *Cap Trafalgar*, a late Hamburg-Sud liner that had slipped out of the Plate estuary and had been armed at sea. Believed to be on her way to join the NDL ships, *Cap Trafalgar* immediately got under weigh but the British ship had the legs of her. Though carrying eight 4·7-inch weapons – these were easily outranged by the German's pair of 4·1's – *Carmania*'s captain closed the range down to 3,000 yards to redress the difference, overdoing it to the extent that both ships were soon well afire. Badly holed and obviously settling, *Cap Trafalgar* broke off the action, with *Carmania* unable to follow because of her need to keep stern to wind to contain her fires. Although the enemy sank, it was something of a Pyrrhic victory, for the British ship was too badly damaged even to rescue survivors and was fortunate eventually to reach safety.

The following month, however, there emerged a new and underestimated foe, the submarine. As already noted, the old Bacchantes of the 7th CS formed a North Sea squadron and, although their aged frames and 21-knot speed had proved inadequate to support the fast flotilla forces as intended, they had shown a capacity for staying at sea in weather that drove the lighter ships to shelter. Early on 22nd September, *Aboukir*, *Cressy* and *Hogue* were thirty miles off the Dutch coast, patrolling the approaches to the strategically important Dover Straits. A sudden explosion stopped the first-named. Suspecting mines, *Hogue* approached cautiously, only to be hit by two further torpedoes from Weddigen's U9 which actually broke surface during the attack. In spite of this *Cressy* stopped and put over all her boats, only to take two torpedoes herself. All three sank, with a loss of over 1,400 lives

HMS Cressy, nameship of a group of six armoured cruisers completed 1899–1901. Together with *Aboukir* and *Hogue*, she was sunk by a German U-boat shortly after the outbreak of war. Note the complexities of the vacated anchor stowage below the forward 9·2.

HMS *Grafton*, a 1st Class protected cruiser of the Edgar class, as bulged for service during the Dardenelles campaign. Note how the sounding and stripping pipework has been led externally up the hull and protected by plating. The structure on the sternhead is a gallows for sweeping the comprehensive A/S net system laid by the Turks.

– a brutal warning that this was a new kind of war.

The lesson was underlined only a few weeks later when *U9* tangled with the 10th CS of the Northern Patrol. In contravention of standing orders in the face of the growing submarine threat, *Endymion* and *Hawke* hove-to to pass mails. When scarcely under weigh again the latter was sunk by a single torpedo. Within a few days the *Highflyer*'s sister, *Hermes*, was sunk by the *U27* off Calais; converted to operate seaplanes, her loss was a set-back to the introduction of aviation at sea.

Early on 3rd November 1914 the gunboat *Halcyon* was off the Norfolk coast when suddenly fired upon by a powerful German squadron that appeared out of the dawn mists. Three of Hipper's battle cruisers, accompanied by the hybrid *Blücher* and three light cruisers, had crossed the North Sea at high speed and achieved complete surprise. As though daunted by their own success, they then behaved with extraordinary indecision, putting a few shells into the beach near Yarmouth before pulling out after only half an hour when they found themselves faced by only two destroyers. Rapid reaction by Beatty could have put his battle cruisers across the enemy line of retreat, but the sheer ineptness of the affair convinced the British High Command that it was only a feint and that the main attack was to fall elsewhere; Beatty stayed his hand and left Tyrwhitt's Harwich force of light cruisers and destroyers to deal with the intruders. Although they sighted the enemy, they were not to be drawn and the first of a series of raids, that were very difficult to counter, came to an unsatisfactory conclusion. Public opinion was predictably incensed at the intrusion, but the navy sat tight and waited.

An early enemy casualty of the war had been the *Breslau*'s sister ship, *Magdeburg*, which had been destroyed by Czarist destroyers after stranding during a sweep in the Gulf of Finland. Codebooks were recovered from the wreck and found their way to London, subsequently proving invaluable in the deciphering of intercepted radio traffic. Early warning was thus gained of another projected raid by battle cruisers, although it was not known that this was to be a coat-trailing exercise designed to lure a vengeful British Squadron into an ambush. The enemy, on the other hand, was equally unaware of British intentions. These depended upon Tyrwhitt's light forces getting straight to any reported incident and tracking and reporting the raiders' movements until they were apprehended by Beatty. Should the force prove too much of a handful for the latter, a Grand Fleet battle squadron would be on call from north or south. All hinged on fast initial reactions.

Whilst the precise German target was not known, the English east coast was so hedged by minefields that the safe passage off the Yorkshire coast from Whitby to Flamborough Head looked a likely approach. In the early hours of 16th December 1914 a powerful Grand Fleet force was at sea on the Dogger Bank when its destroyers intercepted those of the enemy. These were soon reinforced by the light cruiser *Hamburg* whose rapid salvoes again proved the answer to flotilla torpedo attacks. The effect of this skirmish was to convince the German commander that the whole of the Grand Fleet was about to fall on him. Apprehensive, he therefore turned for home, nullifying the whole plan and isolating the as yet undetected German raiding squadron ahead.

At 08.00 this force, formidable in its own right, arrived for a synchronised attack by three battle cruisers on the Hartlepools and by two more on Scarborough and Whitby. With the latter was the light cruiser *Kolberg*, whose duty it was to lay mines rapidly off Flamborough Head. Now that the main plan had been disrupted, Hipper quickly carried out his bombardment and turned for home with the British squarely across his path. As luck would have it, the light forces had been left behind in heavy seas and were intercepted by Goodenough's squadron which immediately informed Beatty. Another signal error from the latter called the Towns off the chase; not only was the enemy group not brought to action but Hipper received advance warning and hauled off to the north and safety.

Smarting from this narrow failure and yet more public approbrium resulting from the bombardments, the Admiralty moved Beatty's battle cruisers south to the Forth, closer to the scene of the next expected visitation. Deciphered signals indicated 24th January 1915, when Hipper's ships were to sweep the Dogger Bank clear of both fishing vessels and naval patrols, although the remainder of the High Seas Fleet was to remain in the Jade. Hipper had three battle cruisers, the *Blücher*, four light cruisers and destroyers; Beatty was at full strength with five battle cruisers and four of Goodenough's Towns, and planned to rendezvous with Tyrwhitt's forces behind the enemy, once they had been reported.

Things worked too efficiently; even as Tyrwhitt approached the appointed position, *Aurora* sighted the *Kolberg* and opened fire. In the grey light of morning the gun flashes were visible to Beatty, who steered for them so that Hipper, slightly to the east, was able to turn for home without more ado and with a slight lead. A tail chase developed, with the British light forces snapping at the heels of the German heavy units, whose attached light forces were now safe beyond. Meanwhile Jellicoe was heading south with elements of the Home Fleet to cut the enemy off and things began to look promising. By 09.00, Beatty's *Lion* could range the German back marker, *Blücher*, at 20,000 yards and – absorbing punishment – the German vessel began to lag.

Her compatriots pressed on but, the British having a good margin of speed and calibre, they might still have been caught and annihilated had not *Lion* been hit severely. In falling out of line, she made a couple of highly ambiguous flag signals which resulted in the whole force falling on the hapless *Blücher*, so allowing the remainder to escape. Faulty communications again, coupled with a blind, unquestioning obedience that stifled all initiative wasted yet another opportunity. The enemy had come so close to disaster that it was another fifteen months before they tried again. In April 1916 an overwhelmingly superior force attempting to bombard Lowestoft and Yarmouth allowed itself to be bundled away unceremoniously by Tyrwhitt's aggressively handled Harwich flotillas.

In 1916, with the completion of the *Chester* (an appropriated Greek newbuilding) the Royal Navy took delivery of the last of the long series of Towns and it may be approp-

The little protected cruiser of the Apollo class of 1890–1, obsolete by 1914, became a reserve of 'expendable' ships for various purposes. Seven, including the *Latona*, here seen at Mudros in 1917, became minelayers. Note the mines on rails laid along the waist, passing below the raised poop and terminating at the aperture in the stern.

Town class light cruisers of the Grand Fleet at anchor in Scapa Flow in 1917. The booms for the mooring of the interminable boat traffic between ships can be seen.

riate to compare them with their German counterparts. From the *Liverpool* of 1910 all had been between 446 and 458 feet overall, with standard displacements between 4,800 and 5,440 tons. Their armament had improved progressively from a mixture of two 6-inch and ten 4-inch guns to a homogeneous nine 6-inch in the last units. All were propelled by steam turbines, with between 22,500 and 25,000 hp on four shafts for about 26 knots, though these powers and speeds were often exceeded under war conditions.

Dresden, of 1909, the first German with steam turbines, was followed by the four Augsburgs, 4,350-tonners carrying twelve 4·1-inch guns on a 428 foot hull and capable of 27 knots with 31,000 shp. In contrast, the four Konigsbergs of 1915/16 had grown to nearly 497 feet with a heavier battery of eight 5·9-inchers. Of just under 6,000 tons displacement, they could make 28½ knots

Elegant but useless, *Courageous* alongside Armstrong's fitting-out quay in 1917. 786 feet overall but only 81 feet in the beam, Fisher's 32-knot 'tinclads' were designed to spearhead his ill-starred Baltic campaign. This idea abandoned, these 18,400-ton 'light cruisers' were converted to carriers.

Furious sports just one of the Royal Navy's largest-ever guns, an 18-inch. The forward turret was superseded before completion by a flying-off deck. The later flying-on deck proved unusable, and conversion to a full carrier began in 1921.

with 45,000 shp. Both side's ships carried torpedo tubes; the German's, invariably, also carried mines. Two specialist 4,000-ton cruiser minelayers, *Brummer* and *Bremse*, were completed in 1916, sacrificing armament for a 34-knot speed and a capacity of 360 mines, a concept later copied by the British in the disappointing *Adventure* of 1924.

After the *Arethusa*, Royal Navy ships had the tremendous advantage of oil-firing, using fuel convenient to load and transfer about the ship, and often conferring a speed advantage not apparent from official figures. The Germans' coal bunkers gave them a similar range but much was stowed in highly inaccessible spaces. The British had fewer, but larger boilers requiring greater headroom but smaller area, and they adopted all-centreline armament earlier, allowing comparable broadsides with fewer guns. Spending comparatively greater time in port, with their crews quartered ashore, German cruisers could get by with decidedly inferior accommodation, but the corresponding advantage of more watertight bulkheads was largely negated by too many apertures pierced in them. To reduce overall weight, the German designers tended to include the nickel-steel protection as part of the ship's structure, at the same time reducing the number of frames, a practice denounced by informed British opinion.

The Royal Navy's Towns were followed by the highly successful 'C'-class, whose first group of eight (the Carolines) were really only slightly stretched Arethusas with an extra couple of 4-inch guns. Their 40,000 shp machinery gave them a speed of 29 knots and were the Royal Navy's first geared steam turbine installations. *Caroline* herself was built in only 11 months and her group was followed by the eight Cambrians, similar except for the 'one-thick, one-thin' funnel arrangement, later to become familiar. Fifteen more were to follow before 1918, all of 4,190-tons and carrying five 6-inch guns (whose centreline disposition gave them the same broadside as the Birminghams, with nine) and eight 21-inch torpedo tubes. Very efficient, if wet, many survived to fight in the Second World War.

For years various war games had explored the possibilities of seizing one of the German islands in the event of hostilities, for use as an advance base. Borkum, Heligoland or Sylt were favourites but, with the submarine demonstrating that close blockade was now impracticable, a fourth alternative was championed by no less than the First Sea Lord, Fisher, and by the First Lord of the Admiralty, Churchill. Their aim was the creation of a 600-strong, shallow draught fleet designed to penetrate the Baltic and land a Russian army on Germany's Pomeranian coast, less than 100 miles from Berlin; to secure the line of approach, an Allied army was to hold Schleswig-Holstein. As the Western Front bogged itself into total impasse, the idea gained currency. A wide variety of specialised craft was duly designed for production, some rational, some odd, some preposterous: among the latter was a trio of big-gun 'cruisers' to give offensive and high speed support to the heavy fire of the lumbering monitors. But the dreadful Dardanelles campaign dampened all ardour for similar adventures; the vociferous anti-Baltic lobby carried the day and the project was shelved. Among its legacies were landing craft, monitors and minesweepers, all of which were to prove useful. And the three big-gun cruisers.

Furious, *Glorious* and *Courageous* had a special uselessness subsequently recognised

Origins

Constitution (USA, 52 gun, 1797). Typical of the big American frigates of the war of 1812. Large enough to carry 24-pounder main battery in place of usual 18-pounders.

Opposite,
Calliope (Great Britain, 2,750 tons, 1884). Among the last sailing corvettes built for the Royal Navy, but among the first small all-metal cruisers. Horizontal protection only.

Undaunted (Great Britain, 4,020 tons, 1860). Last of the Royal Navy's wooden screw frigates. At 250 feet on the gundeck, it was 64 feet longer than Nelson's *Victory*.

Opposite
Mercury (Great Britain, 3,750 tons, 1878). Armament and rig limited in favour of speed. Steel-built prototype of the modern cruiser.

Lifting propeller. Early steam warships spent the greater part of their time under sail. To prevent drag, the two-bladed propeller was mounted in a tracked frame which could be raised into the counter. It engaged with the aligned propeller shaft through a simple dog clutch.

Double expansion engine. Later variety with two low-pressure cylinders flanking the high-pressure cylinder, the easier to deal with increasing pressures and expansion ratios. Required less area than earlier horizontal engines but difficult to include below armoured deck.

by the Fleet, to whom they were known as 'Curious', 'Spurious' and 'Outrageous'. Laid down in 1915, they were beautiful ships – nearly 23,000 tons full load displacement, 786 feet overall and capable of 32 knots on the 90,000 shp produced by two sets of the machinery later installed in the 'C'-class cruisers. As Fisher wished them to 'frighten armies, not battleships' they incorporated only 3-inch vertical protection – earning the label 'tinclads' – and a twin 15-inch turret at either end. These four guns were too few to permit rapid ranging by the methods then in use, but were fitted in the latter two ships, being surpassed by *Furious*, which was supposed to carry two single 18-inch weapons, the Navy's largest ever, firing 3,500-pound shells at an impossibly low rate. Although the 15-inch ships were to serve as such until 1924, the unhappy *Furious* was completed as a hybrid aircraft carrier. All three were eventually fully converted to this use.

Much more use was made of the obsolete protected cruisers. *Doris*'s exploits off the Levant coast will be fully described later but worthy campaigns were waged by others, such as *Juno* and *Pyramus* in the rivurine war in Mesopotamia and the Edgars at the Dardanelles. Four of these, displaced on the Northern Patrol by AMC's, were blistered on the waterline as a measure against torpedo attack. Known as 'bulge ships' (the idea was to gain rapid acceptance in most major classes) the Edgars supported the army most ably; standing close inshore to support an advance with a lyddite barrage, or bombarding at long range with extra elevation of the guns by flooding the opposite bulges.

On the last day of May 1916 began the battle of Jutland, which could have decided the whole course of the war. Why it did not has since been the subject of many an essay, but it certainly profoundly affected the use of the cruiser as a fleet unit. The German C-in-C, Scheer, had evolved a bombardment and ambush plan similar to others before it. When its execution was frustrated by the weather, he used Hipper's battle cruisers as a decoy off the Norwegian coast, with the full High Seas Fleet well out of sight astern. As usual, the British were well aware of an impending movement and Beatty was at sea on the 30th, supported by the splendid new Queen Elizabeths of the 5th BS under Evan-Thomas, steering for a rendezvous with Jellicoe's main force in the general area west of the Skagerrak.

Twelve light cruisers of the 1st, 2nd and 3rd LCS were paired in line abeam across Beatty's bows and the far eastern ship, *Galatea*, sighted a small merchantman, stationary and blowing steam. Closing with the *Phaeton*, she discovered enemy destroyers were present, together with light cruisers of Hipper's left wing.

At 14.20 *Galatea* flashed 'Enemy in sight' and Beatty responded immediately. Unfortunately, he was supported only by Goodenough's 2nd LCS, the 1st and 3rd having been lured away by *Galatea*'s reports. The battle cruisers were supposed to be the main fleet's advance guard, guiding them in to the enemy force; the light cruisers should have formed the tip of this nerve end, also supporting any destroyer torpedo attack on the enemy line and breaking up any similar essay on their part.

Hipper, believing the British battle cruisers to be unsupported, fell back to lure them on to Scheer, and a long run to the south developed with the 5th BS striving to catch up. Despite losing two ships to disastrous explosions, Beatty hung on until Goodenough gave warning of the approach of the HSF. To lead them on to the full force of the Grand Fleet, Beatty turned back, knowing that he must, in his turn, prevent Hipper sighting Jellicoe and warning Scheer. On a day when British communications standards reached a new low, the 2nd LCF of *Southampton* and three consorts proved the exception, bearing a charmed life as they probed the enemy again and again, sending a steady stream of situation reports and surviving the risks by steering for the splash of the last enemy salvo.

But if the light cruiser was to win its spurs here, the armoured cruiser was to meet disaster. Nine were building at the time of the battle cruiser's introduction and completed between 1906 and 1908; of these, eight were present at Jutland as the 1st and 2nd CS, deployed so as to support their own light cruisers in their reconnaissance duties or to frustrate like attempts on the part of the enemy.

The senior officer of the 1st CS was Rear Admiral Sir Robert Arbuthnot, whose urge to engage the enemy bordered on the reckless. Having closed Goodenough's ships in the general fleet action that followed the battle cruiser action, he engaged the already shattered enemy light cruiser *Wiesbaden* and then sighted her three consorts of Boedicker's 2nd Scouting Group. Led by the *Defence*, the four armoured cruisers tore across the bows of Beatty's *Lion* and into the murk of mist and gunsmoke beyond. They emerged suddenly to find themselves only 8,000 yards from the enemy line. Arbuthnot perished with his whole crew as *Defence* erupted under the concentrated fire of at least five battleships; *Warrior* was so mauled

HMS *Southampton*, here coaling, wore the broad pennant of Commodore Goodenough through some of the sternest tests of the war. The pinnace blends into the vivid dazzle scheme.

that she sank the following day. *Black Prince*, although damaged, held on, only to get mixed in the mêlée resulting when British light forces blundered into the Germans retiring later during the night. Well practiced in night fighting, the High Seas Fleet dealt harshly with its assailants. One victim was *Black Prince*, caught suddenly in a web of searchlights and shattered by a dozen broadsides in a scene to be re-enacted almost a quarter century later at Matapan.

Whatever Jutland did or did not achieve, it marked the virtual end of both armoured and battle cruisers. Each had suffered badly from over-zealous commanders involving them in situations for which they were not designed, but the battle disproved the raison d'être of neither. After Jutland, the battle cruiser was still perfectly capable of dealing with the armoured cruiser, while the latter was still an excellent ship for use on the trade routes. Only a few of either class were to be built again, however.

The cruiser also played its part in the development of aviation at sea. In 1913, the *Hermes* had been equipped to operate three seaplanes as headquarters ship for the naval wing, but after exercising with the fleet in that year she was placed in reserve, reactivated for the war, and quickly lost. The launching and recovery of seaplanes meant the parent ship heaving-to, an increasingly unhealthy pursuit as submarine commanders gained experience, and always totally dependent upon calm weather. In addition, the performance of the early seaplane was so limited that it had little hope of catching the Zeppelins that it was supposed to destroy. At Jutland, the first time aircraft were used in a sea battle, their impact was negligible but their promise was such that several policy decisions resulted. One was to put higher-performance wheeled aircraft on to light cruisers. Mounted on an axially-aligned platform forward of the bridge, an aircraft such as the Sopwith Pup could rise easily if the ship steamed rapidly into the wind. That of the *Yarmouth* destroyed the airship *L23* off the Danish coast in August 1917, but that was something of an exception.

Aircraft recovery depended upon 'ditching' alongside ship, relying on floatation bags to keep afloat, but many of them were lost. In an effort to improve the situation, the *Cavendish* – renamed *Vindictive* – was rebuilt along similar lines to the Furious, with a separate flight deck at either end, but

One of the four Weymouths of 1910–11, the *Yarmouth* was equipped with a flying-off platform forward. The ship steamed fast into the wind to enable the non-retrievable Sopwith Pup to rise almost vertically and meet the threat posed by enemy Zeppelins.

Development of the Armoured Cruiser

Northampton (Great Britain, 7,600 tons, 1878). Central citadel ship with high freeboard. More battleship than cruiser.

Nisshin (Japan, 7,300 tons, 1899). One of a successful Italian-built series. Symmetrical layout with optional armaments.

Imperieuse (Great Britain, 8,500 tons, 1883). Last armoured ship designed for sailing. French-style armament layout and tumble-home.

Bacchante class (Great Britain, 12,000 tons, 1899). Development of Diadem class protected cruiser, with battleship-style protection.

Pennsylvania class (USA, 13,700 tons, 1903). Contemporary battleship design, reduced in protection and armament but lengthened for higher power and speed.

Below
Minotaur class (Great Britain, 14,600 tons, 1906). Final expression of the British armoured cruiser before introduction of the battlecruiser.

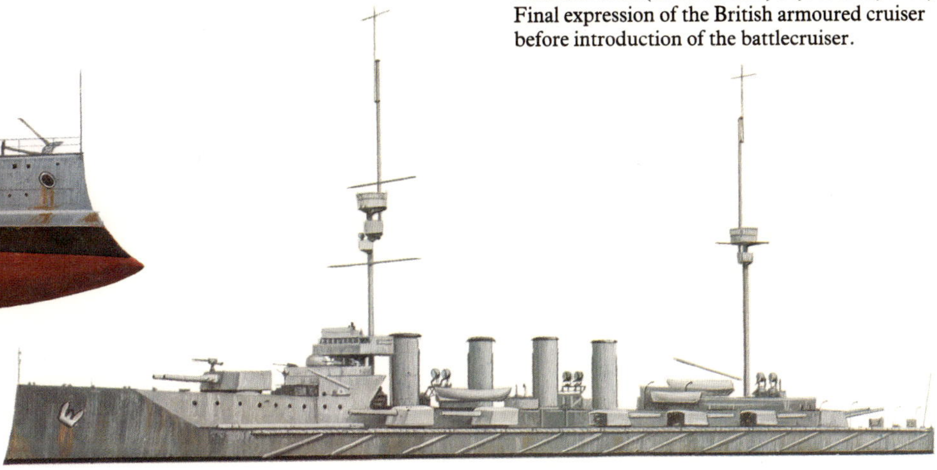

Waldeck Rousseau class (France, 14,000 tons [f.l.], 1910). Ultimate French armoured cruisers. Being post-Dreadnought, had homogeneous main armament.

Below
Scharnhorst (Germany, 11,400 tons, 1906). Smaller than contemporary British equivalents but better protected by virtue of reduction in gun calibre.

Deutschland class (Germany, 11,700 tons, 1931). The armoured cruiser revisited. Not significantly heavier than *Scharnhorst*, but of far larger dimensions and greater hitting power.

was equally unsuccessful.

Meanwhile, the last group of the Cs incorporated the sharply sheered 'trawler bow' to improve their seakeeping, a design later paralleled by the ten Ds. These, the Danaes and Delhis, were about 20 feet longer, incorporating an extra single gun and twelve 21-inch torpedo tubes in triple mountings. Their 40,000 shp was then doubled for the E-type which increased displacement from the Ds 4,650 tons to over 7,500. Beyond boasting a near-destroyer speed of 33 knots and an incredible sixteen torpedo tubes, their capabilities were not increased (except for *Enterprise* mounting an experimental twin gunhouse) and their exact function was hard to define. Only two of a planned three were completed; very distinctive in appearance, with a third funnel set well back from the forward pair, they incorporated an aircraft as a permanent item on a rather primitive rotating catapult.

The last extension of the basic type resulted in the five Effinghams, all of which, except for *Cavendish* and *Hawkins*, were completed after the war. Although extremely imposing ships of nearly 10,000 tons, their 600-foot hulls still contrived to look lean and fast, their rangy appearance nicely complemented by a pair of large, raked funnels, typically 'pusser' in their unequal diameters. There armament was seven 7·5-inch guns in single, handworked mountings, their shells the heaviest that could be hand loaded. They were later exchanged for 6-inch weapons.

In April 1917, Britain's fortunes were at their lowest ebb, ashore and at sea, where the still un-convoyed merchantmen were being slaughtered by the U-boats. The entry of the United States into the war at this point was to prove decisive militarily, but their impact at sea was less pronounced, though invaluable in the provision of escorts, the laying of mine barrages and the allocation of a squadron of Dreadnoughts to assist the Grand Fleet in the great maritime Armageddon that never came.

The US Navy was not particularly well equipped with cruisers, possessing ten armoured cruisers of the Pennsylvania and Tennessee classes of 1905–8, three St. Louis-class protected cruisers of 1905–6, six Denver class small protected cruisers and three Chester class scouts of 1905–6. Authorised but barely commenced were the useful ten-strong Omaha class light cruisers, 7,000-tonners capable of 34 knots and carrying twelve 6-inch guns.

Barely eleven weeks after Jutland, the High Seas Fleet again came out in force in an operation of the time-honoured sort, this time against Sunderland. Understandable caution on both sides resulted in mutual indecision and it was the submarines that made their mark. Two of the British Towns, *Falmouth* and *Nottingham* were lost, the former to four torpedoes, the latter to three, again demonstrating the toughness of the little ships. Jellicoe's criticisms, a few weeks later, of two British torpedoes failing to sink the German *München* are rather hard to justify.

After Jutland, the increasingly air-minded Jellicoe was of the opinion that one Zeppelin, in suitable weather, was worth 'a good many light cruisers' for observation. British airships, however, had never really been accepted because of their poor endurance and, lacking suitable flight decks, the

The 4,000-ton German mine-laying cruiser *Brummer* of 1916. The mainmast could, reputedly, be lowered to enable the ship to pass as a British Arethusa, though the resemblance was not close.

Before there were ship-borne aircraft, the kite balloon was used to spot the fall of shot and observe enemy movement. *Glorious*'s after turret is trained on the port beam, and three of her unusual triple 4-inch mounts are visible.

Navy still had a very real use for both cruisers and towed kite balloons. The US Navy's London representative, Rear Admiral William Sims, took great note of the Royal Navy's pioneering work and caused his policy-makers to become quite adventurous in plans for seaborne aviation. Most were nullified by the obviously approaching end to hostilities, but some ideas survived, such as the conversion of fast cruiser hulls to small carriers, designed to operate with conventional aircraft to increase their efficacy.

In November 1916, Beatty replaced Jellicoe as C-in-C Grand Fleet, in a rather controversial appointment, but the greatly desired 'final solution' to the High Seas Fleet never materialised and the maritime war seemed to lose its momentum. The Navy was still busy, but the advent of the convoy and adequate escorts reduced its other major adversary, the U-boat, to just another problem. Nevertheless, the anti-convoy lobby must have derived considerable satisfaction from the near-annihilation (in October 1917) of a Shetland-Norway convoy by the German minelaying cruisers *Brummer* and *Bremse*, whose approach had been made the easier by their similarity in appearance to the British Arethusa-class. Fearing a rapid British reaction, the German ships acted with considerable brutality resulting in the route being policed by a force of armoured cruisers. As if to underline the uselessness of these tactics compared with a dedicated close-escort, a second convoy was similarly dealt with by enemy destroyers, despite the fact that the patrol group was under sixty miles distant.

In the Mediterranean, things were comparatively quiet, which was fortunate, for the Royal Navy rarely succeeded in securing agreed co-operation from its French and Italian allies and, except for a few joint skirmishes against the Austro-Hungarians in the Adriatic, acted almost alone.

November 1917 saw an attempt to repeat the success of the Heligoland Bight action

The Armoured Cruiser

Drake class armoured cruiser (Great Britain, 14,000 tons, 1901). Dignified ships with great presence, this type of armoured cruiser, with two large guns and a powerful secondary armament in doubled casemates, was rendered obsolescent by later classes with far heavier main calibre batteries. In turn, both were to be made totally obsolete by the arrival of the battlecruiser, and did badly in front-line operations during the First World War. Note in the half-section how the bunkers add to the sloping protective deck, and how the casemate idea echoes the layout of centuries of broadside ships.

with the 'heavies' represented by the 1st CS of the 15-inch *Glorious* and *Courageous*, supported by the new battle cruiser *Repulse*. Four enemy light cruisers were duly surprised but skilfully used both smoke and a feint torpedo attack (*cf Vian* at Second Sirte in the Second World War) not only to extricate themselves, but also to outclass their bigger adversaries with rapid 5·9-inch fire. The 'tinclad' was hopelessly discredited.

By the close of hostilities in 1918 the cruiser contingent of the Royal Navy bore little resemblance to that of only four years before. Only one squadron of armoured cruisers – now increasingly referred to as 'heavy cruisers' – remained but there were now eight light cruiser squadrons. Such other large cruisers as remained were stationed largely in the North America and West Indies Squadron, while the still-plentiful protected cruisers were organised in strategically placed groups in world wide low-hazard zones. Although the fleet was never to get a second chance of a final show-down it beat its enemy by the time-honoured principle of blockade, now conducted at a respectable distance. Deprived of essentials, the German population grew restive: starved of war material and now faced by the Americans, its armies faced a war with no hope of victory. Its superb fleet, still largely 'in being', was devoured by the very factor that had ensured its survival – inactivity. Shaken by revolution, its discipline failed and it degenerated into nothing but a collection of ships whose final, unworthy fate was internment in Scapa Flow after the Armistice, and whose shame was expunged in true Wagnerian fashion by mass immolation on 21st June 1919. They deserved better.

The freebooting cruiser – *Doris* in the Levant

When, on 30th October, 1914, Turkey formally entered the war on the side of the Central Powers, it came as no surprise. From the ruins of the Ottoman Empire, with all its corruption and inefficiency, the new order, symbolised by the Young Turks, was dedicated to the creation of a modern state. German assistance was sought as the very antithesis of earlier Turkish national failings and it was gladly given, both to extend their own influence and to counter the common potential enemy in Russia.

British influence in the area had been weakened by its close identification with the old, discredited regime; it also represented tradition at a time when progress was everything. Britain was still the source of the world's best fighting ships, however, and since producing the *Dreadnought* of 1906, had experienced difficulty in keeping pace with foreign orders and no fleet considered itself reckonable without one. Turkey had two ships under construction in the UK: one, the 23,000-ton super-Dreadnought *Reshadieh*, had been laid down in August 1911; the other had been purchased on the stocks from the near-bankrupt Brazilian government and renamed *Sultan Osman I*.

With war obviously drawing close the British Government decided to appropriate the majority of those warships building to foreign account, at a stroke strengthening the Royal Navy and also preventing such ships finding their way into potentially hostile hands. Turkish public opinion was inflamed by the loss of their ships, for much of the capital had been raised by popular subscription. Their new allies saw their chance and clandestinely agreed to transfer the new battle cruiser *Goeben* and the light cruiser *Breslau* to offset the loss, which was one of the largest single influences on Turkish actions at that time.

The successful delivery by sea of the two ships at the very outbreak of war resulted in a Royal Naval court-martial and considerable augmentation of the small Turkish fleet. Franco-British forces in the Mediterranean were quite extensive at the time, however, and the Austro-Hungarian fleet was rapidly bottled-up in the Adriatic, while the Turks were equally effectively confined beyond the defences of the Dardanelles. In the eastern end of the Mediterranean, a British area of responsibility, there was no stagnation and the Turks were soon being probed by submarines out of the advanced base at Tenedos.

Not that the Turks were quiescent; having control of the whole Levant coast, down through present-day Syria, Lebanon and Israel to a point beyond Gaza, they had only to use part of their considerable army in a swift move across the top of Sinai to reach the Suez Canal. Understandably, this area was particularly sensitive to the British and the local senior officer, Vice Admiral Pierce, sought to establish the enemy's intentions by sending a couple of light cruisers up the coast.

Thus it was that Captain Larken of the *Doris*, engaged in pounding a November beat in the Western Approaches, received a welcome signal to proceed with some urgency to the warmer climes of Alexandria. Launched in 1896, *Doris* was one of the nine-strong *Eclipse* second-class cruisers, carrying five 6-inch guns with three single 4·7s on either side in the waist. Of only 5,600 tons displacement she was small enough to penetrate close inshore and had an enthusiastic crew whose spirit reflected very much the character of Larken himself.

The other ship involved was the Russian light cruiser *Askold*, remarkable for her five spindly funnels which, inevitably, made her known as the 'Packet of Woodbines'. Early in December 1914, she was sent north to the Gulf of Alexandretta (now Iskenderun), leaving *Doris* to the job of patrolling Port Said's approaches. In addition, the latter embarked a French seaplane and crew for the reconnoitering of the hundred-odd miles of waste separating the Canal from the Turkish forward positions. A couple of sorties produced little result and fresh instructions were given to proceed up the coast, observing and causing the enemy the maximum of discomfiture, a virtual carte blanche almost unknown since the end of the sailing navy.

On 15th December, the little cruiser was off Askalon, having flown off the seaplane to look at Beersheba, about thirty miles inland. Whilst its return was awaited, a new earthwork was noticed ashore, together with obvious signs of 'the military'. A few rounds of 6-inch dispersed the latter and Larken set the tone for future events by ordering away a landing party to demolish the position and see what was to be seen. This proved to be little, but when the enemy rallied to bring the shore party under small arms fire the *Doris*, now only a half-mile from the beach, dissuaded them with a few more rounds of lyddite.

Having recovered the seaplane, Larken moved 30 miles north overnight to Jaffa (now a suburb of Tel Aviv). Again the seaplane took off, was duly fired at from the town, created a measure of panic among the populus, but reported nothing of real note.

By the 17th, the *Doris* had reached Haifa, cruising leisurely through waters as yet untroubled by submarines. Far and wide, over country peppered with names familiar from the Bible, the seaplane roamed, reporting little military activity. This, of course, was good news to the military authorities responsible for the defence of the Canal but scarcely exciting stuff to Larken and his crew. That same afternoon, *Doris* spoke with the *Askold*, sighted steaming southward; she had been to the very entrance of the Gulf but had been forbidden to enter owing to the belief that it had been mined. On passage, she had taken three enemy merchantmen, which accounted for the British finding the sea as lacking in interest as the land.

From Haifa northward for about 150 miles to a point beyond Tripoli, both main road and railway hug the coast; at a point near Sidon, another party from the *Doris* went ashore to feel out the ground. Although observed, they were not disturbed as they amused themselves destroying all posts and telegraph lines over several miles. Results, nevertheless, had not been particularly positive and *Doris* was half way up the coast when, on the afternoon of the 18th December, an Italian cargo-passenger ship was stopped. She had just left Alexandretta and reported that it was a hive of Turkish activity. As a railhead, it was receiving all manner of stores, equipment and personnel for onward transit by road to Aleppo which was, significantly, linked to the southern front by rail. Of great interest, in view of the Turkish designs on the Canal, was the

The Eclipse class cruiser *Doris*, whose name was to become associated with her exploits on the Turkish Levant coast in the early years of the war. Note the barrels of the four 6-inch guns in the port waist trained out on the beam.

Scouts

Foresight (Great Britain, 2,900 tons, 1905). Of a type designed to work with destroyers and rather like them in appearance. Note bows are a 'ram' only in shape and large proportion of hull dedicated to machinery.

Attentive (Great Britain, 2,650 tons, 1905). Built to near-identical specification as *Foresight* but by different builder. Note variations.

Quarto class (Italy, 3,500 tons, 1912). Compared well on paper in both speed and armament with both British and German designs, but proved unsuitable to conditions in practice.

Yubari (Japan, 2,900 tons, 1923). Experimental 'one-off' with powerful armament on limited displacement. Influential construction techniques.

Kitakami (Japan, 5,850 tons, 1920). Shown as rearmed in 1941 as Torpedo Cruiser, carrying ten quadruple 24-inch mountings, the most powerful ever carried.

Omaha class (USA, 7,050 tons, 1920). Large size due to oceanic requirements on either American seaboard.

Capitani Romani class (Italy, 3,750 tons, 1942). Fast and heavily armed; if class had ever been completed it would have posed a grave threat to Mediterranean convoys.

Of the four pairs of British Scouts of 1904, only two from the Elswich yard had four funnels, the remainder three. The dazzle painting of *Adventure* gives her something of the appearance of a 'Town', though the 12-pounder looks its size.

report that his material included boats in sections. Like the *Askold*'s captain before him, Larken had been instructed not to brave the suspected mines in the Gulf, but he reasoned that as the Italian ship had just moved without hindrance, it was worth an attempt. His C-in-C agreed with this argument, an added incentive being that Alexandretta was being proposed as an alternative or complementary site to the Dardanelles for a major landing.

Tucked away in the far north-eastern corner of the Mediterranean, the Gulf is roughly rectangular in shape, about forty miles deep with an entrance some twenty miles wide, having also a good depth of water. For the greater part of its periphery, the shore is steep-to, with arid mountains sculpted by a myriad of fast-flowing streams into a series of deep ravines, plunging down to the sea from heights over 5,000 feet. This formidable terrain caused both vital communication links, road and rail, to follow the coast from the town of Alexandretta to the head of the Gulf. It was to cut these links that *Doris* slipped unseen past the town in the early hours of the 19th, closing the shore about ten miles beyond, near the exotically-named Jonah's Pillar, where both targets were vulnerable where they had to cross one of the many ravines by a bridge.

Under the cover of almost total darkness a party from the ship rowed ashore in the best traditions of the 'brethren of the coast', with blackened faces, muffled oars *et al.* The railway line and telegraph were soon cut without incident and the culprits went back on aboard and waited. Barely an hour later, to everybody's delight, a trainload of camels was impressively derailed. *Doris* moved northward and in the gathering light of morning came the cheering sight of a second train, proceeding in the same direction as the first. Forced to stop by the blockage, it was discouraged from going back by a couple of 12-pounder projectiles into the locomotive and Larken then moved along the coast to complete the job by demolishing the next bridge to the north. Although considerably chipped, however, its tough concrete proved equal even to 6-inch fire, and awakening interest ashore meant that a landing would not be feasible.

However, having made his presence felt, Larken appeared off the town itself and sent an ultimatum to the military governor to hand over all British internees who had been caught by the declaration of war, and to surrender all military stores for destruction, on pain of bombardment of the town's official buildings. Playing for time, the Turks demanded twenty-four hours to consider the demand and the cruiser spent an uncomfortable night, anchored in deteriorating weather and with her searchlights playing over the town. Next morning the ship's cutter was sent ashore for a reply, coming back with the American Acting Vice-Consul to act as go-between. He emphasised the gravity of the reply he then brought; for every Turk killed by bombardment, 500 Britons would be shot in Damascus.

Larken stood his ground, pointing out that, whereas the port was a legitimate military target, British civilians were not, and the perpetrators would be held personally responsible, sought out and punished. A further day was given for reconsideration.

This time was filled constructively as it had been observed that a locomotive had taken advantage of the parleying by slipping over the damaged northern bridge and recovering the second train. So an eighty-strong party went ashore under a certain amount of enemy fire but, covered by the full weight of *Doris*' armament, they managed to remove one span of the stubborn bridge with a charge of gun-cotton. One reward for their success was the acquisition of the Armenian staff of an adjacent halt, who pleaded to be taken prisoner on the grounds that the Turks would execute them for allowing a bridge to be destroyed.

During the forenoon of the 22nd, Larken returned to Alexandretta for the enemy's answer, waiting with some concern, for there could now be no going back. Again the US diplomat was the bearer when it came, and he offered a way out of the impasse. All military material had been rapidly spirited away by the Governor, bar two locomotives which were offered for sacrifice. Their destruction would obviously save honour for both sides and the offer was accepted.

Unfortunately, Turkish protocol demanded that they do the job themselves and would the British please send some dynamite? No, said Larken, the job must be done properly by his own men. Turkish intransigence. Further threat of bombardment, and then explanations were given that dynamite was not carried on the ship and that the guncotton which was required needed expert handling. This resolved the crisis and the British were given permission to lay the charges, but not to fire them; only Turks could destroy Turkish property. More anxious consultation followed, with the American as go-between, resulting in the brilliant solution of creating the *Doris*' torpedo-lieutenant an honorary Turkish officer for the day.

The locomotives in question proved to be out of steam, and vast simulated exertions by the military failed to move them. 'Move them' said Larken wearily, and soon afterwards the first pulled out of its shed – and kept going, straight through the town and away to the north. More threats of bombardment resulted in a unit of Turkish cavalry being sent to escort it back and it was late in the day before it was duly destroyed. *Doris*' searchlights were again on before the second joined it in oblivion. Honour was satisfied.

At first light the following morning, another bridge near Jonah's Pillar was destroyed by gunfire from *Doris* and Larken then crossed the Gulf to investigate reports of an immobilised German merchantman. Sure enough, in the desolate Ayas Bay, surrounded by swamp and lagoon, lay the new *Odessa* of the Deutsche-Levant Line, carefully sunk on a sandy bottom in only 15 feet of water, ready for salvage at a later date. Even with her modest 20-foot draught, *Doris* was unable to enter the lagoon, and had to silence an enemy field gun in order to send in her motorboat to investigate. As salvage would have required at least 72 hours, the freighter was destroyed and the cruiser carried on to reconnoitre Mersin (Icel), from whence she was recalled to Alexandria.

Although the materially-minded might question whether these comparatively minor results justified the cruiser's time, the value of *Doris*'s unorthodox patrol undoubtedly lay in the tremendous moral ascendency it established over a new enemy from the very outset. One small ship, appearing at will and without warning, maintained a psychological presence out of all proportion to her size, and the enemy never dared to use this most convenient coastal shipping route thereafter. Although the Royal Navy (and later the French) maintained a presence, the area will always be known as Larken's patch.

The marauding cruiser – *Emden* in the Indian Ocean

Imperial Germany had, by 1914, begun to emulate Great Britain in the use of sea power as a means of territorial acquisition and influence. Although the world was already largely parcelled up by the major colonial powers, German interests were gained in Africa, the Pacific and China, the latter being held to justify a naval presence in the Far East based on Tsingtau, an excellent port about 150 miles south of the Royal Navy's northern base of Wei-hai-wei. Though the latter was isolated, some 500 miles north of Shanghai and the Yangtse entrance and 1,300 miles from the main base at Hong Kong, the Germans were truly alone, and half a world distant from major facilities. Their not inconsiderable East Asiatic Squadron was under the able command of Vice-Admiral Graf von Spee in the *Scharnhorst* which, with her sister *Gneisenau*, was a modern armoured cruiser bearing eight 8·2-inch and six 5·9-inch guns. At 11,400 tons and capable of 23 knots, they were well protected and accompanied by three 3,400-ton light cruisers, *Emden*, *Leipzig* and *Nurnberg*, all of recent construction and each armed with ten 4·1s. The squadron had been worked-up over two years into a very efficient force.

On paper, the corresponding Royal Navy representation was weak, with the C-in-C, Vice-Admiral Jerram, wearing his flag in the armoured cruiser *Minotaur*. In support he had the belted cruiser *Hampshire* (later to gain fame by being sunk with Lord Kitchener aboard) and the light cruisers *Yarmouth* and *Newcastle*. A pre-Dreadnought battleship, *Triumph*, lay unmobilised at Hong Kong. British lack of material strength was offset greatly by a network of interests throughout the area which provided a ready-made intelligence system. Commonwealth naval forces were also available and France kept a small squadron in the Pacific. Russia and Japan could also be relied upon for a measure of assistance.

Jerram had warning of impending hostilities a week before the event and set about reactiviating *Triumph* and making dispositions, although the latter were not simplified by the fact that von Spee's ships were widely dispersed, with only *Emden* at Tsingtau. Both his major units were, in fact, at Ponape in the Eastern Carolines, to be joined there by *Nurnberg* from the US West Coast where *Leipzig* was to remain for the time being.

Von Spee assessed, correctly, that Tsingtau would be attacked immediately in the event of war, *Emden* being under orders to pull out without delay. She did so on 6th August, 1914, joining the flag with the force's colliers at Pagan on the 12th. This breakout was assisted by London ordering a Royal Navy concentration on Hong Kong, by Australia's preoccupation with troop convoys, and by Japan's dilatory declaration of war. As *Emden* arrived at Pagan, however, Jerram was at Yap Island (about 800 miles to the SW) destroying a vital German W/T station.

The German commander called a conference of his captains and there was a general agreement with his plan to cross the Pacific in order to return home, causing maximum disruption on the way. Only von Muller of the *Emden* dissented, saying that a single ship raiding the prolific Bay of Bengal trade routes in the traditions of the French corsairs would stand a good chance of success. Von Spee, rather pessimistic about his own chances, agreed and when his main force sailed eastward for their appointments with history off South America, *Emden* and a single collier sailed southwestward.

Making leisurely progress to conserve fuel, they had by the latter days of August passed west of New Guinea and along the great chain of islands that marks the southern bounds of the East Indies. Loose British W/T discipline warned von Muller of the presence of Royal Naval units searching the islands and he rigged a dummy fourth funnel to give a superficial resemblance to a British cruiser as he crossed the Lombok Strait to enter the Indian Ocean on 28th August. A week's further unhurried progress took the *Emden* along the southern coasts of Java and Sumatra and von Muller now had his first stroke of luck, for the lonely anchorage chosen as a coaling stop had, only the day before, been visited by a British cruiser. Refuelled, he crossed the Bay of Bengal, arriving on 10th September

Converted with separate flying decks, the Effingham class cruiser *Cavendish* was re-named *Vindictive*. She was not a success and re-converted to a training cruiser. The battle-cruiser *New Zealand* is in the background.

at a point NW of Ceylon (now Sri Lanka) on the trade routes to and from the Indian east coast. The up-till-now empty seas were suddenly alive with freighters on their usual tracks – all unsuspecting and with normal steaming lights. *Emden* commenced a systematic execution, although her commander scrupulously observed all agreed codes of conduct and rapidly earned a name for chivalry.

As a coal-burner (like all German cruisers of this date) the procurement of necessary bunkers was an eternal headache for the *Emden*. Reliance needed to be placed on capturing colliers, but there was still the back-breaking task of transferring coal, a job made doubly difficult by the need to do it at sea. The *Emden*'s attached collier, the Hamburg-Amerika ship *Markomannia*, had travelled in company with the cruiser as far as Indian waters. Five other ships taken by *Emden* in three days soon produced a crisis in accommodating their crews, and a passing neutral Italian ship was requested to take them to safety. The captain refused and, lacking radio, turned back for Calcutta to give the alarm, but on the way encountered the Ellerman liner *City of Rangoon*, which broadcast the news immediately. Radio was still far from universally fitted and this was the British authorities' first inkling that a raider was at large, particularly so as von Spee's squadron had, that same day, appeared off Samoa, where it was equally surprised to find the island had already been occupied by New Zealand forces.

Now having an identifiable quarry, the British, French and Japanese units patrolling the Indies split into a definite search pattern, but the *Emden* had not lingered, and by the 18th was in the passage between Rangoon and the Andamans. Von Muller found that, not only had the British cleared the area of normal traffic, but that they had the *Hampshire* in the vicinity. The German accordingly steered westward again across the Bay of Bengal, appearing before Madras on the evening on 22nd September and boldly destroying oil tanks by bombardment, before being driven off by shore batteries. Over centuries of maritime war, resolutely-handled lone raiders have proved notoriously difficult to catch and von Muller had done his homework well, melting away down the east coast of Ceylon as *Hampshire* and a Japanese cruiser converged rapidly on his last reported position. Doubling the island's southern extremity on the 28th, *Emden* passed Cape Comorin to reach the shipping lane which followed the Malabar Coast. Six prizes, one with coal, rewarded this boldness, one survivor being sent into Colombo with the crews of the others on board as melancholy evidence of the German's continuing success.

British reaction was to put cruisers between India and the Maldives and back along the track to Sumatra, along which von Muller might be expected to retire. But this was in vain, for the *Emden*, needing a quiet spot for some self-maintenance, headed south for the Chagos Archipeligo, a place so isolated that the few British inhabitants were as yet unaware of hostilities and even assisted the Germans in the (surely questionable) careening of their ship for a bottom clean.

Meanwhile, patrolling British cruisers had discovered and destroyed *Emden*'s colliers off Sumatra and divined that the enemy was still somewhat to the south, a likely spot being the old imperial coaling station of Diego Garcia. *Hampshire* and an AMC moved down from Colombo, missing the enemy closely as he again headed north to the Cape Comorin area where, as was obvious from wireless traffic, trade had returned to normal. All too easily, seven prizes were taken between 16th and 19th October, five being sunk, one with 6,000 more tons of coal being retained, while the seventh was sent in with the crews.

Slowed by his collier, von Muller stayed too long in the vicinity and early on the 21st was lucky not to be sighted, as he was certainly no more than ten miles from pursuers in an area of heavy rain squalls. Sensing that things were warming up, he resolved on clearing the area once again, detached the collier, and proceeded via the Nicobars toward Penang, on the West Malaysian coast. Intelligence had warned of the addition of French and Russian ships now in the hunt and he hoped to catch the French *Dupleix*. His boldness was considerable for this ship, although built in 1899, was very much superior to *Emden* in all but speed.

Penang Roads were always crowded and busy with ships coming and going, so when, out of the dawn of 28th October, a four-funnelled cruiser was seen approaching she caused little comment being thought to be, as likely as not, *Hampshire* or *Yarmouth*. She was neither. With no fixed shore defences to concern him, von Muller's use of a dummy funnel worked well, but he surprised not the *Dupleix* but the 3,100-ton Russian *Zhemchug*. Incredibly slow to react, *Zhemchug* reeled under a torpedo smashing into her port quarter and she commenced flooding progressively through ruptured bulkheads, her crew trying desperately to get to their action stations through a cyclone of shot unleashed at a quarter-mile range.

Von Müller's *Emden* was completed in 1908, a sister ship of *Dresden*. Of 3,650 tons, she mounted ten 4·1-inch guns, but unlike her turbine-driven sister, had triple-expansion machinery.

Shattered, burning and doomed, the wretched ship was finished off with a torpedo into a magazine.

Less than fifteen minutes had elapsed and the still unmarked *Emden* made toward the entrance, only to meet a British cargo liner entering – in spite of the turmoil – as though nothing was happening. Von Muller, equally cool, stopped in the fairway, and was in the act of lowering boats to take the merchantman when interrupted by the French destroyer *Mousquet*, returning after a night patrol. Of only 300-tons and armed with a brace of 65 mm (2·56-inch) guns, the Frenchman attacked without hesitation, only to be sunk after a fierce seven-minute action. The cargo liner made good her escape, as did the Germans who, having picked up the French survivors, were pursued unsuccessfully by other minor units. Had she dallied, *Emden* could easily have cleared the roadstead, but the resulting disruption to sea traffic was almost equally damaging.

Three more British and three Japanese cruisers were sent to the Bay of Bengal but long before their arrival their quarry disappeared to the SE, made as if to sail through the Sunda Strait into the Java Sea and then reversed course, having instructed its colliers to rendezvous near the Cocos Keeling Islands, where von Muller proposed to destroy the important Cable and Wireless station to draw the hunt before switching to the Red Sea approaches.

When, on 9th November, the station's duty staff sighted a four-funnelled cruiser approaching, they paid her more than usual attention, having been warned to expect a visitation. The dummy funnel was soon spotted and a raider warning was sent *en clair* from the powerful transmitter, repeated until finally silenced by a German landing party. Some two hours of destruction later, the shore party was puzzled to hear *Emden* sound her siren and put to sea.

Her luck had run out, for an important convoy was passing, bound from Australia to Colombo; its senior officer detached the Australian cruiser *Sydney* to investigate the calls. Only fifty miles distant, she soon approached close enough for her smoke to be sighted and she met *Emden* coming out. At 5,400 tons, *Sydney* was larger; she was a new ship and her eight 6-inch guns were heavier and of longer range. Still clean, she could also make use of her full 26 knots.

Nevertheless the German rapidly found the range and damaged the Australian whose captain, Glossop, used his speed to dictate the range, keeping a cool, deliberate fire laid on the enemy, who manoeuvred in the fifteen-mile gap between the main atoll and North Keeling island. In ideal conditions, *Sydney*'s fire began to tell, damaging her adversary's steering and, with it, ending any real chance of a German torpedo attack. The serious loss of the *Emden*'s main rangefinder was followed rapidly by that of the forefunnel and foremast. Splinters scythed down on the German gun crews at their open mountings and Glossop, encouraged by their slackening fire, closed to fire a torpedo, which missed. It hardly mattered, for the effect of the 6-inch lyddite was terrible; down came the after funnel, the centre one leaned drunkenly, and after an hour the bridge and both control positions were destroyed. His position hopeless, von Muller made for North Keeling and grounded the remains of his command. At this point, *Sydney* left the scene to deal with an escaping collier; when she returned, it was to find *Emden*'s flag still flying defiantly. Glossop had no choice but to reopen fire until she struck, then left again to assess the situation on the main island.

Under the leadership of the *Emden*'s first lieutenant, von Mucke, the shore party had seen the hopeless fight and, commandeering an ancient 100-ton inter-island schooner, *Ayesha*, sailed immediately. Having called at the East Indies, they made an eventual landing in the Yemen, and marched across country to join German forces in Turkey after a saga that makes a story in itself.

Sydney, meanwhile, returned to the wreck in the teeth of a heavy surf to remove the surviving crew. *Emden* had been fought to a standstill, suffering 155 dead. Of the 211 left, a quarter were wounded. The Australians had lost four killed and a dozen wounded in ending the career of this most successful of the enemy raiders. Although the German had inflicted material losses in her cruise, these were small when compared with the disruption caused to essential traffic and the diversion of many ships to the hunt that could have been better employed elsewhere.

The fighting cruiser – Coronel and the Falklands

As has already been related, the main force of von Spee's East Asiatic Squadron made eastward across the Pacific after the departure of *Emden* for the Indian Ocean. Their progress toward the American continent was marked by a series of brushes with the defenders of various islands not anxious to share either fuel or supplies. Strangely, the British Admiralty seemed determined to believe that these appearances were deliberately staged to mislead them about von Spee's true intention, to reverse course and attack vital Australian troop convoys. Only when the British intercepted and decoded a message from *Scharnhorst* early in October 1914 were they convinced of her true destination, for she stated that she was bound for Easter Island and wished to arrange a further rendezvous with colliers. At Easter Island, the whole of von Spee's scattered force of two armoured and three light cruisers concentrated, sailing for Mas a Fuera off the Chilean coast on 18th October.

One man, however, had never been in any doubt: Rear-Admiral Sir Christopher Cradock commanding the 4th CS, had been tracking both *Dresden* and *Karlsruhe*, the former gravitating slowly southward and appearing in the Magellan Strait early in September, after sinking a few merchant ships. In spite of London's indecision, Cradock sent *Monmouth* and *Glasgow*, together with the AMC *Otranto* to cover the Strait, having passed through the South Atlantic zone of Stoddart's responsibility. Leaving the old pre-Dreadnought battleship *Canopus* to cover the vulnerable Falklands, Cradock himself in the *Good Hope* entered the strait in mid-September and soon uncovered evidence of *Dresden* and supply ships. Returning to the Falklands in October, he

Short but successful, the raiding career of the cruiser *Emden* ended on a reef in the Cocos Keelings to avoid further pounding from the guns of the *Sydney*. Heavy surf made the rescue of survivors difficult.

finally left on the 22nd for the South Pacific, via the Strait, to be followed by *Canopus* at her best speed. London's assumption was that he would keep the old battleship in company for heavy support, but had reckoned without Cradock's impetuousness.

As the British progressed deliberately northward along the inhospitable Chilean coast, von Spee's force was approaching from Easter Island. On the 29th, *Glasgow*, which had been sent ahead to the small port of Coronel to exchange despatches with London, reported German W/T transmissions from close at hand. These were believed to emanate from *Leipzig*, in company with store ships, and Cradock duly put on speed to intercept them.

The Admiralty, tardily convinced that Cradock had a tiger by the tail, now sent reinforcements and instruction by telegram to stay with the *Canopus*, but if Cradock ever received it, there is little evidence that it influenced any of his subsequent actions.

Having rendezvoused with *Glasgow* in the early afternoon of 1st November about fifty miles off Coronel, the squadron turned NE by E on a line of search in a lumpy, quartering sea from the SE. At 16.20 *Glasgow* sighted smoke and soon reported that at least two armoured cruisers and a light cruiser were present, rather than the expected lone *Leipzig*. Von Spee, too, was surprised as he was bent on intercepting the *Glasgow*. What went on in Cradock's mind we shall never know; he was well aware of the fighting inferiority of his squadron but he also knew that, if he took the time to fall back on *Canopus*, the enemy squadron might well disappear again. They simply had to be damaged, if not sunk.

With the Germans heading generally SW, the British squadron steered a converging course. The oldest naval power and the newest, each ironically bent on preventing the other from escaping. It was a sunny but storm-laden evening; Cradock had the lowering sun behind him, illuminating the enemy well and also blinding their gunlayers. Now that the British ships were heading into the wind and working up speed, they were being washed down heavily and the lower casemated guns were useless. But Cradock could not close the canny von Spee until shortly after 19.00, when the red ball of the sun dipped below an angry horizon and the positions were reversed. The British were now sharply silhouetted against the after glow, whilst the Germans rapidly became indistinct in the gathering gloom to the east. Von Spee had gauged things perfectly and a dozen 8·2s bore against only two 9·2s, his gun crews with a Kaiser's prize for gunnery pitted against new-mobilised reservists.

Otranto had been packed off to the disengaged side and *Good Hope* led *Monmouth* and *Glasgow*. Ship for ship they engaged *Scharnhorst*, *Gneisenau* and *Leipzig*. The enemy flagship put *Good Hope*'s forward 9·2 out of action with the third salvo and *Monmouth*'s 6-inch did not even get into range of the *Gneisenau* before she was heavily damaged. *Leipzig* was joined by *Dresden* against the *Glasgow*.

Half an hour after fire had been opened, von Spee allowed Cradock to close range from 12,000 to only 5,500 yards, for the issue was no longer in doubt. The wildly plunging *Good Hope*'s scuttles glowed from internal fires; *Monmouth*, yawing in her wake, was ablaze forward from an explosion

Opposite top
After Coronel, von Spee's squadron entered Valparaiso, and this splendid picture of *Scharnhorst* conveys something of the urgency of the occasion. Note the 8·2s in the waist, carried above the casemated 5·9s.

Opposite below
The four 14,000-ton Drakes, completed in 1901, were enlarged Cressys. Here *Good Hope* typifies the fine appearance of the armoured cruiser. She was sunk at Coronel. Note the very low situation of the lower casemates.

Bristol, one of the first group of four Towns of 1909–10, differed in having two screws to the others' four. At the Falklands, her function was the destruction of von Spee's auxiliaries. Two single 6-inch guns can be seen. There were five 4-inch along each side.

The German *Köln* rusts at Scapa after the surrender of the fleet in 1918. Not to be confused with her predecessor, sunk at the Heligoland Bight in 1914, she was a 6,000-tonner of the Königsberg class.

that had blown her fore turret overboard. Only *Glasgow* was still relatively unscathed, exchanging salvo for salvo with opponents now visible only by their gun flashes, and her crew watching the two cruisers ahead, as the funnels and upperworks flickered eerily in the gathering strength of the fires that were consuming them. They fought on until 19.50, when *Good Hope* erupted with a violence that extinguished all fires, falling back into the water, silent and visible to the passing *Glasgow* as a dark profile glowing dully from deep within. She sank shortly afterwards with all hands.

The battered *Monmouth*, down by the bows, pulled out to the west with *Glasgow* and the guns fell silent as contact was lost. *Monmouth* then steered north to present her undamaged stern to the heavy seas while *Glasgow* left for the south to find *Canopus*, still 250 miles away, and warn her of the danger.

Some 20 miles astern of von Spee, *Nurnberg* had not succeeded in catching up in time for the action but, running through the fitfully moonlit sea, sighted a darkened ship at 21.20. Listing so heavily to port that her guns could not be depressed sufficiently for use and with steam issuing from great rents in her hull, *Monmouth* had her fires under control and was desperately unfortunate in being sighted. She refused to surrender and was easily finished off at 21.25, *Nurnberg*'s gunflashes being clearly visible to the retreating *Glasgow*. Due to the conditions, no lives were saved.

Scharnhorst had been hit twice, neither shell exploding. *Gneisenau* suffered four hits, being damaged only superficially. There were no German dead and the sole result of Cradock's supreme sacrifice was that the enemy had expended over half of his irreplaceablc ammunition. As the victorious squadron were being greeted as heroes in Valparaiso soon afterwards, the British Admiralty seethed with activity; a severe moral defeat had to be wiped from the slate and Cradock avenged.

While von Spee dallied in Chilean waters, preparing for his breakthrough into the Atlantic, the survivors of Coronel were ordered to rendezvous off the Plate with the ill-fated *Monmouth*'s sister ships, *Kent* and *Cornwall*, together with the armoured cruisers *Defence* and *Carnarvon*. More significantly, in the UK Jellicoe had been ordered to detach the two battle cruisers *Inflexible* and *Invincible*, which left for the

South Atlantic (after feverish preparations) on 11th November, ten days after Coronel, under the flag of Vice-Admiral Sir Doveton Sturdee. The battle cruiser had been evolved to deal with the armoured cruiser and now was the first chance to prove the theory, although it was almost wasted by the incredible lack of urgency with which Sturdee ambled south.

Defence, Stoddart's flagship, was detached to the Cape of Good Hope, her place being taken by the light cruiser *Bristol* and the AMC *Macedonia*. Luce of the *Glasgow*, having suffered already at the enemy's hands, counselled haste as he knew instinctively that von Spee was about to enter the Atlantic. But Sturdee was not to be hurried; having sent the mechanically deficient *Canopus* to ground herself on the mud inside Port Stanley to act as a stationary fort, he was still off the Plate on 3rd December, when the Germans actually rounded the Horn. They were fighting against appalling weather, which created something of a fuel crisis so that the capture of the British barque *Drummuir* with a full cargo of anthracite was a godsend, and three days were spent off the Beagle Channel in transferring it. On the 6th, they sailed for the Falklands to destroy installations and any of Stoddart's cruisers found there, though by now *Canopus* was firmly aground, covering the approaches and with a signal station established on a neighbouring hill. Sturdee's squadron finally arrived in the late forenoon of 7th December and his ships were instructed to coal as quickly as possible from the two colliers available so as to sail within 48 hours, and be able, as they thought, to prevent von Spee entering the Atlantic. Von Spee, in fact, was then only twelve hours steaming away and, alone of the British, *Macedonia* was on patrol. Sturdee was corked and helpless but, fortunately, neither side realised it.

At 07.56 on the 8th, coaling was proceeding at a frenzied rate when *Glasgow* fired a gun to draw attention to a signal fluttering from *Canopus*' halliards. It read 'Enemy in sight'.

Gneisenau and *Nurnberg* had been detached to take care of the port and were due to rejoin their squadron afterwards. At 09.00, an hour after they had been sighted, they were some eight miles offshore, studying the great columns of smoke arising from the as-yet invisible British ships. They were still appraising their admiral of the situation when *Kent* was seen coming out.

Although she had not actually been coaled, she had had steam at one hour's notice; otherwise only *Carnarvon* and *Glasgow* were refuelled and the urgency with which the squadron raised steam was heightened by a further report of smoke from the enemy main force.

Laid blind by the signal station, *Canopus* fired two two-gun indirect salvoes and, incredibly, hit *Gneisenau*'s after funnel with a ricochet. Making as if to attack *Kent*, the two Germans suddenly sighted the great tripods of the battle cruisers and sheered

Sturdee's squadron surprised in Stanley Harbour in the Falklands by von Spee in December 1914. *Glasgow* is already away, and *Kent* on the left will shortly follow. The battlecruiser *Inflexible* is also seen in this view from the foretop of her sister, *Invincible*. Frapping on the maintopmast shrouds is to confuse enemy ranging.

The German fleet in the dreary wastes of Scapa before the mass scuttling of June 1919. Cruisers (left to right) are: SMS *Frankfurt*, *Köln*, *Bremse*, *Brummer* and *Emden* (II), the latter housing the senior German naval officer, Admiral von Reuter.

away. At this point, had von Spee closed the harbour, he could have destroyed the British force completely as they emerged, but, like somebody about to cork an angry wasps' nest, his nerve failed and he ordered a retirement. However, from this point there could be no escape either by fighting or fleeing for, on an uncharacteristically clear morning von Spee could clearly see the great ships as they left, one by one, as steam was raised.

Glasgow, like an avenging terrier, overtook *Kent* to establish a visual link and, with all day at his disposal, Sturdee ordered 'General Chase'. Crews washed off coal grime as the British ships worked up speed, steadily overhauling the weed-fouled Germans. Something of the spirit of a foxhunt was in the air when at 12.51, *Inflexible* ranged on the enemy back-marker *Leipzig*. Slowly and inexorably, the British closed the range and the tall 12-inch splashes soon marched the length of the enemy formation without reply. At 13.20, realising the futility of the situation, von Spee selflessly ordered his light cruisers to scatter and escape while the two larger ships delayed the British. This ploy might have worked with a less experienced commander on the other side, but Sturdee was a cool tactician who had already issued fully detailed battle orders. As the Germans' light cruisers turned from SE to S, they were followed by *Cornwall*, *Glasgow* and *Kent*; there was no way out.

The two armoured cruisers, meanwhile, had turned NE to face Sturdee's two battle cruisers, which kept to 14,000 yards to capitalise on their superior gun calibre. As the enemy 8·2- and 5·9-inch weapons could range 13,000 and 12,000 yards respectively, the manoeuvring between the two sides turned on von Spee's attempts to close the range while holding the lee gauge so that the British were blinded by their own smoke. By 15.00 both German ships were hard hit, *Gneisenau* flooding and lacking her third funnel and burning. Although holding the advantage of wind, von Spee had presented only his port side to the heavy 12-inch projectiles, but damage was lessening his fire power. When, at 15.30 he reversed course to bring his starboard battery to bear, Sturdee slipped through his wake and could, for the first time, shoot clearly. *Scharnhorst*, now riddled and glowing from internal fires, signalled *Gneisenau* to keep going and, just after 16.00, ceased to fire, lurched toward her tomentors and at 16.17 plunged under the sea with all hands. The weather had deteriorated and *Gneisenau* held on grimly through a mist of fine rain, under fire not only from the battle cruisers but also from the *Carnarvon*, which had finally caught up. By 17.30, slowed to 16 knots and with only one gun still firing, the end was near and the British bombardment slackened. Twenty minutes later, she slipped quietly under, her flag still flying. Many of the crew perished in the icy waters and only 200 were rescued. The battle cruiser idea had been triumphantly vindicated and Sturdee had wisely expended ammunition rather than take risks and close his enemy for a quick kill.

Meanwhile the light cruisers were settling their own affairs. At about 13.30, when they turned south for the dubious cover of the Magellan Strait, the Germans were in approximate line abreast, *Dresden*, *Nurnberg* and *Leipzig*. Nominally faster than the pursuing British ships, they were slowed by want of docking, except for *Dresden*, which steadily drew ahead even of the fleet *Glasgow*. As the sky flattened to a sullen grey, Luce saw his best chance in slowing *Leipzig*

The first 'production' steam turbine cruiser in the German fleet, *Dresden*'s extra power enabled her to survive the Falklands trap of 1914. She is seen here fired and abandoned after surrendering three months later at Juan Fernandez. Note the foremast white flags.

sufficiently for the two armoured cruisers to get within range. It must have been of some satisfaction to him that his 6-inch splashes bracketed the *Leipzig*, whose 4·1s were not yet in range, for here was the ship that had been firing on him at the nightmare that had been Coronel.

Sustaining damage, *Leipzig* was goaded into changing course to close the range; in doing so, she succeeded in hitting the dogged *Glasgow* but lost so much ground that *Cornwall* could range her at 16.17 – the time that *Scharnhorst* was sinking to the north. The German ship was now under fire from both quarters, splitting her own fire. Through the curtain of drizzle her shape changed constantly with the smoke of her fires and, by 18.00, her resistance was slackening. High explosive, bursting on impact from only 8,000 yards, lanced her thin decks with splinters and caused fearful casualties. Her last gun fired at about 19.00 as ammunition ran out, but she still maintained a low speed although blazing at either end and lacking two funnels and her mainmast. The British ships closed, expecting to save lives, but were greeted by a salvo of three torpedoes, a defiant gesture that cost many lives. The *Glasgow* and *Cornwall* had to re-open fire even though many of the German crew were now topsides with the ship's seacocks open. Shortly before 21.00, the British approached on a safe stern bearing and put boats into the water, but, soon afterwards *Leipzig* rolled over to port, leaving only a cloud of smoke drifting downwind. Again, most of the crew succumbed to the icy waters and only 18 were rescued alive. One British seaman had died, and only *Dresden* was safe for the time being.

As *Cornwall* first fired on *Leipzig*, her sister *Kent* was off to port, making the previously unheard-of speed of 25 knots in her efforts to catch *Nurnberg*, even burning her woodwork in her furnaces. At 17.00, in deepening gloom, she was mortified to be straddled by her quarry's 4·1s, although her own 6-inchers were still out of range. In a final effort, *Kent*'s wardroom furniture was sacrificed and the range closed relentlessly. An early shot plunged from extreme range and shattered the German's steering gear, a disaster which, followed by the failure of two of her neglected boilers, reduced her speed to only 19 knots. At 17.45, *Nurnberg* turned rapidly to port to bring her full broadside to bear; *Kent* followed suit on a forward bearing to reduce danger from torpedo fire. Heavily armoured and with a much heavier broadside, *Kent* somewhat ungallantly pressed in to only 3,000 yards, accepting hits in order to smother the enemy. She was in fact, struck no less than 38 times but by 18.25 had reduced *Nurnberg* to a wreck, blazing and settling by the stern.

Though the drifting rain, her flag could still be seen aloft and *Kent* was forced to re-open fire until she struck, sinking at 19.30. Only seven men survived, while *Kent*'s tougher hide had kept her own fatalities to only four.

The completeness of the victory was complemented by the extreme gallantry with which the enemy fought and tempered by the escape of the *Dresden*, which led a fugitive and useless existence until run to earth the following March at Mas a Fuera by *Kent* and *Glasgow*. Von Spee's squadron had perished but had bequeathed standards that earned the respect of friend and foe alike; no fledgling fleet was ever set a finer example.

The expendable cruiser – Zeebrugge and Ostend

Seeking to paralyse Britain's most vulnerable limb, her commerce, Germany used her U-boats to the utmost, and by 1917 looked like succeeding where the French, Dutch and Americans had failed in earlier years. The offensive was cost-effective, not only in the direct losses it was causing, but also in forcing the construction of large numbers of escorts. Even though efficient means of detection and destruction of submarines were not yet to hand, the convoy system was instituted with consequent delays to traffic, and costly schemes such as mine and net barrages were introduced.

Those submarines bound for ocean patrols tended to follow the deep water routes north of the British Isles but smaller craft, minelayers and coastal boats, often used the Dover Strait, a twenty-mile gap of shallow water heavily patrolled by the Royal Navy out of Dover. From a point almost on the Belgian border, where the stagnant Western Front met the sea, to the neutral Dutch waters in the Wielingen, the enemy had control of the coast, including the ports of Ostend and Zeebrugge, connected by canals to the inland port of Bruges. Submarines were based in the latter, their reinforced concrete pens immune to the light airborne bombs of the day and too close to the town for naval bombardment to be feasible.

Also based on Bruges were small enemy destroyers, whose periodic forays against the large number of drifters tending the fixed anti-submarine (A/S) defences of the Strait were a considerable nuisance, tying down large numbers of British ships. The elimination of this threat, too, was something that needed urgent attention.

With the stalemate between the land forces, taking Bruges was out of the question and the Navy looked for means of denying the port its access to the sea. The most vulnerable point of the system lay in its sea-locks and a precedent had been set long before when (in 1798) Popham had landed a military force to destroy the Ostend lock gates. This type of solution was considered impracticable and a suggestion by Admiral Bacon of the Dover Patrol to torpedo the gates from CMB was dismissed, though it was used at St Nazaire in 1942. Blockships scuttled in the approaches were favoured but Bacon seemed lukewarm to the project and was reluctant to expedite it.

Towards the end of 1917 an estimated 38 submarines and 28 destroyers were based on Bruges, a force whose neutralisation by that time received a higher priority. Fortunately, this coincided with the appointment of Rear-Admiral Roger Keyes to Dover, a man of proven spirit and dash, well suited to an enterprise whose success would provide a lift to national morale at a difficult period.

Zeebrugge was the more important outlet from Bruges, the connecting canal being both shorter and deeper. Offshore approaches were difficult, shallow, strewn with sandbanks and scoured by swift tidal streams, problems compounded by the enemy's habit of moving or removing navigational marks. The actual sea-lock emptied into a short tidal exit debouching between

The scuttling of the High Seas Fleet at Scapa took the British by surprise. One of a handful saved by towing them into shallow water was *Frankfurt*, seen here awash with a British boarding party aboard. She was later expended in American bombing trials in 1920.

two piers, protected from tidal scour by an enormous granite-faced mole, some 1,850 yards in length. About eighty yards in width, it curved in a great quadrant, its inner wall low enough to serve as a quay but some sixteen feet higher on the outer (exposed) face in a vertical extension ten feet wide. Another narrow, 350-yard extension terminated in a lighthouse and the whole edifice was linked to the shore by about 300 yards of elevated viaduct bearing a road and double railway tracks on to the mole but allowing tidal flow along the shore. On the seaward extension was mounted a battery of 4·1-inch naval guns and others were sited along the shore, two batteries being particularly close and including both 5·9s and 8·2s.

The British plan was to approach at high water, under cover of darkness and smoke screens, and lay an elderly cruiser alongside the battery on the mole extension, which would then be taken by a landing party. When this threat had been removed, three old cruisers would pass and be scuttled across the approaches to the lock. An old submarine, packed with explosives, was to blow up the viaduct and prevent enemy reinforcements reaching the mole, the installations on which were to be destroyed as far as possible by the landing party. Numerous CMBs and MLs were to be attached for laying smoke screens, rescuing blockships' crews, etc. The whole operation was meticulously planned to be completed in about one hour, but it depended upon absolute surprise.

To storm the mole, Keyes chose the cruiser *Vindictive*, one of the strong and handy Arrogant class, dating from 1897. Two Mersey ferries, *Iris* and *Daffodil*, were commandeered for the purpose of keeping her pushed hard against the outer wall in the exposed tideway. *Vindictive* had a false deck built up to the calculated height of the mole, the intervening gap to be spanned by eighteen hinged gangways, or brows, to be let down when once alongside. *Vindictive*'s normal 6-inch armament was removed and replaced by heavy howitzers for high-angle fire, along with Lewis guns, pom-poms and even two large flamethrowers.

For blockships, three of the little 1891 Apollo-class, *Brilliant*, *Intrepid* and *Iphigenia*, were selected because of their limited 18-foot draught. They were packed with cement and rubble to render their subsequent removal by the enemy more difficult.

Once the landing parties had been trained in the necessary martial arts, the whole squadron, together with accommodation ships and two further Apollos – *Thetis* and *Sirius*, the latter ship destined to block Ostend – was, to preserve secrecy, moved to an isolated anchorage at the Nore early in April 1918. Two attempts to go into action were cut short by weather, but after weeks of waiting the final departure was made on 22nd April, in spite of a full moon. Small craft led the main force to lay special navigation marks so that the attack proper would go in during the small hours of the 23rd, St George's Day.

For some days previously, the coastal batteries in the area had been bombarded by the Royal Navy monitors and that night's special 15-inch barrage on the two Zeebrugge batteries provoked no special attention. By 23.30, Keyes in his destroyer-flagship *Warwick* was just five miles off the mole and being overtaken by CMBs racing in to lay the first smoke. Puzzled, the enemy fired starshell and shot blindly into the smokescreen until, at 23.56, *Vindictive* emerged clear of it, some 300 yards short of the mole. As she crossed this last shell-torn stretch she suffered heavy damage and severe casualties to the storming party mustered on the upper deck. Nevertheless she was alongside only one minute behind schedule, but, unfortunately 350 yards short of the battery – not a great distance but it was protected by barbed wire and machine guns to such good effect that the objective was never taken. For the next hour there were prodigies of valour as the bluejacket force battled, not only with the garrison troops, but also with the crews of seven enemy destroyers berthed inside the mole.

Vindictive's vitals were protected by the wall but her upperworks were struck by continuous hits that sent splinters scything down on anyone who showed himself. Severed fuel lines prevented the flamethrowers from working, the 7·5-inch howitzers were silent, surrounded by their dead crews, and only the better-protected 11-inch howitzer kept up a steady stream of projectiles to discourage the batteries ashore.

Early in the proceedings a massive explosion signalled the end of the viaduct. According to plan, the old submarine C3 wedged herself between the piles and her skeleton crew, having set a short fuse, took to their small motor boat, only to find its propeller was jammed. Pulling frantically on oars against a growing tidal stream, the threat of the impending explosion made heavy rifle fire from the shore seem a small nuisance indeed. In fact, only 200 yards of water separated them when 100 feet of viaduct and their tormentors were blown into oblivion. Holed and sinking, their little boat just reached the coastal craft which was seeking it and only the darkness prevented its gallant crew observing the cheering sight

St George's Day, 1918. The starboard, undamaged, side of *Vindictive* after return from Zeebrugge. Her hull, protected by the mole, was relatively unscathed. Note the temporary flame-thrower hut by the bridge structure.

of a whole cycle-mounted German rifle company pedalling, lemming-like, into the void in the viaduct roadway.

At about 00.50 the blockships were seen emerging from the smoke into the ruddy glare of battle and the recall was sounded to the men on the mole. *Thetis*, leading the line, surprised the enemy, and she suffered little damage on the approach, swinging around the lighthouse and steadying on a course for the lock entrance. Unfortunately, the tide set her into a boom of barges, and in slicing through this obstacle she fouled both propellers. Engines seized, she slewed, now under fire from both mole and shore, where the 8·2s were a bare 1,000 yards distant. Holed and settling she carried her way over shallows and approach channel, grounding finally near the western pier marking the entrance. Her scuttling charges were fired and the crew decamped rapidly in an ML, the complements of which vessels took incredible risks that night.

Although *Thetis* had sunk short of her planned position, she had drawn the enemy's fire to such an extent that *Intrepid* and *Iphigenia* passed easily through the gap that she had torn in the boom and they approached up the dredged channel.

Intrepid was scuttled beyond *Thetis*, with her stern against the western bank; the young commander of *Iphigenia* spent time backing and filling to plug the remaining gap as far as possible before blowing his charges. Afterwards, the two MLs that picked up the crews were in hazard as much from the risk of capsize through the massed humanity on their decks as from the enemy gunners.

Vindictive pulled clear by 01.10 and, accompanied by the faithful ferry *Daffodil*, vanished into the smoke. *Iris* has spent the hour trying to land a further party but was defeated by the height of the wall. Still untouched and crammed with personnel, she left with the others but had the bad luck to emerge from the smoke right in front of the shore batteries, which smothered her with fire, killing 77 and injuring 105 in minutes. She was fortunate to survive, as the destroyer *North Star* was sunk whilst trying to round the head of the mole to torpedo the German destroyers on the inside.

A hero's welcome awaited the force on its return to Dover; some 220 decorations were awarded, no fewer than eleven of them VCs. In fact, the blockage was not complete, with small submarines still able to pass via the undamaged lock at high water. But Britain badly needed a victory and the tremendous fillip of Zeebrugge boosted morale, hiding the failure that had occurred at Ostend.

Here, in a similar type of operation, *Brilliant* and *Sirius* had steered for the piers on a bearing taken from an anchored ML, marking the Stroom Bank buoy, but in thick, confusing smoke they found themselves in rapidly shoaling water. Before action could be taken, both had grounded; their crews were removed and their charges blown. As the smoke cleared, the wrecks came under heavy fire and the truth was made obvious – the enemy had shifted the buoy about 1½ miles to the east of its correct position.

It was cruel luck to be defeated by so simple a ruse and Keyes determined to make another attempt before the defenders could regain their full composure. *Vindictive*'s shattered topsides were patched up and she was made ready for sacrifice, together with the *Sappho*.

On 9th May, the expedition sailed from nearby Dunkirk but immediately lost *Sappho*, one of whose boilers blew up, forcing her to return. No preliminary bombardment was to alert the defenders but ominously the CMBs that approached at 01.35 to lay smoke screens were fired on. Although the offending batteries were immediately plastered by four monitors and by Army guns, surprise had been lost. Nevertheless, other CMBs darted in and out of the smoke to shake up the defenders by torpedoing the pierheads. Then, as *Vindictive* shaped up for her approach, the surrounding smoke screen was suddenly thickened by a clammy sea fog and, in spite of desultory fire, extra eyes were needed topside to spot the pierheads. Apprehensive of suffering the fate of *Brilliant* and *Sirius*, however, *Vindictive*'s commanding officer turned west to parallel the beach, missing the entrance by so small a margin that accompanying CMBs found and again torpedoed the pierheads. As she was obviously heading the wrong way, the old cruiser was hauled around and crept back to the east. With visibility scarcely a ship's length and her speed reduced to nine knots, she missed the entrance again, and turning sixteen points to starboard, she must have been perilously close to grounding as she tried once more. Flares were fired and as their pale light flickered back from the billowing vapour, something more tangible could at last be seen. *Vindictive* began to swing to port under full helm and the batteries on the piers brought her under fire, only to be rattled yet again as another CMB streaked in to launch two more torpedoes, though the open construction of the piers seemed proof against their efforts.

Under a hail of fire, an early casualty was the *Vindictive*'s commanding officer, whose death was followed instantly by a heavy shell striking down all at the con. Still under helm, the cruiser swung until her bows touched the downtide side of the channel, the stream immediately taking her stern in as well. Grounded axially with the channel but to one side of it, there was no way of getting her off to improve her position and the scuttling charges were fired. Unbelieveably, two MLs succeeded in braving the enemy fire to take off the surviving crew and return with news of the failure.

In material terms, the Royal Navy had sacrificed six old cruisers, one destroyer and a submarine in these operations, apparently to little effect, but to the Allied camp the audacity with which they had been carried out engendered a surge of pride in what was seen as the fleet's ability to act still with a courage equal to anything in its history.

Having survived the Zeebrugge operation, *Vindictive* was expended in an attempt to block Ostend. The remains of her splinter-pocked superstructure are seen here against the backdrop of Ostend piers.

BETWEEN THE WARS

That period following a major war is always a depressing time for a fleet, be it victor or vanquished. The latter has its remains fought over for cession among the victorious powers and the former, swollen by war to proportions unsupportable in peace, faces major surgery.

Cruisers, as a class, suffered as the remainder of the Royal Navy. After a spell on weed-grown buoys, their once-busy decks alive only with the raucous quarrelling of gulls, they were sold out of service in 1920 and 1921 in numbers so large that British breakers could not handle them, many ending up in the Netherlands or, ironically, falling to the cutting-torches of their late enemies, the Germans. By the end of 1921 all 21 survivors of the discredited armoured cruisers had gone, and about 50 protected cruisers and scouts as well, the only surviving examples being those on detached duties, usually with Commonwealth navies. 'Light cruisers' were now the accepted type and undergoing development so rapid that the early Towns and Arethusas, the latter scarcely six years old, were also disposed of, leaving the later and better-armed Towns, and the continuing programme of C, D, and E classes, together with the big new Hawkins class, with their 7·5-inch armament and extensive protection.

Paradoxically, at a time when warships of all types were worth little more than their scrap value, a new race began in capital ships between the late allies. Though both the USA and Japan had played comparatively minor roles in the late war at sea, each had seen at first hand how a major sea power, could still successfully apply the age-old lessons of war to even the most powerful of land-orientated states. Nelson's observations that 'He who controls the sea, controls the world' seemed as true as ever and here were two new contenders ready to

The six Carolines of 1914–15 were improved versions of the Arethusas, and were the first class to adopt geared as opposed to direct-drive steam turbines. *Caroline* still survives as a static RNVR ship at Belfast. Note the lofty, fidded topmasts for W/T aerials.

extend their influence across the Pacific that divided them. With four 32,600-ton Colorado class battleships with eight 16-inch guns apiece recently completed, the Americans commenced the six-strong South Dakota class (43,200 tons). These had twelve 16-inch guns and were followed by six 16-inch armed Lexington battlecruisers with incredible 180,000 shp machinery. In reply, the Japanese began work on two Kaga class battleships and four Amagi class battlecruisers, all with a ten 16-inch main battery, to be followed by a further four modified Amagis and a quartette of 47,500-ton battleships with 18-inch guns. Out of habit rather than necessity, Great Britain followed suit with the planned '1921' Battlecruisers and a class of near-49,000-ton battleships carrying nine of the already proven 18-inch guns.

Though each contestant doubted the wisdom of his vast commitments in money and resources, none dared withdraw and it took a change in the US Presidency, with a pledge to cut this kind of expenditure, to bring the powers to the conference table. Each was aware of how much the recent rivalry between Great Britain and Germany had contributed to the late war; each knew that a formula had to be agreed to control this new madness.

The conference that began in Washington in November 1921, also included France and Italy, and eventually agreed a treaty which defined the relative ratios of tonnage in capital ships and aircraft carriers allowable to each power. It resulted in the immediate scrapping of 45 existing ships, and the scrapping or conversion of 19 others under construction to the yet undersubscribed carrier tonnages. Cruisers had not been the main concern of the conference, which satisfied itself with limiting any future design to 10,000 tons, with guns not exceeding 8-inch calibre, figures largely determined by Great Britain's new Hawkins class ships. Including those under construction, the cruiser strength of the Royal Navy was now only 65, compared with 126 in 1914. Japan had reduced from 27 to 20 in the same period, but the USA still had 29, a reduction of only one.

The results of the Washington Treaty were interesting, if predictable, for where it successfully limited the capital ship by being specific, it encouraged the growth of the cruiser by being vague. In imposing maximum parameters to which none had yet aspired, it set new standards which became the target; each power's designers vyed to pack the maximum offensive power inside the limits of gun calibre and displacement. In a given size of ship, three variables were interdependent, viz: speed, armament and protection, any one of which could be improved only at the expense of the others. The cruiser was now to enter its most interesting phase as each power juggled the equation so as to suit its own needs. Some were to succeed only by deception.

Still viewing the cruiser in the largely classical role of fleet support and reconnaissance, in addition to independent operation, the British designers held that, as protection could not be provided on a scale to be proof against anything more than small calibre fire, it was largely wasted. Weight saved on extensive protection would better be devoted to more powerful machinery to enable the ship to keep out of trouble. Medium vertical armour and light horizontal protection were accepted. With regard to the calibre of the main battery, it was felt that it should be superior to the average battleship's secondary armament yet have the rate of fire necessary to repel a destroyer

One of the prolific 'C' class cruisers, *Ceres*, in 1918. Note the low freeboard foreward, the disposition of the five 6-inch guns, and the prominent, post-Jutland, searchlight tower.

attack. At a time when guns were still hand-worked, both requirements presented problems and led directly to powered mountings, turrets now being preferred to the earlier open mountings for everything over 4·7-inch calibre.

Another essential ingredient for a British cruiser was endurance, with bunker capacity and habitability receiving special attention. It was known that facilities for the stowing and launching of aircraft were being built into French and US designs then being prepared, but this paraphernalia was to be included in British ships only if it in no way interfered with fighting capacity. Interestingly, the Royal Navy's first post-war ship was a 'one-off', the mine laying cruiser *Adventure*, a 6,750-tonner looking like an enlarged 'D' with a high freeboard aft housing two long galleries accommodating up to 340 mines, which could be laid through doors in her transom stern. Her

The 'D's of 1917 were very similar to the later 'C's, from which they were derived, but with an extra centre-line gun abaft the bridge. Note the 'trawler' bow and abrupt sheerline to reduce wetness forward.

The distinctive profile of a British 'E' class cruiser, in this case *Emerald*, notable for their twelve torpedo tubes and 33-knot speed. The early aircraft catapult can be seen.

In the white-and-buff 'foreign station' livery, *Effingham* leaves Portsmouth. At nearly 10,000 tons displacement, the design was largely responsible for the maximum size of cruiser permitted by the Washington Treaty. *Effingham* was wrecked in the Norwegian campaign of 1940.

Though termed 'Scouts' by the US Navy, the ten Omahas of the early 1920s were of more than 7,000 tons. Of the two seen here, *Marblehead* (CL12) is the nearer. Note how six of the ten 6-inch guns are mounted in casemates, one of the last class so fitted.

geared steam turbines were supplemented by a diesel-electric plant for controlled speed movement whilst laying, but she was greatly underpowered. Armament, a paltry four 4·7s, was purely defensive.

In 1922, France laid down the first of a trio of Duguay-Trouins, whose design pre-dated the treaty and was not affected by it. They were very lightly-built with a 33-knot speed on a designed power exceeding 100,000 shp. Displacing 7,250 tons and mounting eight 6-inch guns they also boasted a catapult and aircraft. Their first 'treaty' cruisers were the two Tourvilles, begun in 1924 and designed to the maximum 10,000 tons, with an armament of eight of the larger permissible 8-inch calibre guns. Again, they were poorly protected, their designers using the larger hull to install machinery of about 130,000 shp for a pace-setting 36 knots.

The Italian counter to these were the two of the Trento class, the lead ship of which was laid down in the following year. Of similar displacement and armament to the Tourville class, they worked-in a measure of protection at the expense of structural strength, the scantlings of their lean, 656-foot hulls being very light. They had the advantage of three aircraft to the French type's one but required 150,000 shp for the same speed. Neither class, being designed chiefly for Mediterranean service, had very great endurance.

In the Pacific, meanwhile, the other rivalry continued with both Japan and the US laying down classes, displacing about 9,100 tons, well inside the limit. Here, the greater experience of the Americans showed with their two Pensacolas being far superior to the Furutakas. As though they had some pre-knowledge of the Americans design, the

Japanese ships were very similar, with a length of 602 feet against 586 and a power of 103,500 shp compared with 107,000. At 65¼ feet however, the *Pensacola* had a beam nearly ten feet greater than the *Furutaka*, enabling her to carry ten 8-inch guns compared with six. She was, however, undoubtedly over-armed and, like many US designs of the period, showed signs of insufficient stability.

With other naval powers contenting themselves with construction of pairs of ships, Great Britain kicked off with a respectable and confident seven, the Kents being funded under the 1924 estimates. As might have been expected with a weight-critical design, there were several castings. Though only 80,000 shp were planned, the boiler spaces were so sub-divided that three funnels were a factor common to all, although foreign equivalents had only two. On the Furutakas and Trentos this was achieved by trunking the forward pair of uptakes into one casing but both French and American ships, though with higher installed power, had their boilers in two, widely-spaced groups. Against this, the British Nelson-class battleships were being designed on the all-or-nothing principle, where vital spaces were closely grouped so as to be protected by as small an area of armour as possible. By the same thinking, one County draught design had three funnels closely-grouped well aft, with the secondary 4·7-inch armament, separated by a Nelson-style tower bridge structure from three triple 8-inch turrets forward. Twelve torpedo tubes were to be carried in place of the E-class' sixteen.

In the event, a more orthodox layout was adopted, resulting in a majestic profile that was instantly recognisable anywhere. Four large, powered 8-inch turrets and the great hull, with its enormous freeboard, devoured so much of the allowable displacement that protection was on a very light scale. However, though of far lower power than her foreign contemporaries, a County could still manage a respectable 32 knots and maintain it in poor conditions, whilst having bunkers for the great endurance required for Imperial duties.

By the terms of the Armistice, Germany had been left with only a rump of a fleet, retaining eight near-useless pre-Dreadnought battleships and eight cruisers, of which six were of the small 2,700-ton protected type. Those modern cruisers that were not scuttled at Scapa Flow were shared out among the Allies. France commissioned four into her own fleet and scrapped a further one, a replacement *Emden*. Three hoisted Italian colours but the six assigned to Great Britain were scrapped. Japan, also, disposed of the only one ceded to her and the Americans expended the *Frankfurt*, along with the battleship *Ostfriesland*, in a series of aerial bombing trials staged off the Virginia Capes in 1921. These were to test the vigorously-pursued theories of Brigadier-General 'Billy' Mitchell, who maintained that the aircraft had rendered the conventional warship practically obsolete. Both ships were eventually sunk, but under the ideal weather conditions it actually proved nothing except that even near-misses could seriously damage a ship by rupturing plating from a concussive 'mining' effect.

With no reason for competing in the 'treaty' cruiser rivalry and with the Deutschmark giving reason for some concern,

One of three ex-German light cruisers ceded to Italy after the First World War, *Strassburg* became *Taranto*, seen here at La Spezia about 1940. She was altered to carry seven 5.9s in place of her twelve 4·1s. Scuttled by the Italians in 1943, salvaged by the Germans only to be sunk by bombing, she was raised yet again but sunk for the last time by aircraft action in 1944.

Britain's first Washington Treaty cruisers, the Counties had a dignity of their own, stemming from their vast freeboard and three lofty funnels. One of the later ships with internal bulges is seen here in her original state, unmodified by tripod masts, hangar, etc.

USS *Indianapolis* (CA 35), probably shortly after her completion in the early 1930s. Except for the first of the treaty cruisers, the two Pensacolas, all American heavy cruisers have kept to the three triple 8-inch layout.

Germany's first postwar cruiser was of 5,600 tons, once again bearing the name of *Emden*. Built in Wilhelmshaven Naval Dockyard her displacement was much reduced by using newly-introduced welding techniques, enabling plates to be butt-jointed where rivetting demanded laps or buttstraps. In spite of this advanced construction, she had coal-fired machinery developing only 46,000 shp, though mounting a comparatively powerful armament of eight 5·9-inch guns. Her main tasks were to train crews for future ships whilst showing the German flag again world-wide.

In the County class the Royal Navy had a design well suited to its purpose and a further six near-identical sisters were ordered in 1925–6. Though the Japanese followed the Furutakas with a very similar pair of six-gunned Aobas, spurred on by the thought of the Pensacolas with ten guns, they rapidly produced the similarly armed four-ship Nachi class. The Americans had, unusually, triple turrets super-firing twins but the Japanese installed five twins, necessitating a 662-foot hull and giving space for machinery uprated to 130,000 shp. Being also well protected, carrying three aircraft, twelve (later sixteen) torpedo tubes and an eight 5-inch secondary armament, it was hardly surprising that these fine ships displaced 13,400 tons, their designers thus ignoring the treaty almost from the very beginning.

America's follow-on were the six Northamptons, slightly larger than the tender Pensacolas, with a raised forecastle for improved seakeeping but with weight reduced by part-aluminium topsides and armament reduced to a nine-gun battery in three triple turrets. They, in turn, were followed by an improved pair, *Portland* and *Indianapolis*, which utilised the full 10,000 ton maximum, and which were launched in 1931–2. Much the same situation obtained in the Mediterranean, with the French observing the limitations and the Italians paying lip-service. Where, following their first pair, the French built four improved Suffrens with slightly better protection at the expense of a 20 per cent reduction in power, the Italians commenced with light cruisers. The first four Condottieri were laid down in 1928 as an answer to the Duguay-Trouins and were to set new records, not only with the length of their names but also in speed, clocking about 42 knots at 120,000 shp on a light trials displacement. Soon after, and before completion of the improved Suffrens, the Italians laid down in 1929–31 the four-ship Zara class and the Bolzano, an improved Trento. All were reasonably well protected and all displaced between 11,000 and 12,000 tons. Acknowledging the extreme fragility of their lead ships, the French then tried a new approach in their lone *Algérie*. About one quarter of her displacement was consumed by armour and, for good measure, she was given improved protection and stability by bulges. She was 30 feet shorter than the *Suffren*, but beamier; only 84,000 shp was installed, requiring three shafts in place of four. With her completion in 1934 the French had a ship able to absorb punishment, but from that time finished with heavy cruisers and concentrated on 6-inch cruisers, the Italians following suit.

This great activity in construction had led to the 1927 Geneva Conference, called to plug some of the loopholes left by the Washington one, but with the Mediterranean rivals refusing to attend and Japan already ignoring previous limits, it was a futile gathering. Its keenest member had been Great Britain who, concerned at the cost of the Counties, had cut the design to the six-gunned *York* of 1928, followed by her sister *Exeter*. With a low quarterdeck, a 3-inch belt could be worked-in over the vitals whilst keeping the displacement to only 8,400 tons. The Kents, the first group of Counties, had been built with three short funnels and the Yorks were to follow suit, but were altered by having the forward pair trunked into one and both heightened, as were those of the Kents, to combat smoke nuisance.

Though growing recession forced the cancellation of five Counties and three Yorks, the Spaniards built two of the former to a modified design under licence. Named *Baleares* and *Canarias*, they sported a single, gigantic funnel of singularly unlovely aspect but, though the former was a casualty of the Civil War, *Canarias* survived until 1978.

Two of the cancelled Counties were of an improved type and had been provisionally named *Northumberland* and *Surrey*. With only a two-knot penalty, machinery could be reduced to only 60,000 shp (equivalent to a 1942 Battle class destroyer) releasing tonnage for improved protection. Two catapults were to have been included, one on B-turret roof. In appearance they resembled four-turret Yorks and there was debate as to whether masts and funnels should be raked (like *York*) or vertical (like *Exeter*). It was noted that raked funnels kept smoke further from the bridge and assisted in the estimation of a ship's course at a distance – something which could also profit an enemy.

With these cancellations, the Royal Navy too, turned to the light cruiser, a decision

Top
USS *Quincy* (CA 39) in May 1942, less than three months before her loss at the disaster off Savo Island. Note the clutch of four aircraft and their substantial hangar, which were to be a terrible fire hazard, and the searchlights, so strangely ineffective on the night of the action.

Above
Designed for long-range forays against an enemy's commerce, the three German 'pocket battleships' of the early 1930's provided a revolutionary new slant on the armoured cruiser concept. This picture of *Graf Spee* shows their austere elegance. Note the Arado floatplane and the torpedo tubes on the quarterdeck.

which had been reinforced by yet another conference, this time held in London in 1930. Great Britain did badly from the agreement which, whilst not limiting numbers of hulls, set a ceiling on total tonnage. If nothing but the large 8-inch ships were built, the navy would have had too few to discharge its responsibilities; more, smaller cruisers were therefore needed. And as agreement had also been made on a minimum age at which a ship could be replaced, many smaller and obsolete units soldiered on toward their second war, a process made more necessary by the financial problems of the time.

If the 1920s had been the decade of the 8-inch cruiser, the light cruiser came into its own in the 1930s, with only the USA and Japan continuing with heavies. In 1927–8 the latter laid down four Takaos, improved Nachis, once more of 13,000 tons. The Astorias, the American reply, were seven slightly improved Portlands; with aircraft increased from three to four, they had a large hangar around the mainmast, which was to prove a real fire hazard in action.

In her turn, Italy laid down a second pair of Condottieri in 1930, resulting in France, which had recently built only a brace of cruiser/training ships, to build the one-off *Emile Bertin*, whose very high-powered design was then given more protection and de-rated machinery to serve as the basis for the six splendid ships of the La Gallissoniere class, of 7,600 tons and nine 6-inch guns. This size was then followed up by the Italians in the two Montecuccolis, which though 2,000 tons greater than the preceding Cadornas, were still termed Condottieri.

After the *Emden*, the new German navy received the three Konigsbergs which, on only 6,600 tons, mounted nine 5·9s in three triple turrets, one forward and two aft, staggered about the centre-line to improve ammunition handling. Their machinery was interesting in incorporating a pair of small cruising diesels of 1,800 bhp, in addition to the more orthodox steam turbines, which developed 68,000 shp. These twin-funnelled Ks were followed by the single and marginally larger *Leipzig*, whose uptakes were trunked into only one funnel and which adopted a third, centre-line shaft for the four cruising diesels, whose power was considerably increased to 12,400 bhp.

The distinctive trunked funnel of *Leipzig* was echoed in the Royal Navy's first new class of light cruisers, the Leanders, five attractive little 7,150-tonners with a nicely balanced armament of eight 6-inch, eight 4-inch and four torpedo tubes, powered adequately for 33 knots. Their distinctive funnel betrayed, however, a weakness in adjacent boiler spaces and three follow-ons for the RAN had staggered machinery compartments and, consequently, two wide-spaced funnels. Though of no great size this design was then, surprisingly, cut down even further to the four six-gunned Arethusas, of 5,250 tons.

These European ships looked quite puny when compared with the first Japanese essay into light cruiser design. Their four-ship Mogami class, though nominally of 8,500 tons, mounted an incredible fifteen 6-inch guns in five turrets, requiring a hull of the same length as the Nachis, into which their designers managed to accommodate machinery of 150,000 shp. Not surprisingly, the first pair were found to be seriously unstable and required a two-foot bulge to be added on either side; the second pair were modified in a similar way and, when completed, displaced 1,250 tons more than the agreed limit for heavy cruisers. Inevitably, the Americans replied in kind, the nine Brooklyns mounting a similar armament on a hull as beamy but about 55 feet shorter, and with more realistically-powered machinery of 100,000 shp for 34 knots. They proved excellent ships, four still serving under South American colours in 1979. Gun crews of their secondary 5-inch were badly exposed in open mountings, but the class introduced the later standard high freeboard hull, with aircraft stowed in a hangar below the quarterdeck.

Completing also in the early 1930s was the first of a new German class, formidable ships aimed at commerce raiding but very difficult to categorize formally. The Deutschlands were called Panzerschiffe, or Armoured Ships, by the Kriegsmarine and, later, heavy cruisers but, in essence, they were a resurrection of the armoured cruiser in the original sense, as represented by the French *Jeune Ecole* in the 1890s and the Russian *Rurik* and *Rossia*, capable of waging a commercial war whilst possessing the gunpower to deter opposition. Though the earlier threat had resulted in the British Powerfuls, the new challenge was felt to be

A view looking forward along the port waist of USS *Quincy*. Note the open, exposed mountings of the 5-inch secondary armament and the inflammable wood-planked decks.

The Brooklyn class *Honolulu* (CL 48) under repair. The five triple 6-inch armament resulted from the Japanese Mogami design, but was disposed forward after the fashion of the British Nelsons. White circles indicate areas where the shipyard had made modifications or repairs.

adequately covered by the three remaining battlecruisers of the Royal Navy. Though the 'pocket battleships', as they became popularly known, exceeded their advertised 10,000 ton displacement by about 20 per cent, they were still an ingenious package built around two triple 11-inch mountings. With a secondary battery of eight 5·9s and six 4·1s, together with eight torpedo tubes, they could pack a fair punch. Welding experience, gained in the construction of the light cruisers, was put to good use, saving enough weight to add a belt of 100 mm armour. Seeking maximum endurance, the designers incorporated diesel propulsion, with eight engines on two shafts. This allowed units to be opened up at any time to prevent the maintenance problems that had plagued earlier steam-driven raiders operating from far distant dockyard support. Unfortunately, however, these 7,000 bhp diesels proved unreliable and caused much vibration whilst still providing power for only 26 knots. In retrospect, a combined plant would have been a distinct advantage.

Certain classes at the lower end of the scale were also rather difficult to rate in the cruiser scale. Once the Scouts of the Royal Navy were sold out soon after the First World War, interest in them died as their function was largely overtaken by the big destroyer leaders then being built, together with plentiful small cruisers of the 'C' class, fast and little larger. That the Americans did not produce a smaller type of 'scout' than the Omaha class can be explained by the fact that any potential enemy would be an ocean away, making size, and thus endurance, of paramount importance. Japan, on the other hand, was very keen on the type, possibly with an eye to operations nearer home in the island-studded waters of the Far East. Their first pair were the Tenryu class, contemporary with and inspired by the British 'C' class. Their 3,250 tons were apparently insufficient as the five Kumas that followed in the early 1920s were of 5,850 tons, more suitable for a large ocean concept than that required for the British ships and enabling them to carry a respectable seven 5·5s. Furthermore, Royal Navy scouts had carried only a nominal pair of torpedo tubes where the Japanese had four pairs of tubes for their newly introduced 24-inch monsters, weapons so effective that the navy developed their use into a speciality that was to prove deadly in action. Though Japanese destroyers tended to mount eight tubes, similar to their foreign contemporaries, their cruisers commonly mounted twelve.

To anticipate a little, *Kitakami* and *OI* of the Kuma class were later converted to specialist torpedo cruisers. In this guise, they lost most of their gun armament and were sponsoned in the waist to take no fewer than forty torpedo tubes, five quadruple mountings on each side. It was to be expected that these formidable ships would

Top
One of America's 'treaty cruisers', the *Indianapolis* (CA 35) was launched in 1931 and is seen here before the war. Her loss in 1945 remained undetected for several days, and resulted in the US Navy's highest death toll. Note the 8-inch guns in common sleeves, sided catapults, searchlights around the after funnel, and the general built-up appearance aft.

Centre
The Royal Navy's return to the light cruiser in the 1930s began with the five Leanders, unique in being single-funnelled. This shows *Neptune* in 1937 in a rather unorthodox colour scheme. Mined in the Mediterranean in December 1941, she was the only one of the class to be lost.

Lower
The Italian *Armando Diaz* off La Spezia in 1938. With the *Luigi Cadorna*, she formed the second group of Condottieri, recognizable by the mainmast having been moved forward of the after funnel. They managed nearly 40 knots on trials.

have been put to good use, but they were presumably over-ambitious in design, for they were soon converted again, this time into midget submarine carriers.

The capabilities of the Japanese scouts was later enhanced by fitting an aircraft catapult, though there was no space for a hangar for a seaplane. This problem was solved in the six follow-on Nagaras in the same way that the Royal Navy had employed earlier on cruisers such as the *Dauntless*, where a flying-off platform was sited forward of the bridge and a hangar below it. A further class, the Sendais, were also built in the twenties but only three of a planned six were completed. A machinery rearrangement rather unusually increased the earlier ship's three funnels to four.

The 5,200 ton Sendais still had the earlier armament of seven 5·5s in single mountings, five centre-line and two flanking the bridge. All were at upper deck level and the greatest number for a broadside was six. Thus, when the 2,900-ton *Yubari* was launched in the same year with two twins superfired by singles, the Sendais were outclassed, though by a ship that could well be termed a super-destroyer. Though the

Yubari is credited with greatly influencing the character and construction of the first Japanese 'treaty' cruisers, the Furutakas, she marked the end of the line for their scout designs.

France and Italy, whose horizons were bounded largely by the Mediterranean, might have been assumed to be enthusiastic builders of small cruisers but, though Italy had built the trio of 3,500-ton Quartos as far back as 1911, they sat back and watched French developments, which favoured the super-destroyer. In 1922–3 the six Chacals were laid down, to carry five 5·1-inch guns and six 550-mm torpedo tubes on a working displacement of about 2,600 tons, little short of the *Yubari* and equalling her speed of 35½ knots. Though still definitely destroyers, the Chacals were twice the displacement of the usual run of such craft and encouraged the French to build a succession of classes, termed Contre-Torpilleurs, culminating in the Mogadors of the 1930s. These were decidedly over-ambitious, cramming eight 5·5s and ten large torpedo tubes into a 447-foot hull of 3,550 tons displacement. In addition they found room for 92,000 shp machinery for sustained speeds of better than 40 knots, but only two were ever built.

Italy moved to a rather half-hearted reply in 1927–8 with a dozen Navigatori which, at 1,950 tons, were large for their day but did not encourage further developments. It took the arrival of the Mogadors to provoke an answer in the very similar Capitani Romani, which shipped eight 5·3s on a 3,750-ton displacement and, whilst scarcely 15 feet longer than the French class, incorporated 125,000 shp on only two shafts for bursts up to 43 knots. They could have caused great headaches to later Mediterranean convoys but only four of the planned dozen were ever completed. As it was, they typify how the large destroyer and small cruiser designs merged almost imperceptibly.

Only slightly up the scale were the two Dutch Tromps of the late 1930s, 4,200-ton 'pocket cruisers' developed from the 'Kanonneerboote', colonial gun-boats with 5·9-inch armament. Designed to carry six of these, along with four 75 mm weapons and no torpedo tubes, they had machinery of comparatively low power and a speed of 30 knots, so cannot be termed 'scouts'.

It was to be the Germans who were to have the last word in scout design. After a succession of large 5-inch gunned destroyers in the years proceeding the Second World War, they increased the calibre to 5·9-inch in the Z37 type of 1940. Contemporary with these were a trio of 4,550-ton ships, originally given the destroyer pennants Z40-42, but which were later reclassified SP1-3, short for Spähkreuzer, or scout cruisers. Suffering from low priorities, they were never completed but would have been elegant ships with a destroyer-like profile and carrying six 5·9s. They were designed for triple screws, steam turbines on the wing shafts, and cruising diesels on the centre-line.

It should not be assumed that innovation was the prerogative of the major fleets, as witness the *Gotland* of Sweden, laid down in 1931. That country's traditional neutral stance required not a fleet capable of ocean warfare but of securing her coast and creating a measure of sea control at any required point on its approaches. Skerry-ridden and shallow, these waters had encouraged the development of the Pansarskepp, ships somewhat akin to the German Deutschlands in layout as well as in name, but geared to coastal defence. The Royal Navy had demonstrated the exciting possibilities of seaborne aviation during the First World War, though for the greater part it had been deployed only from cross-channel packets converted to operate seaplanes and wheeled fighters, which were flown from ramps without any facility for landing-on. Swedish naval appropriations, never generous, had often led to multi-purpose ships, most of them fitted for minelaying and, when a small carrier was proposed for use with flotilla craft, the idea was rapidly changed to that of a combination cruiser/carrier. Completed at the end of 1934 she was of only 4,750-tons and 427 feet in length, fairly conventional forward with six 6-inch guns, two in paired gunhouses and two flanking the bridge in casemates, probably the last instance of such mountings. Her last 100 feet or so were occupied by an elevated deck where six Hawker Osprey floatplanes could be stowed on trolleys in the open, to be transferred by rails to a revolving catapult level with the deck and forward of it. In fact it was found later that aircraft could be more efficiently operated from shore bases and *Gotland* was converted to a pure A/A cruiser, but she was noteworthy for influencing Japanese design particularly and for foreshadowing the helicopter cruisers of today's fleets.

Paying only token attention to treaty agreements, Japanese designers were producing probably the best cruisers of the 1930s, though their dedication to big ships with maximum firepower did limit the number of hulls that they could lay down before 1936, when their country renounced all limitations. A further agreement was cobbled together in London in 1936 but it was

Top
The Japanese cruiser *Mogami*, as built, in 1935. Extremely fast at 37 knots, the class had a heavy armament of five triple 6-inch turrets, later exchanged for five twin 8-inch. Compare the layout with the American Brooklyn class, built as a counter.

Above
La Galissonnière typifies the French light cruiser of the 1930s. The secondary armament, was wisely of high-angle weaponry. The large aircraft catapult on the after turret can be seen.

Left
The late 1930s in Taranto. Four Spica and one old Pilo class 'torpedoboats', with beyond them one of the first group of Condottieri, and a second in the distant far left. Bows on, beyond the two tugs, is the *Bari*, an ex-German cruiser which fought at Jutland as the *Pillau*.

An early wartime picture of *Newcastle*, a British 'Town', arriving at Plymouth. Virtually 'as built', she boasts only a D/F loop at the foretop, but has acquired the un-loved URP mountings on 'B' turret and quarterdeck. A D/G girdle has been rapidly tacked around the hull, following the mine offensive of 1940.

clearly the beginning of the end and re-armament programmes, overt or covert, moved into top gear.

First fruits of this defection were the two 11,200-ton Tone class units which started as two further 6-inch Magamis but, in an arrangement unusual even by Japanese standards, received four twin 8-inch turrets, forward of the bridge structure, with the after end given over to the operation of five floatplanes. These were sited in the open at quarter-deck level, precariously close to the water, and needed to be transferred by ramp to one of two catapults flanking the mainmast and one deck higher. In spite of her limited size, *Gotland* would seem to have been the better design, though the Japanese pair were used effectively. The Imperial Japanese Navy never took to the 6-inch cruiser and even the fifteen-gun Mogamis later traded their triples for twinned 8-inch. The Japanese did, however, complete the oddly under-armed Agano class during the Second World War. Four were single-funnelled 6,650-tonners mounting only six 6-inch guns but were followed by the *Oyodo*, an 8,200-ton derivative with two superfluous Mogami 6-inch turrets forward and a large catapult and hangar aft for up to six reconnaissance aircraft. It is worth noting in passing that the battleships *Ise* and *Hyuga* were also converted to hybrid carriers late in the Second World War in much the same way.

Italy launched two final pairs of Condottieri in 1934–6 similar to their predecessors only in name. The first pair, the Aostas, weighed in at about 8,700-tons, having the same armament and machinery as the previous ships but being better protected with a 4-inch belt and turrets and a light 1½-inch deck. They were followed by the Abruzzis which, on 9,400-tons, squeezed in ten 6-inch guns by superimposing pairs over triples, an arrangement which required extra beam and which was used to good effect by increasing the above protection by a further inch in thickness. Though the same 105,000 shp was installed the speed penalty was only three knots and they were undoubtedly fine ships. Almost all Italian cruisers were fitted for mine-laying, up to 150 being carried in later units, and that they could make good use of this facility was to be demonstrated in December 1941, when the Royal Navy's Malta-based Force K was devastated off Tripoli.

As the 1930s progressed, Germany's in-

From the foredeck of the Italian *Zara*, broad-banded for aircraft identification, her three sisters *Fiume*, *Gorizia* and *Pola* are seen at high speed target practice in the summer of 1940.

creasingly aggressive stance won her ever greater concessions and, able at last to negotiate from a strong position, she gained from the Anglo-German naval agreement of 1935 the go-ahead to reconstruct her fleet, up to 35 per cent of that of the Royal Navy by tonnage in all classes except submarines, which were to a maximum of 45 per cent. As many as five 'treaty' heavy cruisers could thus be built and the fact that these were nearer to 14,000 tons apiece was just one more factor in this period of make-believe. Thus, where other major fleets had progressed from heavy cruisers to light, the Kriegsmarine reversed the process, laying down the five Hippers in 1935–6. Not much longer than a British Counties they were, as usual in German construction, beamier in comparison, enabling them to incorporate 5-inch vertical and 4-inch horizontal armour. Their more portly lines required 132,000 shp to drive them at the same 32½ knot speed that the Counties could manage on only 80,000 shp. In secondary armament, the Hippers managed a 50 per cent improvement in twelve 4·1s and their compartmentation was reported superior, though the only one of the class ever to be severely tested, the *Blücher*, capsized in Oslofjord after being torpedoed in April 1940.

As the larger fleets now built seriously for war, Britain put in hand the fine seven-ship Southampton class. Not repeating the mis-

Laid down in 1927, the Swedish cruiser *Gotland* provided the model for Japanese Second World War conversions through the ships of our own time such as *Jeanne d'Arc*, *Andrea Doria* or *Moskva*. The two 6-inch guns at the corners of the bridge structure are probably the last example of the casemate. The second picture shows three of her Hawker Ospreys and part of the catapult.

The Australian cruiser *Canberra* was to be sunk in August 1942 in the debâcle at Savo Island. She was built, with her sister *Australia* on Clydebank in 1927, and was identical to the Royal Navy's Kent class ships.

Seen here at Beirut after problems with Vichy French naval units in 1941 is the *Carlisle*, one of the Cs converted for A/A duties. Note the 4-inch mounting and 2-pounder pom-pom forward and improved director. She fell victim to the German 'Stuka Club', at Scarpanto in October 1943, and was used as a base ship at Alexandria until 1949, when she was scrapped.

take of the undersized Arethusas, the designers gave them a displacement well in excess of 9,000 tons so that they could ship twelve 6-inch and eight 4-inch guns and machinery for 32½ knots. By involving seven separate shipyards, all went into the water in the space of only 22 months. It became apparent that they were a little overarmed for their size and the 9,100 tons of the first four was increased by 300 tons with a six-inch increase in beam. Even this was apparently not the full answer, for the third group, the *Edinburgh* and *Belfast*, were only just inside the still-observed 10,000-ton limit, with an increase of yet another foot in beam and of 22-feet in length, from 591½ feet to 613½. Much improved vertical protection was worked-in, though horizontal was no better than 2-inch. War experience, as a later account of *Edinburgh*'s sinking will show, proved the design to be generally excellent and with adequate stability but some slight doubts must have remained for, when *Belfast* was severely damaged by magnetic mine early in the war, her reconstruction included the bulging of the hull by an extra six feet.

By 1937, with the sands of time running out, it was apparent that the high quality of the Towns militated against rapid series

The eleven Atlantas were among the smallest cruisers in the American fleet and were based on the British Didos. All were armed with the standard twin 5-inch 38 gunhouses, and *San Diego*, shown here, was one of the earliest units with eight. Their powerful A/A support was valuable to the carriers in the Pacific war, but they had little post-war usefulness and were short-lived. Note the radiused sheerstrake.

Unique with their three forward turrets on different levels, the Didos were the Royal Navy's only purpose-built A/A cruisers. The 5·25-inch mountings were the same as those used for the secondary armament of later battleships. Of particular interest in this picture are the prominent degaussing girdle, RAS hoses by 'B' and 'C' turrets, and the paravane rig right forward.

production and a 'utility' version was introduced in the Fiji, or Crown Colony class. As beamy as the Towns, they retained their full armament though 36 feet shorter, which was partly accounted for by their transom sterns, a feature at once more economic and efficient, and also reducing vibration. Their austerely perpendicular top-hamper always nicely complemented the rakish good-looks of their predecessors but, like them, they were to land X-turret to save top-weight. Later units of the class, together with its derivatives were completed without it.

Finally, brief mention should be made of the Russians. Keen on the cruiser idea in pre-revolutionary days, the Soviet fleet had only a handful of First World War-vintage units to take it through to the early 'thirties and, when new tonnage was authorised in 1935, there was no design experience equal to the task and they bought it from the Italian firm of Ansaldo. The 8,800-ton Kirov class were, not surprisingly, closely similar to the later Condottieri, though only two were destined to be completed before the Soviet Union was overtaken by war. Their nine 7·1-inch guns were mounted in poorly designed turrets that did not allow the barrels to be separately elevated and the ships were of light construction for northern conditions.

This massive commitment in cruisers was, of course, only a part of the total strength with which the naval powers eyed each other in the last breathless days of the summer of 1939. In the ensuing five and a half years their relative strengths and weaknesses were to be fully exposed.

THE CRUISER IN THE SECOND WORLD WAR

The Second World War at Sea began as a European affair, involving initially only the major fleets of Britain and France on the one hand and that of Germany on the other. Following the collapse of France in May/June 1940, however, her fleet was removed as a coherent fighting force, the balance being tilted further by Italy declaring for the Axis, its vainglorious leader alive to the chance of easy pickings, only to turn the Mediterranean from a peaceful backwater into the cockpit that was to prove his undoing.

With the passing of the Grand Fleet, the Royal Navy's capital ships now numbered only fifteen; these were to work independently or in small groups and the function of the cruisers had therefore also changed somewhat. Though still organised into squadrons, they were to act very much more individually except when involved in specific operations. Even in 1914–18, the High Seas Fleet never thought in terms of challenging the Grand Fleet in straight combat, but the Kriegsmarine of 1939 was far weaker comparatively, developing slowly through the ambitious Plan Z towards a war in 1944 or thereabouts, in which year it would have been balanced and formidable.

Though the Royal Navy could still muster a respectable number of cruisers on paper, it was never to have enough to fulfil its commitments, there being far too many small and over-age units which had survived because of lack of funds in the recession of the 'thirties and also by virtue of the disarmament treaties. There had been a 'total tonnage' limit and, had Britain built modern units, this tonnage would have been absorbed by far too few cruisers for her needs.

Available to the British were fifteen 8-inch ships, thirteen Counties (two of them Australian) with the two smaller Yorks.

Large, 6-inch cruisers comprised eight Southamptons and the two larger Edinburgh class derivatives, together with eleven smaller Fiji, or Crown Colony, class under construction. Modern smaller 6-inch units included the Arethusa and Leander groups, twelve strong and again including two Australian ships. Three serviceable Effinghams remained, with their oddly-assorted armament, two Es, eight Ds and thirteen Cs, of which eight had been remodelled around a high angle 4-inch A/A armament. Eleven specialist A/A cruisers of the Dido class were also building, armed with dual-purpose 5·25-inch armament.

No less than 28 assorted cruisers were based in Home waters at the outbreak of war, in suitably balanced forces designed to deal with any major sally on the part of the German fleet, to intercept outward-bound raiders and to establish a blockade in the time-honoured fashion. For sea control in a wider sense, forces were based on Halifax, the West Indies and Gibraltar with, initially, a modern French squadron working out of Brest. The long-legged Counties in particular were to prove invaluable against the proliferation of supply ships stationed in the Atlantic by the enemy to increase the endurance of his U-boats and raiders. Though a force based on Gibraltar could also cover the western Mediterranean basin, this area was looked upon as a French responsibility, with her forces, based mainly on Toulon, Mers el Kebir (Oran) and Algiers, adequate to meet any Italian threat.

In the economically-important Far East there were 15 cruisers, part of a balanced fleet covering the East Indies and China, an area where range was important. These units included three elderly Ds, long on the station, and RAN and RNZN ships, one of which was the *Adelaide*, an Australian-built 'Town' of First World War vintage. This overall disposition of cruisers proved equal to the tasks envisaged pre-war but was to undergo drastic change as the pattern of hostilities developed. Not having sufficient regular warships to pursue an effective war against commerce, the enemy again employed Auxiliary Cruisers (Handelsstorkreuzer), chosen this time rather more judiciously, not from among the ranks of express liners but from powerfully-built merchantmen, picked for their endurance and ability to adopt disguise easily. However, it was to be 1940 before these ships could be available and the Allied fleets' immediate task was to deal with two so-called 'pocket battleships', *Deutschland* and *Graf Spee*, that had sailed in late August 1939. Charged to destroy commercial traffic 'by all available means' they were well supported by supply ships to extend their endurance but anxious to avoid action with warships, lest they be damaged far from dockyard assistance.

Deutschland operated in the North Atlantic until November with conspicuous lack of success, sinking only two ships of 6,902 grt., but *Graf Spee* was to be more adventurous. Her first sinking, off Pernambuco, caused the British and French to form no less than eight hunting groups, absorbing four carriers, three battlecruisers, ten 8-inch and six 6-inch cruisers, demonstrating once again how a single raider could occupy the attentions of vastly disproportionate forces.

During October the *Graf Spee* was to claim four more victims in the South Atlantic, her captain, Langsdorff, acting with scrupulous fairness and transferring crews to his auxiliary, *Altmark*, before sinking their ships. With the chase hotting-up, Langsdorff doubled the Cape to appear in the Mozambique Channel briefly before returning quickly to his old haunts. Several sinkings early in December plotted his steady progress toward the rich pickings off the Plate, which area was the responsibility of Commodore Henry Harwood with Force G, comprising the two 8-inch cruisers *Cumberland* and *Exeter* and two 6-inch Leanders, *Ajax* and *Achilles*. Convinced of *Graf Spee*'s intentions, yet with *Cumberland* away at the Falklands, Harwood concentrated his three remaining ships. When, at first light on the following day, December 13th, 1939, his quarry appeared, dead on cue, each of his command knew precisely what to do.

The plan was to divide the fire of the enemy's two 11-inch turrets by attacking in two divisions, the two light cruisers and the lone *Exeter*. Though showing some indecision, the German's fire was excellent and, within 40 minutes, two out of the *Exeter*'s three turrets were out of action, despite the terrier-like tactics of her two compatriots which came also under heavy 5·9-inch fire from the *Graf Spee*'s secondary armament. Neither 6- nor 8-inch projectiles could hope to cause mortal damage through the enemy's 100 mm side armour but this was offset by the dash and courage of Harwood's ships which kept their great adversary on the defensive. With *Exeter* forced to withdraw, heavily damaged, the others tried a vain torpedo attack, only to have *Ajax* lose two turrets to a severe hit. Yet, as though four months at sea had numbed his sense of resolution, Langsdorff fell back on neutral waters, allowing his still-belligerent shadows to dog him into safe anchorage off Montevideo. Limited by convention to a maximum time to be spent in a neutral port, she did not dare to come out to face Harwood's reinforced cruisers and she was scuttled. Though cheated of the satisfaction of a clean kill, Force G had won a fine victory by any standards and, had Harwood's tactics been adopted by Holland against *Bismarck* nearly eighteen months later, the result of that action could well have been very different.

Early recognising the potential threat posed by the aircraft, the Admiralty put 4-inch HA guns in increasing numbers into every cruiser from the Counties onward, later ships mounting eight in four twin

Battle of the Plate – the final act. At sunset on 17 December 1939 the *Graf Spee* destroyed herself. *Ajax*, two turrets inoperative from damage, was still on station with *Achilles*. Together with the newly-arrived *Cumberland*, she comes inshore to allow her crew a glimpse of the burning enemy.

Gutted by fire and explosion, the remains of the *Graf Spee* settle into the mud of the Plate estuary. Note the early radar antennas on the main director.

mountings. A most successful gun, it serves to this day in ex-RN ships serving under foreign flags, and in escorts as well. The far-sighted A/A conversions of the 'C' class had led directly to the Didos, with homogeneous armament of ten 5·25s. Certainly among the most beautiful cruisers ever built, their lean gunbarrels, fine masts and perfectly proportioned funnels were complemented by a slender hull, presenting an elegant whole that entirely belied their fighting potential. Involved in some of the war's most contested operations, five of the eleven were to be lost. However, on balance, the 5·25 was less than successful, being too heavy for concentrated and rapid A/A fire yet not carrying sufficient punch to be lethal to a surface target. Though the 6-inch/4-inch mix was undoubtedly superior, the Didos, in turn, inspired the American Atlantas, again eleven-strong and slightly larger to mount no less than sixteen (later twelve) 5-inch weapons in the US Navy's standard twin 38-calibre gunhouses.

War experience was to demonstrate quickly the vulnerability of warships, even the most agile, to aerial attacks, in the most dangerous of which aircraft came in sufficient numbers to saturate the A/A armament and could combine the threat of both dive and torpedo bombers. An early example occurred during the doleful Norwegian campaign of April 1940, when the A/A conversions *Curlew* and the modern 'Tribal' class destroyer *Gurkha* were lost to a synchronised attack by over 80 Ju 88s and He 111s.

Fully committed to the Norwegian invasion, the Kriegsmarine suffered badly, losing, among others, three cruisers that it could ill afford. Their British opposite numbers were heavily involved in escorting, carrying and, later, evacuating a large part of the army, and serving a hard apprenticeship in the arts of three-dimensional war. On 17th April 1940 for instance, *Suffolk* severely damaged an enemy seaplane base at Stavanger by 8-inch bombardment, but was fortunate to survive the resulting attentions of Ju 88s of II/KG 30, arriving home with her quarterdeck awash after seven hours of continuous attack.

Success attended German arms on all fronts in 1940; the fall of the Low Countries, Norway and Denmark was hardly surprising, but that of France was numbing. With her fall, affiliations were sharply divided and her fine fleet never given a chance to prove itself. Some ships joined the British, others were interned and disarmed; some remained true to the Vichy regime, becoming associated with the sad affairs at Mers el Kebir or Dakar, or later to be scuttled at Toulon. Lost to the Allied cause were many ships, needed the more desperately after 10th June, when Mussolini, encouraged by the debacle at Dunkirk, threw in his lot with the Axis. His fleet, including six battleships, nineteen cruisers and 125 flotilla ships, no longer being contained by the French, became the responsibility of Admiral Cunningham's Mediterranean Fleet. Already reinforced, the latter, based

Carrying part of the force intended for the occupation of Oslo, the German heavy cruiser *Blücher* sets sail in April 1940. In attempting to force the Drøbak Narrows in Oslofjord she capsized with heavy loss of life, after being badly damaged by shore-based guns and torpedoes.

on Gibraltar, Malta and Alexandria, took the offensive from the outset, putting considerable pressure on the Italians, who were bent on running supplies to their North African armies, which were already retreating westward before British land forces from Egypt.

With its superior speed, the Italian fleet declined action off Calabria on 9th July 1940 but were surprised only ten days later to lose the *Bartolomeo Colleoni*, one of two 6-inch cruisers lured by destroyers off Cape Spada on to the guns of the lone Australian cruiser *Sydney*.

Though Malta's vulnerability was apparent, it was still no real problem to keep it supplied as Mussolini, undaunted by his North African reverses, began an equally disastrous adventure in Greece in October of the same year. This episode had the doubly unfortunate result of involving British land forces and brought about German support for their ally in the Balkans and Africa. Elements of what was to become the famed Afrika Korps crossed the Mediterranean in February 1941, preceded to Sicilian airfields by the Luftwaffe's Fliegerkorps X (X Fl. K), an experienced anti-shipping strike group that had already demonstrated off Norway that effective fleet operations were no longer possible without command of the air. In the Mediterranean it was to prove the fact conclusively.

Carriers, and lack of carriers, were to influence the sea war in all theatres. In November 1940, a model air strike devastated an Italian fleet secure in its Taranto base – an attack noted for future reference by eyes in the Far East.

During March 1941, the Italians were persuaded by their partners to put a large force to sea to intercept British convoys between Greece and Alexandria. Caught off Cape Matapan by carrier aircraft, their battleship *Vittorio Veneto* and the heavy cruiser *Pola* were torpedoed. Cunningham's fleet caught up with its limping adversaries after dark and, although missing the capital ship, despatched *Pola* and two sister ships in a hurricane of close-range major-calibre fire. The action taught no real lessons other than the value of training in night fighting, already demonstrated at Jutland and due to influence the war in the Pacific at a later date. Malta remained the key to domination of the Mediterranean but, though determined assault by airborne troops could have taken it, the Germans had suffered severely in a similar operation in Crete and sought to reduce the island by bombing. From mid-1941, the sea war in the area polarised into battles for supplies, with convoys the prime targets for either side; the enemy armies depended upon the Italians' getting ships through to Tripoli or Benghazi, a course disputed largely by British forces based on Malta which, in turn, existed through the Royal Navy's ability to fight through convoys from east or west. Though the enemy route was fairly short, his losses topped one million gross registered tons by the end of 1941 and cruisers were then being used for overnight dashes, usually with deck cargoes

The Italian heavy cruiser *Zara* during the indecisive action of 9 July 1940 against the British off the Calabrian coast. Her 8-inch guns are near maximum elevation, with the forward turrets on the extreme after bearing.

The British cruisers (from left to right) *Berwick*, *Newcastle* and *Southampton* in hot pursuit of Italian forces off Spartivento in November 1940. Heavy return fire from the Italian's two battleships damaged *Berwick*. Walrus amphibians can be seen on the cruisers' catapults.

of fuel. Several of the early Condottieris were used, *Luigi Cadorna* making several successful runs. Her sisters, *Alberico da Barbiano* and *Alberto di Giussano* were unfortunate enough to run foul of a brilliantly-executed destroyer ambush close under Cape Bon, torpedoes detonating their volatile cargoes and incinerating both ships together with the larger part of the crews. The Royal Navy's great advantage of radar was further exploited by the Force K cruisers *Aurora* and *Penelope* out of Malta which, on one occasion, destroyed a complete seven-ship convoy under the noses of an escort that included a brace of 8-inch cruisers.

By far the greatest discomfiture to the British convoys came from the air, land-based because of the teachings of Douhet and because a plentiful supply of airfields convinced the Italians that they had no need of carriers. Matapan and Taranto changed all that and a crash programme was commenced to convert two liners to carriers, following the example of the British *Argus* and Japanese Taiyo classes. Painfully slow progress on them prompted the naval architect to an interim proposal, that of razing the torpedo-damaged heavy cruiser *Bolzano* and using it to carry twelve Reggiane Re 2000 fighters, which were to be ranged unprotected along the upper deck and launched from two bow catapults. Neither project was destined to be completed.

With the arrival of the Luftwaffe in Sicily began the period of Malta's struggle for survival, with every movement by sea contested and the island scourged by relentless bombing. On 10th January 1941, the British carrier *Illustrious* had nearly succumbed to a beautifully-coordinated attack by the newly-arrived Junkers 87s and 88s which, on the following day, severely dealt with two cruisers running in troops to the island, the *Southampton* being sunk. Her loss, as was that soon afterward of the *Gloucester* off Crete, was due largely to the saturation of her A/A armament by a concentrated assault. More disturbing was the loss in the same area of the *Fiji* and the A/A cruiser *Coventry* which, after days of unremitting action, each fell victim to only two aircraft.

Space does not permit the detailing of all the bitterly-opposed Malta convoys and the description of Vian's action off Sirte, which will be told later, must suffice. From early 1941 until August 1942 convoys kept the island alive, and then from Alamein onward the situation eased. Opposition to them had come, like the Devil, in many forms – surface attack, high and low level bombing, torpedoes from aircraft, fast attack craft and submarines, even mines.

In June 1941, Britain found herself in unlikely alliance with the Soviet Union who had suddenly been savaged by her erstwhile German partners. This reeling colossus had manpower but no equipment and the Royal Navy found itself stretched even further in covering a new series of convoys to the Arctic, enfiladed from enemy-occupied Norway and assaulted by some of the world's worst weather. Where it was customary to give east-bound Malta convoys a close-in heavy escort which turned back at the Narrows, northern practice was to provide a close escort of flotilla ships and a distant cover of Home Fleet heavy units positioned particularly to safeguard the vulnerable point off North Cape where out and homeward-bound convoys crossed.

In December 1941, the yet-uncommitted United States was pitchforked into the conflict by the Japanese pre-emptive strike at Pearl Harbor. Whatever its ethics, it was brilliantly executed but left Japan, like Germany in Russia, with a war that she could not possibly win.

The sea war in the Pacific was vast in scope and fought with very different objectives from that in the European theatre. Japan needed both space and resources, and intended to annexe the main island groups of Indonesia and the Philippines, backed by territory on the Asian rimland and protected by a fortified outer line of strategically sited Pacific islands. The plan was to be carried-out speedily by a series of coordinated operations and it was assumed that the Western Powers would accept a *fait accompli* rather than face a war on another front. A lot of fighting was needed to convince them of the error of this assumption.

Where Germany had few cruisers and those of Britain were employed mainly on commerce protection and fighting the convoys through, the powerful cruiser forces of both Japan and the US were available for more offensive deployment. In the integrated fleet context, however, the aircraft carrier emerged rapidly as the new capital ship, so dominating the war at sea as to relegate both battleship and cruiser to the role of consorts, screening her so that she might exercise her power to the full.

Though, at their entry into what was now a world war, the US Navy had only 37 cruisers (half of them with 8-inch armament), Congress had for some time taken the view that war was only a matter of time and had initiated a vast fleet expansion programme. With great vision, it produced the maximum number of hulls by the series production of a few successful designs, recognising that, in war, there is no time to waste in producing 'tailor-mades', a fact all too often forgotten in Britain. The late 1930s had seen the introduction of the ten-strong Brooklyn class, 10,000 tonners, mounting fifteen 6-inch guns as an answer to the Japanese Mogamis. One of the class, *Wichita*, was given three triple 8-inch turrets in a successful up-grading and, between them, the two designs formed the basis of the 13 8-inch Baltimores and the incredible run of 29 Cleveland/Fargo class cruisers, essentially four-turret versions of the Brooklyns. Nine further Cleveland hulls were bulged and completed as light fleet carriers (CVL), realising the suggestion made at the end of the First World War. Stowing 45 aircraft and capable of a speed of 33 knots, they were to prove valuable when fleet carriers were not available.

The only really original class produced by the Americans during hostilities was the, already briefly mentioned, eleven-strong Atlanta group. At 6,000 tons they were small by usually standards and carried no aircraft. They were designed purely as A/A platforms, carrying sixteen 5-inch guns in eight standard gunhouses, reduced to six later to save topweight. As aircraft became the major threat in the Pacific, the tophamper of all warships became festooned with 40 mm guntubs for throwing up curtain barrages. The secondary armament of the Atlantas, for instance, increasing from 10 to 24 40 mm guns at the expense of torpedo tubes. When, later in the war, the Kamikaze made its appearance there developed an urgent need for a gun capable of disintegrating an aircraft before it could crash into a ship, and the 3-inch 50 was introduced.

Until the US Navy could reorganise itself after Pearl Harbor, the Japanese ran rampant, taking strategic islands almost at will, from which they could mount further operations to secure the adjacent area. Their plans worked faultlessly because they were able to take seemingly appalling risks, due as much to the total disorder into which the Allied camp had been plunged as to its lack of material.

Among the last armoured cruisers to be built were the two Italian San Giorgios of 1910–11. The nameship (shown here) was rebuilt as an A/A ship in 1937–38, but was damaged by shell-fire from British cruisers at Tobruk in June 1940, to be scuttled on the capture of the town in January 1941. Note the main 10-inch turret, 7·5-inch wing turrets and a modern 100 mm twin mounting on the forecastle. Her back appears broken.

Japanese cruisers, half of the 36 available being 8-inch gunned, proved to be formidable antagonists. In addition to their powerful gun armament they carried anything up to sixteen 24-inch 'Long Lance' torpedoes, weapons which they were always ready to use in large numbers. Though their fire-control was basic and they lacked radar for a long time, they were doughty fighters by day and truly fearsome by night, an aspect of war that the US Navy had neglected.

Such Australian, British and Dutch naval forces as were available in the Far East were engaged initially in the protection of troop convoys and then in a bitter series of evacuations and rearguard actions. Nothing was secure, Hong Kong fell on Christmas Day 1941 and Singapore only seven weeks later. It seemed only a matter of time until Australia, India and even East Africa would follow.

The Allied defensive 'build-up' on the important island of Java was set back badly by a massive air strike on the Australian port of Darwin, mounted largely by the same enemy carrier group that had ravished Pearl Harbor. Such Allied naval forces as were available were split in two owing to the size of the island and, on paper, the Soerabaya force of two heavy and three light cruisers, together with ten destroyers,

Immaculate against the pyres of 'Battleship Row', the Brooklyn-class cruiser *Phoenix* (CL 46) slips out to sea at the height of the attack on Pearl Harbor in December 1941. Her secondary 5-inch guns are elevated but uniformly aligned as the Japanese offer only fleeting targets.

looked formidable, but they were of four nationalities and unpracticed in working together. Already exhausted, they also lacked aerial reconnaissance and, in trying to repulse enemy landings in late February of 1942, were badly defeated by Japanese cruisers in a series of actions that came to be known as the Battle of the Java Sea. Though few enemy cruisers were, in fact, present two, *Haguro* and *Nachi*, were devastatingly accurate at nearly 30,000 yards in daylight. Another action by night was stopped dead by enemy torpedoes and the survivors largely destroyed piecemeal the following day, including the British *Exeter* which sank while fighting four Japanese heavy cruisers. This battle effectively ended the Allied naval presence in the Far East for the time being.

Having consolidated their outer defensive ring from Sumatra to Timor, though still contesting New Guinea, the enemy sent his main carrier group into the Indian Ocean. The Andamans were taken to cover the newly-acquired Burma and the nascent British Far East Fleet, forming on Ceylon, was hard hit in air strikes on both Colombo and Trincomalee in April 1942, losing not only the veteran carrier *Hermes* but also two County-class cruisers, overwhelmed by 53 dive bombers. Scouting had been by aircraft from the Japanese cruiser *Tone*, a hybrid ship with four twin 8-inch gunhouses forward and space aft for five floatplanes.

In attempting an invasion of Port Moresby the following month the Japanese were given a rude shock by the re-grouped Americans, both sides losing a carrier at the Battle of the Coral Sea, an action that set new standards because, although powerful cruiser forces were available on either side, it was the aircraft from the carriers that did the fighting and the gun, which had dominated the war at sea for over five centuries, had begun its rapid decline.

Early in June there followed the Midway action where the almost totally committed enemy fleet lost four carriers against the US one in a crushing defeat. Again it was land and carrier-based aircraft that did the execution. In addition, four of the Japanese heavy cruisers that had proved near-invincible only weeks earlier, ran into trouble on a bombardment mission, the *Mikuma* being sunk and the *Mogami* badly mauled. The battle established the aircraft carrier firmly as the new capital ship.

The American landing on Guadalcanal in August 1942, which led to the disastrous Battle of Savo Island, described later, began a weary trial of strength, with the invaders dominating the area with aircraft by day and the Japanese running in men and supplies by night in operations which were so regular that they became known as the 'Tokyo Express'. Ill-trained in night fighting, the US Navy gradually repaired the deficiency to the extent that an enemy bombardment group was soundly defeated in the night battle off Cape Esperance in October. On the night of 12th November 1942 the Japanese battleship *Hiei* was sunk, together with two US cruisers, but the enemy was undeterred and a sister ship, *Kirishima*, was sunk by battleship gun-fire only two nights later, one of only three capital ships so sunk during the Second World War.

In straight night combat, unchallenged by air attack, the Japanese cruisers still proved extraordinarily hard to tackle, cost-

Prelude to Matapan. The Italian 1st and 8th Cruiser Divisions near the island of Gaudo on the day of the action, 28 March 1941. *Zara*, *Pola* and *Fiume* are seen, leading the *Abruzzi*, from the destroyer escort. The first three were to be sunk.

ing the Americans the cruiser *Northampton* to a torpedo spread at Tassafaronga. Further actions at the Kula Gulf and Kolombangara in July 1943 disrupted the enemy but were in the nature of Pyrrhic victories. Not until August at the Vella Gulf, were the Japanese trounced by their own favourite weapon, the torpedo, rather than the gun. In the November, the actions of Empress Augusta Bay and Cape St. George brought the 'Express' to a halt.

Guadalcanal itself had already been evacuated by the enemy early in 1943, but had triggered two fleet actions, the battles of the Eastern Solomons in August 1942 and Santa Cruz in the following October. Each centred around carrier forces dedicated primarily to each other's destruction, their heavy escorts reduced to no more than A/A platforms. The whole theatre was now dominated by the aircraft with, for instance, no less than five of the enemy's redoubtable 8-inch cruisers being heavily damaged in one strike on their base at Rabaul in November 1943 by 97 aircraft from the US carriers *Saratoga* and *Princeton*.

Early in 1944, Japan was in retreat, being pushed relentlessly from one island to another but disputing each in a war of attrition that could have but one result. The tide really turned at the Philippine Sea battle of June 1944 where the enemy, bent on disrupting the American's re-conquest of the Marianas, mustered a considerable force that flung itself in vain against the inadequately-named Task Force 58, an armada with a solid core of fifteen carriers. Already low on aircrew, the Japanese lost another 350 aircraft and three carriers in what became known as the 'Great Marianas Turkey Shoot'. Under constant pressure from then on, they were never able to replace them.

October 1944 saw the American landings at Leyte Gulf in the Philippines, stimulating the final fleet showdown in a complex series of actions resulting from the Japanese plan to attack the beachhead simultaneously with forces from both north and south. To enable them to do this, Halsey's mighty Third Fleet was to be lured away by four enemy carriers which, though devoid of aircraft, would prove irresistible to the impetuous American admiral.

One Japanese striking force, under Kurita, with five battleships and ten cruisers, ran into American submarines, losing the battle-hardened heavy cruisers *Atago* and *Maya*, with a third, *Takao* dropping out in a sinking condition. Kurita battled on against a series of American carrier strikes, which cost him the super-battleship *Musashi*, for he had to rely only on land-based aircraft for his own cover. Though these aircraft suffered badly, they did succeed in hitting the CVL *Princeton* which was rapidly swept by uncontrollable fires. Such a crippled encumbrance would have been put down in the Royal Navy but, since Lawrence in 1814 started the 'Don't Give up the Ship' tradition, the US Navy has striven to bring lame ducks home. Thus is was that the cruisers *Reno* and *Birmingham* were close aboard fighting *Princeton*'s fires when she detonated in a series of devastating explosions. *Birmingham* was swept by fragments, fire fighting crews and 'rubber-neckers' being mown down in hundreds.

Midway, in June 1942, marked the watershed of the Pacific war, when the American fleet switched to the offensive. The Japanese heavy cruisers *Mogami* and *Mikuma* collided and were then hit by an American carrier strike. *Mikuma* sank after being reduced to the condition shown in the picture.

Meanwhile, the ploy to entice Halsey away worked only too well, Kurita being able to penetrate almost to the beachhead before being fooled into retreat by a resolutely-fought group of escort carriers. Fortunately, the southern arm of the Japanese pincer ran into a veteran American battleship force covering the Surigao Strait and was shattered in a gun action by night. Victory thus was absolute though Halsey's rash pursuit of the carriers – all of which were to be destroyed – had put the Americans on the very brink of disaster.

After Leyte, the once-proud Imperial Japanese Navy virtually ceased to exist and a new foe, the sinister Kamikaze, took the stage. The dubious distinction of being the first target for this weapon was the Australian heavy cruiser *Australia* off Luzon; her three funnels were to prove an irresistible target, for she was struck by three more Kamikazes on successive days in the following January in the Lingayen Gulf. She survived but had to pull out.

It was off Leyte in the closing days of the war that the US Navy was to suffer its heaviest loss when the heavy cruiser *Indianapolis* was sunk by torpedo with a death-toll of 900. She had just delivered parts of the nuclear bombs that were instrumental in

PQ13 convoy of March 1942. Attacking German destroyers were surprised in low visibility by the British cruiser *Trinidad*. In disabling the Z26, here seen sinking, the cruiser was badly damaged by one of her own torpedoes, which had circled out of control.

the termination of the Far Eastern war. In the west, meanwhile, the balance had shifted measurably after about the third quarter of 1942. Priorities had been directed toward fighting the convoys through and containing the enemy fleet.

With the availability of more and more specialist frigates and long range aircraft, the U-boat was being gradually countered, releasing fleet destroyers for work better suited to them. Techniques were developed whereby a convoy would have a close 'fighting escort' of destroyers, covered at a distance by a small cruiser force. The effectiveness of this was demonstrated on the last day of 1942, when a northbound Russian convoy was attacked by two groups of German warships, each of three large destroyers and led by the 'pocket battleship' *Lutzow* and the heavy cruiser *Hipper*. Six British destroyers under the splendid leadership of Captain R. St. V. Sherbrooke in the *Onslow* kept the uncertain enemy guessing by going on the offensive, and, though pitting their 4 and 4·7-inch guns against a mixture of 11, 8, 5·9 and 5-inch, kept him at bay until he was forced to retire by the welcome arrival of the 6-inch cruisers *Sheffield* and *Jamaica*. Hitler's rage at this lack of resolve by his forces resulted in some of the major German units being paid off. This in turn, provoked the resignation of Grand Admiral Raeder.

It was fortunate that it was customary to use heavy units of the Home Fleet as distant cover when available for, nearly a year later, on Boxing Day 1943 and again off the North Cape, the fast battleship *Scharnhorst* made contact with the Arctic gloom with another Russia-bound convoy. Interposed, however, were the three cruisers *Belfast*, *Norfolk* and *Sheffield* and, in extremely bad conditions, the County put an 8-inch shell into *Scharnhorst*'s main gunnery radar position. The blinded Cyclops fell back but continued shadowing the convoy, dogged by the cruisers which frustrated his every approach whilst shepherding him in the direction of the *Duke of York*, whose presence he never suspected. Yet, even with 14-inch shell damage from the battleship's guns, *Scharnhorst's* superior speed would have enabled him to escape but for a classic four-destroyer attack that put four torpedoes into him (an action to be repeated in the sinking of the Japanese heavy cruiser *Haguro* in May 1945). When finally closed again by the *Duke of York* and the cruisers *Scharnhorst* was doomed but, like her namesake of 1914, fought to the end.

The northern route to Russia was to be secured by the commissioning of more flight decks as the opposition declined to a scattered collection of enemy surface ships, low on both fuel and morale. Declining standards in U-boat commanders as earlier 'aces' were eliminated also contributed, as did a whittling away of the Luftwaffe strength in the north to meet the growing needs of the Eastern Front and the increasing bombing offensive against the German heartland. In the Mediterranean, the combined onslaught by the RN and RAF virtually severed the Afrika Korps supply route, even as the cautious Montgomery gathered strength by the Great Sand Sea. Ensuing victory at el Alamein was a virtual certainty and, as the Eighth Army rolled westward, it captured those airfields from which the enemy had disputed the passage of the convoys. Landings at the other end of the North African coast sealed the enemy's fate.

But the work of the navy was far from done, for Europe itself was now to be

The powerful air strikes of the Japanese carrier forces exposed the weaknesses of older Royal Navy warships. Here the heavy cruiser *Cornwall* sinks after an attack by 53 dive bombers. Notice how the useless 8-inch main battery is trained fore and aft.

assaulted by a series of amphibious landings in which the cruisers of both the Royal and US Navies were to be busily employed in gunnery support, 'softening up' the zones before the actual landings and subsequently firing under instructions from forward, land-based observers. Sicily, Calabria, Salerno, Anzio and the South of France – each landing was different, each signified a further stage in the progress of the war.

Salerno and Anzio were particularly disputed by the defending Germans, determined to demonstrate that their ally's capitulation on 8th September 1943 was not significant. On the day of the Salerno landing, five British light cruisers and one American landed a complete Airborne Division at the important naval port of Taranto to prevent the enemy digging in.

These landings were also notable for the slowly-moving bombardment ships offshore being assailed by a new weapon, the air-to-ground missile. Two of these in the form of the Hs293 and FX1400 glider bombs had been developed and, deployed by Do 217s of the specialist KG100, had already been used to disrupt a British A/S sweep in the Bay of Biscay and to sink the newly-surrendered Italian battleship *Roma*. A/A fire against such small targets was usually ineffective, the controlling aircraft being left unmolested far above. Off Salerno, the

Anzio, January 1944. Offshore shipping with the British 'Improved Dido' *Spartan* in the foreground in a support role. On 29 January she was sunk by a German glider bomb. The shorter, vertical funnels and only four turrets compared with the original Dido's five are points to notice.

The 11,800-ton Italian cruiser *Gorizia* racing to intercept Vian at the Second Battle of Sirte in March 1942. Already weather conditions were severe enough to encourage the Italians to train A-turret on to the beam.

British cruiser *Uganda* and the American *Savannah* were heavily damaged by bombs plunging deep into their vitals, as was the veteran battleship *Warspite*. At Anzio, the improved 'Dido', *Spartan*, was to be sunk. Countering these difficult weapons required fighter support to intercept the parent aircraft, a problem that exists to this day, though it is interesting that attempts were made at the time by the Americans to jam the radio control transmissions, an example of what would now be termed electronic countermeasures, or ECM.

These new weapons were, however, to prove rather ineffective against fast, free-manoeuvring targets as when the British cruisers *Enterprise* and *Glasgow* were attacked in the Bay of Biscay on 28th December 1943. On this occasion, eleven German destroyers were out to escort the blockade-runner *Alsterufer* into the Gironde, only to have her sunk by aircraft and then run into the cruisers. Had conditions been calm, the British would have had a problem against so many ships but, in the heavy sea that was running, their steady platforms and rapid, accurate fire proved, as had been the case in the First World War, that flotilla attacks could be thwarted. Three of the destroyers were sunk. When a cruiser's armament was too widely spread, however, destroyers could still pick her off, as when five British ships sank the *Haguro*.

In the great armada supporting the Normandy landings in June 1944 were 23 cruisers in an active role while others, old units damaged or infirm, were scuttled to form part of the Gooseberry breakwater for the vital supply ships. Firmly on the bottom in shallow water, these ships, British, Dutch and French, still wore their ensigns proudly in their last assignment.

With the reduction in the effectiveness of the Luftwaffe, British ships returned in strength to Norway's waters and, in November 1944, the cruisers *Kent* and *Bellona* sank two out of a convoy of four off the Lyster Light, together with five of their six escorts, a neat reversal of earlier misfortunes in the First World War.

Europe was now becoming something of a backwater and more and more British naval units headed east to join the Americans. Unfortunately the latter regarded the Far East largely as 'their' war and the Royal Navy was hardly equipped with the necessary 'fleet train' to operate so far from their main bases in Australia. The equivalent to one of the US Navy's large Task Groups was formed, however, though tending to be used in secondary operations. As with their American counterparts, the British cruisers were used largely in carrier escort and shore support duties. Nevertheless in waging this most widespread of sea wars, the cruiser forces of the combatant fleets paid a stiff price for their achievements and a breakdown of their losses may be of interest.

Nationality	In Surface Action	To Submarines	To Aircraft	To Mines	Other Causes	Totals
Great Britain (inc. Commonwealth)	8	9	11	1	3	32
Germany (inc. Panzerschiffe)	2	1	6	–	1	10
Italy	6	3	3	–	5	17
Japan	4½	16	20½	–	–	41
United States	7	2	1	–	–	10
					Grand Total	110

In the follow-up to the Normandy landings in June 1944, cruisers were employed in a vital fire-support role. Here *Glasgow* looses a salvo against enemy shore batteries near Cherbourg. Beyond is the American heavy cruiser *Quincy* (CA 71), not to be confused with the earlier *Quincy* (CA 39) sunk at Savo Island.

The armed merchant cruiser – Jervis Bay

As already mentioned, the Royal Navy counted many small and over-age cruisers in its total strength at the outbreak of the Second World War, but still did not have the numbers necessary to meet its commitments, even allowing for new tonnage nearing completion. Anticipating this shortfall, the Admiralty commenced requisitioning before hostilities broke out suitable tonnage for rapid conversion into Armed Merchant Cruisers. These had proved their value in the First World War, where their large bunker and storage capacities gave them great endurance for their primary task of replacing regular cruisers in blockade and long distance patrol duties. No fewer than 56 twin-screw passenger liners were taken over, but such was the toll taken of them, particularly by U-boat torpedoes, that most had been withdrawn by the end of 1942. In the early days of the North Atlantic convoys, escorts too, were in short supply and AMCs were sometimes used, though the protection they afforded was minimal as they had no A/S weapons and insufficient gun armament to engage a surface raider effectively. Such a ship was the *Jervis Bay*.

Of 14,184 gross registered tons, she had been built to the account of the Australian government's Commonwealth Line in the early 'twenties, the last of five 'Bay' class emigrant and cargo carriers. Cursed with recurrent labour problems, the company was unable to attract sufficient custom and was soon in dire straits. In 1928 its ships were sold and acquired by the British White Star Line, but they were run as a separate entity by grafting their operation on to that of the old Aberdeen Line, whose handsome Brunswick green hulls and buff funnels they now adopted. However, shipping was heading for one of its periodic downturns and the mighty White Star itself fell on hard times, in 1934 being forced by the Government into a shotgun marriage with Cunard, the Aberdeen and Commonwealth passing under P & O/Shaw Savill control.

In practice, all this upheaval made little difference to the 'Bays', which, throughout the 1930s, voyaged successfully but unspectacularly on the UK-Suez-Ceylon-Australia run.

In August 1939, *Jervis Bay* went round to the Tyne to be stripped of superfluous combustible fittings and for the mounting of armament suitable for her new role as an AMC; she sailed shortly afterward for the South Atlantic station, drab in a new overall coat of 'crabfat' and with eight old 6-inch guns in single mountings. Any peaceful existence in southern climes was to be short-lived however, for the convoys to the north were being severely ravaged in 1940 by submarine, aircraft and surface raiders. By October, six German auxiliary cruisers were operating in the area, their numbers due to be supplemented at the earliest opportunity by regular warships. These would come forward after repair of damage many had suffered from action during the Norwegian campaign of the previous spring.

The armoured cruiser *Admiral Scheer*, one of the trio of Deutschlands, purpose-built for commerce-raiding, sailed from Gotenhafen (now Gdynia) on 23rd October 1940, called briefly at Stavanger, and entered the Atlantic through the Denmark Strait, passing the latitude of Cape Farewell on 1st November. She passed undetected, due not only to the poor visibility that was so much a feature of the area, but also because of the withdrawal of the usual British cruiser and air patrols, because of a very real invasion threat at that time. Operating initially about midway along the UK – Cape Race route, *Admiral Scheer* claimed her first victim on 5th November, the Elders and Fyffe's reefer *Mopan*. Though it was required procedure for all merchantmen thus accosted to broadcast a general raider report, this ship did not succeed in so doing, which was unfortunate for, just west of the point where she was eventually sunk was the 37-ship convoy HX84, eastbound and recently out of Halifax, Nova Scotia. Its sole escort was the *Jervis Bay* commanded by Captain E. S. Fogarty Fegan, scion of a family that had produced generations of seafaring men.

For an early winter day in the North Atlantic it was uncharacteristically calm and, fortunately, already becoming dark when ships in the port wing column of the convoy sighted a strange warship, hull down on the northern horizon. Any doubts regarding her nationality were dispelled when an 11-inch salvo dropped neatly into the centre of the formation, perfectly sighted by the enemy's long-based optical range finder which was accurate at out to 50,000 yards, well beyond her gun range. Things looked bleak, but Fegan's reaction was unhesitating as he cut across the convoy directly toward the stranger, working up to the *Jervis Bay*'s full speed of 16 knots. Meanwhile directed by the convoy Commodore, Rear Admiral H. B. Maltby, all ships made funnel smoke and dropped smoke floats as they scattered throughout the quadrant from SW to the darkening SE, hastened by three-gun salvoes whose startlingly white columns rose mast-high against the charcoal sky.

Enemy fire was clearly attracted by the big *Rangitiki* of the New Zealand Shipping Company, but was being frustrated by the advancing *Jervis Bay*, whose guns, such as were bearing, were still well out of range. *Admiral Scheer* shifted target with contemptuous ease and accuracy, shells from her second salvo drilling through the thin skin of the AMC's port side, shattering the machinery space behind. The next set the bridge afire and a fourth wrecked the steering gear; she staggered on however, now firing and buying precious minutes for her charges as they scattered into the rapidly deepening gloom. But it was soon apparent that *Jervis Bay* was out of the fight and the enemy began to range on other targets, missing the wildly manoeuvring *Rangitiki* but hitting several others, five of which were sunk.

As it grew darker, experiencing difficulty in laying her guns, *Admiral Scheer* fired a starshell, which did not help her very much as its light merely reflected back from the thin smoke bank rolling toward her from the convoy on the light SE wind.

The one-sided action now took another incredible turn as the defensively-armed Canadian Pacific cargo liner *Beaverford* made directly at the enemy, ignoring the awful warning of the glowing hulk of her late escort. Inevitably, she paid the supreme penalty for her reckless courage, gaining a little more time at the expense of the lives of 77 of her crew. Darkness was now almost total, covering the *Jervis Bay*'s end as she slipped below, colours still flying and taking with her three-quarters of her 245-strong complement. Her survivors were saved by another act of courage as the neutral Swedish *Stureholm* returned in the black of night to see if any of the crew still lived; their number did not include Fegan.

Stureholm remained in the area until the early dawn glowered through rain and rapidly rising sea, but unfortunately did not

A Russian light cruiser, probably *Krasni Kavkaz*, built in 1916 as the *Admiral Lazarev* of the Czarist fleet, in action during the Second World War, though the ship in the foreground looks un-committed to say the least. Of 8,030 tons, she mounted four 180 mm and twelve 100 mm guns.

The American cruiser *Pensacola* (CA 24) lies at the advanced fleet base of Espiritu Santo after becoming another victim of Japanese torpedoes in the bitterly contested waters around Guadalcanal. Note the temporary patch just forward of X-turret.

sight a further boatload of survivors. These were from the Eagle Oil tanker *San Demetrio* which, with 11,000 tons of crude oil below, was hit both forward and in the amidships bridge structure. Well ablaze, she had been understandably abandoned. Her boat fought on through the deteriorating weather, its weary crew heartened beyond measure, when, about noon on the following day they sighted a ship downwind. It is hard to imagine their feelings when, on closing her, they discovered that she was the partly gutted hulk of their own ship. Largely for reassurance in the hostile waste of ocean, they lay close aboard the smouldering derelict for another miserable night in the near gale now running. Next morning, *San Demetrio* was still there and the sixteen men reboarded her by the trailing ladders by which they had left. How, with no steering gear, no charts and the barest essentials of navigational equipment they raised steam and brought their ship and cargo into the Clyde on 19th November is another story.

Meanwhile, the hue and cry that followed the HX84 incident passed the *Admiral Scheer* by as she wisely made southward, spending almost a month cruising the Gibraltar-Panama track. Because of the activities of several other raiders, few victims were available to her and only two were taken but, though each gave a clear warning of attack, Allied patrol groups failed to apprehend the *Admiral Scheer*, which gravitated further down to the Atlantic narrows. This area was so utterly devoid of shipping that a rendezvous was arranged with the auxiliary cruisers *Thor* and *Pinguin*, to render the armoured cruiser assistance in a self refit at sea, necessary for ships where dockings could only be few and far between.

In the early days of 1941, *Scheer* went briefly north, claiming three more foreign merchantmen by pretending to each that she was British. After a mid-ocean refuelling rendezvous, the raider then doubled the Cape of Good Hope to enter the Indian Ocean in mid-February, passing east of Madagascar to hit the traffic at the northern end of the Mozambique Channel. She spent a month in the area though, even using her Arado floatplane for scouting, she sank only four ships, the last of which sent an *en clair* signal that was intercepted by the British cruiser *Glasgow*, only 150 miles distant. Promptly catapulting her own aircraft the latter soon established visual contact and, with a comfortable margin of speed over her heavier adversary, should have had little difficulty in tracking and reporting until assistance was to hand. It was a great disappointment that the enemy evaded her almost immediately in an area of low visibility, doubling back before the British could effect the required concentration.

After a leisurely and uneventful return passage through the length of the central Atlantic, *Admiral Scheer* slipped through the overcast Denmark Strait and reached Germany on April 1st, 1941, after about five months at sea. She had sunk a useful 100,000 gross tons of shipping in addition to the *Jervis Bay* and, in conjunction with the other raiders, had caused widespread disruption and occupied the time of many British warships which could have been more profitably employed.

The last, tragic fight of the *Jervis Bay*, for which her captain was awarded a posthumous Victoria Cross, highlighted the shortcomings of these temporary AMC expedients, for which no amount of heroism could compensate. A year previously, in fact, the P & O liner *Rawalpindi* had suffered a similar fate in a hopeless gun duel,

HMS *Enterprise* differed from her sister *Emerald* in mounting a prototype twin 6-inch turret forward. She is seen here early in 1944 after her successful action in the Bay of Biscay where, with *Glasgow*, she defeated a powerful force of German destroyers.

A 1943 picture of the French sister cruisers *La Galissonnière* and *Jean de Vienne* after salvage at the Toulon base, where they had been scuttled in November 1942 rather than accept German take-over.

and submarines continued to exact a toll. One of the first results of the swelling numbers of specialist escorts was, therefore, the early retirement of the AMCs to duties more suitable to their abilities, remaining as escorts only in the peaceful Far East seas. For the rest, most found employment in the interminable movement of troops about the world and it is to be hoped that never again will merchantmen be pitted against warships.

The fighting cruiser – Second Battle of Sirte

Following Italy's ill-advised declaration of war, under the inspired leadership of Admiral Cunningham the Royal Navy established rapid domination of the

Mediterranean, an initiative that hinged on the use of the strategically important bases at Gibraltar, Malta and Alexandria. Mussolini's reeling North African army, meanwhile, was buttressed by Rommel's Afrika Korps to such good effect that the British land forces were being pushed relentlessly back to the Nile Delta. For the enemy armies, however, every last bullet and jerrican had to cross the Mediterranean from Italy or Sicily, a route commanded by Malta-based Allied ships and aircraft. Realizing that to muzzle Cunningham was the key to the situation, the Germans moved the X Fliegerkorps to Sicily. This was made up of anti-ship specialists who had demonstrated already in Norway that a modern fleet could not operate effectively without air superiority. This elite unit was reinforced by bombardment groups whose function was to pound Malta, its dockyard, its airfields and its populace to the point where it would be ripe for direct assault.

Depending upon its few carriers, the Royal Navy was badly handicapped when first *Illustrious*, and then *Formidable*, were disabled by precision dive bombing, followed by the loss of *Ark Royal* to a single torpedo from a submarine. Without these carriers or friendly airfields beyond the Egyptian frontier, the naval forces based on Alexandria were virtually beleaguered, yet without regular convoys and replacements for her fighter defences, Malta was doomed. This simple truth was well realised by both camps and a bitter contest began, with the island as the ultimate prize.

February 1941 had seen the beginnings of convoys passing to both Malta and to Rommel on the African coast, uneventful operations that were not to be repeated. Cruisers, having both capacity and speed, ran troop reinforcements in, but a convoy from Alexandria in March 1941, the month of Matapan, was opposed. Operation 'Substance' in July brought a large convoy through from Gibraltar, repeated by 'Halberd' in September. Though losses were acceptable, opposition was noticeably increasing and two groups of merchantmen were fought through in January 1942 only by a powerful surface escort. Finally in mid-February a three-ship convoy lost two of its number and had the third disabled, a deteriorating situation that was aggravated further by detachment of vital warships to meet new commitments in the Far East and Atlantic.

The unsuccessful February operation had been under the direction of Rear Admiral Vian, who had caught the public eye during the Norwegian campaign by taking his destroyer, *Cossack*, into a fjord to cut out the German *Altmark* and her cargo of prisoners. Described accurately by Cunningham as 'a fighting sailor', it was predictable that the failure would serve only as a spur to Vian, though he was to experience a further setback on 11th March 1942, when his flagship was sunk under him by a U-boat after an attempted interception of an Italian convoy.

On 20th March, the MW10 convoy of four fast cargo liners left Alexandria with a close escort of the A/A cruiser *Carlisle* and six destroyers, soon to be joined by Vian with three more Didos and four further destroyers. Six Hunts embarked on an A/S sweep along the convoy's planned track, ominously losing one of their number to the torpedo of an intended victim. Looked at as a whole, the light calibre of the escort's armament put it at a disadvantage in view of the fact that the Italian fleet was now becoming a little more enterprising following the removal of the carrier threat. Submarines based outside Taranto and Messina, together with Malta's few remaining reconnaissance aircraft, had to suffice as distant cover.

After thirty-six uneventful hours' steaming, MW10, augmented by the Hunts, was west of Tobruk when two Italian submarines and a German transport aircraft made the first sighting reports, midway between the African coast and Crete. However, the expected bombing did not follow as the Allied army, in a linked operation, was successfully worrying the enemy's forward airfields. Soon after 05.00 on the following morning, the 22nd, the watchful submarines warned Vian that the 15-inch gunned battleship *Littorio* and six destroyers were sailing from Taranto. At the same time a severe pounding of Maltese airfields prevented any aerial reconnaissance; had there been any, it might have reported a second force, of the 8-inch cruisers *Gorizia* and *Trento*, the 6-inch *Giovanni della Bande Nere* and four destroyers leaving Messina, bound for a rendezvous with the first group off the Gulf of Sirte on the convoy's projected route. Fortunately, for Vian, he was reinforced by the cruiser *Penelope* and a further destroyer at 08.00. This additional cruiser's 6-inch guns were the heaviest in the escort.

Following Nelson's example of holding a pre-engagement council of war of all his commanding officers aboard his flagship, Vian outlined his plans so that each would know his duties without further instruction. The fighting escort was to be grouped into five separate divisions for an action where speed and manoeuvre would need to compensate to a large degree for lack of firepower. *Carlisle* and one Hunt were detailed-off to provide continuous smoke cover for the

Operation 'Pedestal', the famous August convoy of 1942, was fought through to Malta at high cost. The Italian fleet had insufficient air cover to attack in force as planned, and the sortie ended disastrously when it encountered the submarine *Unbroken* near the Aeolian Islands. Both *Muzio Attendolo* and *Bolzano* can be seen torpedoed and heavily damaged.

convoy, which was also to be closed by the remaining Hunts as a 'last-ditch' defence, their armament being H/A 4-inch weapons and lacking torpedo tubes.

On an exhilaratingly blustery afternoon, with a rapidly falling glass and a rising gale pushing an increasingly lumpy sea from the port quarter, the force was corkscrewing its way westward when, at 14.10, *Euryalus* reported smoke to the NW, followed by a sighting report. It was the Messina group.

With the advantage of the weather gauge, Vian's fighting divisions tore off toward the enemy whilst the convoy, with close escort, turned SW, only to be immediately embroiled in a brisk air attack in which high-level Italian bombing was synchronised with a strike by torpedo bombers of II Fliegerkorps. This was met by the massed barrage of the escort and the characteristic and ear-splitting cracks of the short-barrelled 4-inch. Meanwhile, the flagship *Cleopatra*, together with the *Euryalus*, tried hard to close the enemy in visibility already poor enough to make identification uncertain. That the Italians were not battleships was resolved at 14.36 when the splashes of 8-inch ranging salvoes suddenly erupted from the water; still 20,000 yards distant, they comfortably out-ranged Vian's 5·25s, whose long barrels, at maximum elevation, still remained silent, describing arcs against the torn clouds.

Straining like thoroughbreds, the cruisers, now backed by a wall of smoke in every shade of grey rolling before the brisk south-easter, finally made the range at 14.56. After only a brief exchange of fire, however, the Italians opened the range again to the northward, possibly through uncertainty, possibly to lure Vian away from his prime responsibility, the convoy. Not to be so easily drawn, the cruisers fell back, joining their still-unscathed charges by 16.30. The lack of damage thus far had been bought at the price of prodigious expenditure of A/A ammunition, for accurate gunnery was impossible in conditions where the length of the ship's upper decks was being swept by green seas. In addition, 'C' class conversions were more efficient in firing ammunition than in carrying it and *Carlisle* was down to less than 70 per cent of her total with some of the Hunts having only half remaining.

And the show had scarce begun. At 16.37, the destroyer *Zulu*, leading the 3rd Division, signalled that the enemy was again in sight to the north and this time both his groups were acting together, steering SW at high speed to get between the convoy and its destination. Again Vian interposed his cruisers, again the merchantmen bore off to the SW, its escort generating vast quantities of smoke and commencing a series of feint attacks from it. Lacking gunpower, the British had to threaten with the torpedo but, as these were 'once-only' weapons, they could not be loosed indescriminately and the object for the moment was to intimidate the enemy with 'fierce-face' tactics.

The Italian commander, Iachino, with unhappy memories of Matapan still fresh, declined to enter the screen, preferring to lay off and bring under heavy fire any British ship that chose to show itself. To keep up the psychological pressure forays had to be frequent, each being greeted by a positive hail of medium and heavy calibre salvoes. Fortunately by dint of fast manoeuvre, only splinter damage was sustained by the British ships until *Havock* collected a 15-inch shell from a bracket whose monstrous columns of water dwarfed her. Badly damaged, she fell back to add her smoke to that of the convoy's close escort.

The situation now developed dangerously, with the Italian heavy units trying to force their way around the limit of the smoke to get at the merchantmen. With the destroyers of the 5th Division engaging the giant *Littorio* at ranges down to 13,000 yards, things were looking unhealthy when Vian's cruisers emerged from the smoke, firing at maximum rate and letting go some of their precious torpedoes. Accurate spotting was near-impossible. It was a trial of nerve, of will, against Iachino's four large ships, whose destroyers lay well back. Then at only 6,000 yards, *Kipling* took a 15-inch projectile. *Cleopatra* herself was hit on the bridge by a 6-inch and all were thoroughly peppered by fragments. A desperate last effort was made with most of the remaining torpedoes but the Italians evaded them, and turned away. It was just after 18.00 and the convoy still uncomfortably close.

One of the few Capitani Romani to be completed, *Giulio Germanico* is here seen late in 1942 fitting out at Castellammare di Stabia. Scuttled in September 1943 at the capitulation, she was later salvaged and served, rebuilt as the *San Marco*, for another thirty years.

As the drenched and weary British gun-crews gratefully saw the smoke close around them once more, the enemy broke off at a tangent and then made to break through again. To face them there were now the four destroyers of the 1st Division, lurching through an unpleasantly heavy sea to a range of some 6,000 yards and on a suitable bearing to use their remaining torpedoes. From that distance the detail on the battleship's tophamper was pin-sharp and from the flash of her guns to the fall of shot was a few short seconds, raising a wall of water above the wildly gyrating mastheads of the destroyers or roaring over them with the noise of a freight train. *Lively* shuddered as a heavy calibre shell slammed home but another and final, twenty-five torpedoes sped out toward the enemy. Again he turned away to avoid them, but this time to the NW, setting his course for home; his resolve had been finally broken. It was nearly 19.00; the battle was over.

Owing to the total domination of the Luftwaffe over Malta at this time, it was not policy to take major units in to the island and Vian, his task discharged, turned for the long haul back to Alexandria. He left two of his heavily damaged destroyers to supplement the close escort, as in the weather conditions it was less hazardous for them than would have been the course home. Though subjected to some bombing, both were to reach Malta safely, though two larger and undamaged destroyers of the returning Italian force foundered in the turmoil of the sea east of Sicily.

Convoy MW10 sailed on. Its arrival had originally been timed for pre-dawn darkness on the 23rd, but delayed by both the action and weather, it was clear that it would now inevitably be harassed for the last few miles by the bombing that would come as surely as the day itself. As a precaution, the group dispersed, each of the four precious merchantmen proceeding independently with its own escort of Hunts that were themselves desperately short of fuel and ammunition. Fortunately the weather was still thick and blustery and Malta's fighters were airborne.

The Royal Mail ship *Pampas*, damaged by bombs, and the *Talabot* of the old-established Norwegian concern of Wilhelmsen passed the Grand Harbour breakwaters soon after 09.00 cheered by the excited populace lining the baraccas. Only a few miles further out the Glen liner *Breconshire*, which had already completed several trips, was disabled by a bomb hit in the machinery space. Swept toward the shore by a strong wind in spite of the efforts of her crew to get her towed, she finally managed to come to anchor. Badly bombed again two days later, she capsized, her loss added to that of the *Southwold*, a Hunt that ran on a mine whilst standing by her.

The last ship of MW10 convoy was the *Clan Campbell* which still had 25 miles to go when she was hit in a low-level attack, foundering rapidly in the confused sea. Ironically, having survived so much, the two ships that did reach Valletta safely were both sunk at their moorings before more than a fifth of the cargo had been discharged, but this scale of loss was typical of the Malta operations at this time. It was to become yet worse until the final showdown during the immortal August convoy of a few months later. Nevertheless, Vian's action is one that stands out as brilliant as any in the Fleet's history. Nelson himself would have approved.

The light cruiser *Penelope* was obliged to spend a brief period in drydock in Malta during the height of the siege. Though repeatedly bombed she was not seriously damaged, but the marks of countless shell fragments on her sides earned her the nickname 'HMS Pepperpot'.

One of the numerous Cleveland class of light cruisers, the *Santa Fe* (CL 60) is seen here in Task Group 38.3 off the Philippines in December 1944. The battleship beyond is either *North Carolina* or *Washington*, and the CVL left is *Langley* or *San Jacinto*.

Cruiser v. Cruiser – The Battle of Savo Island

Japan's tide of success after Pearl Harbor rolled inexorably forward. The key to these operations was the Imperial Fleet, landing invasion forces in rapid succession on strategic islands, from whence they took control of each neighbouring area. For months the machine seemed invincible, defeating anything that the Allies could muster until, in May 1942, the Americans reorganised themselves sufficiently to give the enemy a surprise at the indecisive battle in the Coral Sea, followed a month later by a sound thrashing at Midway. Aimed ultimately at Samoa and Fiji, the enemy's land offensive had brought him to New Guinea, threatening Australia itself and the vital staging post of the Solomons. In New Guinea, however, the Japanese army was hard pressed by Australian forces and was prevented from an early advance to the southward by the mountainous jungle-clad hinterland. Leapfrogging the greater part of the Solomons, meanwhile, the Japanese established a base on Tulagi, at the SE end of the chain, from which he could monitor, and threaten, American activity on nearby Espiritu Santo. He also established an airfield on neighbouring Guadalcanal. However, now buoyant with the success of Midway, the Americans resolved to dislodge the enemy before he could get too firmly entrenched.

Lacking the availability of any ports worthy of the name, the US forces decided to try amphibious landings, later to become the accepted norm in this theatre, though the necessary range of specialised landing craft and transports did not exist at that early time. Their creation, together with the necessary training of the assault forces, was not completed until August 1942.

The operation that then took place, code-named 'Watchtower', involved powerful naval forces with the 23 transports of the assault group, known as Task Group 62.1, supported by two separate groups. TG 62.2 comprised the Australian cruisers *Australia*, *Canberra* and *Hobart*, the American *Chicago* and nine destroyers. TG 62.3 was all-American with the cruisers *Astoria*, *Quincy* and *Vincennes*, accompanied by four destroyers. Also available was the A/A cruiser *San Juan* and two destroyers as TG 62.4.

Overall cover for the operation was the responsibility of Vice-Admiral 'Jack' Fletcher's Task Force 61, split into three groups but totalling three carriers, one battleship, six cruisers and sixteen destroyers.

The landings were on 7th August 1942, and, in spite of the Tulagi garrison fighting to the end, Tulagi and Guadalcanal were in American hands on the following day, with the Marines working at a frantic pace to prepare the incomplete airstrip re-christened Henderson Field. Fletcher's two hundred-odd fighters had created almost total air superiority, though their admiral grew increasingly uneasy about hazarding his three precious carriers – all that remained to the US Pacific Fleet at that time – in waters that would soon attract submarines. The result was that, on the evening of the 8th, Fletcher stated that he was pulling out, ostensibly to refuel and replenish his aircraft, though neither need could yet be said to be urgent. Deaf to all protests that Henderson Field was not yet operational and that the mass of anchored shipping would be without air cover, he left. It was to be a fateful decision.

A Japanese naval force was based on Rabaul in New Britain under the command of Vice-Admiral Mikawa. Known as the 8th Fleet, they comprised five 8-inch cruisers of the 6th CS, his flagship *Chokai*, the *Aoba*, *Kinugasa*, *Kako* and *Furutaka*, supported by four destroyers and two Tenryu class scouts. On learning of 'Watchtower', Mikawa concentrated all available units and sailed, less three destroyers, by 16.30 on the 7th, bent on a night attack which would create maximum surprise while shielding him from the attentions of the American aircraft carriers, which had not then left. The enemy move was reported almost immediately by a passing B-17 and then by a submarine. A further report placed the force as steering along the north side of Bougainville Island.

At the night action of Tassafaronga in November 1942, torpedoes from Japanese destroyers created havoc, hitting four American heavy cruisers. One was sunk and here the *Minneapolis* (CA 36) is seen at Tulagi after the SeaBees had affected a palm-log repair, her bows having been blown off.

USS *St Louis* (CL 49) in March 1942 at Mare Island, California. Notice particularly the 50-calibre machinegun on the top superstructure deck and others on the main deck. Also the 1·1-inch Anti-aircraft mount and the main and secondary battery directors on the superstructure. The portholes in the hull are plated over.

Early on the cloudless morning of the 8th August, four of the Japanese cruisers launched reconnaissance floatplanes of which *Aoba's* returned with a detailed report of the Allied forces, including the vital information that they were split between Tulagi and Guadalcanal. Mikawa cracked on speed to 24 knots and, despite being reported twice more, transitted the Bougainville Strait by 16.00, entering the wide channel known as 'the Slot' that divided the Solomons into two parallel chains. The last sighting report wrongly identified Mikawa's ships as 'seaplane carriers', though even if this influenced Fletcher's decision to withdraw, it still did not explain his failure to send reconnaissance aircraft to confirm the report.

Keeping strict radio silence, the Japanese admiral semaphored his intentions to his

As part of Task Group 77.2, the County class HMAS *Australia* helped to cover an assault in the Lingayen Gulf, Luzon, and her three funnels proved a persistent attraction to the Japanese Kamikaze.

commanders. Dividing the strait between the two beachheads was the small island of Savo; approach was to be via the south (Guadalcanal) side, attacking one Allied guard force and then rapidly swinging around the island to repeat the dose on the northern (Tulagi) force. The main weapon was to be the 24-inch Long Lance torpedo of which the squadron carried 66. Sunset was at 18.16 and the tropical darkness fell quickly, covering the enemy's final approach, still unchallenged after a 700-mile passage.

Overall command of the Allied guard forces was vested in Admiral Victor Crutchley, RAN, who as a lieutenant had been awarded the Victoria Cross for his part in *Vindictive*'s valiant attempt to block Ostend in 1918. Having resolved that the transports, bereft of air cover, must be withdrawn the following morning (the 9th), he posted *Canberra*, *Chicago* and two destroyers in the six-mile-wide southern channel. In the northern channel, with deep water eight miles wide, were the *Astoria*, *Quincy* and *Vincennes*, again with two destroyers whilst *Hobart* and *San Juan* were placed to prevent surprise from the east. Both Savo approaches were covered further out by a single, radar-equipped picket destroyer. At first glance, Crutchley would appear to have made the best dispositions possible with the forces available to him, but he had in fact weakened them by dividing the areas of responsibility. He himself was in his flagship, *Australia*, anchored off the Guadalcanal beach for a conference to decide policy following Fletcher's precipitate withdrawal. One item to be considered at the meeting was a report that had come in by a circuitous route, referring to a powerful enemy cruiser force. From the position, course and speed given, and the fact that the sighting was some eight hours earlier, this force could not be far distant.

Soon after 23.00, Mikawa launched three floatplanes into the dark, humid night, which was heavy with squalls and lightning-charged tropical cloud. Their task was to drop channel markers and flares as required. One was seen by the northern picket destroyer *Ralph Talbot* but, though correctly identified, its significance was not comprehended and her routine sighting report neglected to mention the plane's type.

At 12.40, the looming mass of Savo was sighted from *Chokai's* bridge as a silhouette etched against the faint red glow from a freighter burning off Tulagi. Simultaneously, the *Blue*, the southern picket, was seen crossing their bows some five miles distant. Oblivious, in spite of her radar, of the weaponry trained on her, she slowly reversed course, allowing Mikawa's squadron to slip silently through her wake. Throttled-back to lessen the chance of their wakes being sighted, the Japanese had Savo on their port beam at 01.30, at which point they sighted the southern force. Mikawa ordered revs for 30 knots, sent his single destroyer back to take care of the sleeping sentry, *Blue*, and had his aircraft drop flares.

As the flares ignited, the enemy let fly with both torpedoes and guns. *Canberra*, leading *Chicago*, staggered under two torpedo hits right forward while her crew were still running to their action stations. As she yawed out of line with her main battery still fore-and-aft, she was hit by about two dozen 8-inch shells in complete salvoes and began to settle. *Chicago*, close astern, was similarly smitten, a torpedo opening out her bow plating and releasing both anchors to the full scope of their cables. Slowed by these dual brakes, she opened up with her secondary armament at targets, real and imaginery, for her radar and searchlights showed nothing, and all star-shells failed to ignite. Her main armament remained silent as the phantom enemy hauled rapidly round to the NE. In the shocked aftermath of the attack, nobody thought fit to report it. . . .

The flashes and sound of the guns during the six minutes' action had been clearly observed in both beachheads and by the Northern Force, but as no reports had been received it was assumed that somebody had been 'letting off' at aircraft, a common-enough occurrence. The all-unsuspecting Northern Force had viewed the proceedings through heavy squalls which had dimmed its significance and, unperturbed, continued on its box course, turning eight points to starboard in succession at 01.40 from SW to NW. Savo's black bulk lay some five miles distant on the port bow, while not much further away on the port beam their undetected enemy bore on. However, Mikawa's formation had lost cohesion in the first phase and, leaving the wandering *Chicago* in its wake, headed NE in two groups, *Furutaka* trailing the two scouts close under the island, paralleling the course of the other four heavy cruisers. Though probably accidental this formation was to prove devastating.

Within minutes, Mikawa opened fire, again simultaneously with the release of aircraft flares. Incredibly, the Americans assumed that they were being attacked in error by the Southern Force and their delay in firing proved fatal. *Astoria*, the third in line, took a full salvo amidships,

The Japanese *Nachi* manoeuvres desperately under massed air attack over the sun-dappled waters of Manila Bay in November 1944. The attack was part of a co-ordinated American offensive by no less than three task groups, with twelve carriers.

Either *Mogami* or *Suzuya* at the receiving end of a 1,000-pound AP bomb dropped by a Helldiver from the US carrier *Hancock* during the battle around Leyte Gulf in October 1944. Both ships were sunk.

which immediately triggered an near-uncontrollable fire in the aircraft hangar. Close ahead, the *Quincy* had her main armament ready and loosed a salvo as the Japanese drove past, but it was to be her last as she was raked in turn by each, losing all three turrets in as many minutes. Blazing, she lurched out of line, almost colliding with the stricken *Astoria*.

Vincennes in the lead was still trying to make out the enemy when she was brought under fire from both sides and hit by two, possibly three, torpedoes. As her hangar, like that of *Astoria*, erupted it provided the aiming point for every calibre of Japanese gun from ranges so low that she was even being scoured by machine gun fire. However, in the glow of her own fires she loosed off at *Kinugasa* and hit her, though this brief success was short-lived as two more torpedoes crashed home. Reduced to a shambles by over fifty hits she had to turn to matters of her own survival as the victorious Mikawa turned NW and away, though still continuing to fire astern until 02.15.

Only his own *Choka* had been at all badly hit, 34 men dying when *Quincy* put three rounds into her bridge structure; between the rest there was only one dead. The Allies had lost over 1,000, but it was now that Mikawa made his first error. Either dazed by his own success or aware of a possible dawn airstrike from Fletcher's carriers (which he believed still to be in the area) he pulled out instead of ripping into his primary target, the transports lying off the beaches.

There remained the lone picket *Ralph Talbot* in the enemy's path. Almost predictably on this night of disaster, she misinterpreted the gunfire and was swamped by Japanese shot, surviving only by vanishing into a fortuitous rain squall.

Quincy and *Vincennes* sank soon afterward and it was decided to scuttle *Canberra*, which however died hard. During the early hours she, and assisting destroyers, had been sighted, and fired upon by *Chicago*. Already burning strongly, she was later abandoned and 370 rounds of 5-inch fired into her without great effect. Embarrassed, the destroyers tried torpedoes, several of which were fired before one ran true enough to hit her. *Astoria* lost a long battle for survival, foundering a few minutes after noon on the 9th.

Crutchley, marooned on his flagship, could never be more than an uninformed observer to the debacle, which was over long before he could take action. In its first real surface action the US Navy had fared badly, but even on the morning after, scores could have been settled if Fletcher had chosen to intervene. Still within range and in receipt of reports, he could have overwhelmed the retreating Mikawa but the strike was never flown. At the subsequent enquiry he justified his inaction, but was never again to be given command of a large carrier group.

It was left to the American submarine S44, of a type so ancient as to be called 'pig-boats', to exact some revenge when she sank the returning *Kako* with a salvo of torpedoes just outside her Kavieng base.

On the 9th, all shipping was withdrawn from Guadalcanal, leaving the Marines as sole occupants. Their tenancy was to be disputed bitterly for the next year, and before the Japanese conceded defeat, thousands had to die and many more ships to lie on the sea bottom off Savo – so many that it fully earned its grim soubriquet of 'Ironbottom Sound'.

The cruiser at bay – *Trinidad* and *Edinburgh*

Germany's sudden savaging of Russia in June 1941 presented Britain with a new and unlikely ally – and a whole series of problems. Not the least of these was the carriage of immense quantities of urgently needed war material to the Arctic ports, the only available access to the Russian continent. This route was compressed between the variable limits of northern ice and the upper end of the Norwegian mainland, an occupied coast with unlimited deepwater anchorages for enemy surface ships and plentiful airfields from which to strike at passing convoys. In winter the weather was indescribably vile, but the greater danger came in the summer months with tranquil seas and near-perpetual daylight.

The first convoy was run in August 1941, a bare couple of months after the invasion, followed by numerous others during the year. All these arrived without loss due to the German preoccupation with the new eastern front, but the gathering strength of enemy submarines, surface ships and mixed Luftwaffe units in the north was disquieting.

Northbound convoys were coded PQ and southbound, mostly returning 'empties', QP. As Admiral Sir John Tovey, C-in-C Home Fleet, lacked sufficient strength to provide heavy escort for all movements, sailings, where possible, were synchronised so that convoys, coming and going, passed

At Tjilatjap in February 1942, the crew of the American Omaha class cruiser *Marblehead* (CL 12) repair damage from Japanese bombing. This was so severe that it caused the ship to miss the disastrous Java Sea action that was to follow. A Nederland Line 'T' class freighter is in the background.

The British *Glasgow* suffers a hit whilst engaged on counter-battery work near Cherbourg in June 1944. The lack of elevation of the guns testifies to a comparitively short range. Notice the battle ensign at the fore and the chemical smoke screen in the background.

about the latitude of North Cape, the point offering the greatest danger but also the best opportunity for economical cover by having the 'heavies' cruising the area. It was not, in fact, until PQ12 of March 1942 that an operation was seriously threatened by a sortie of the new battleship *Tirpitz*, though foul weather frustrated the efforts of both sides with the enemy and attendant destroyers and PQ12 and the reciprocal QP8 playing at one stage a grim Blind Man's Buff within a circle of 40 miles radius. In clearing weather the following day an air strike from *Victorious* failed completely but gave the *Tirpitz* a nasty scare, as she had been unaware of the carrier's presence. Both camps resolved to do better on the next occasion.

The Royal Navy's prime task has always been the protection of the merchant shipping upon which the country has depended, but Tovey now considered that the destruction of *Tirpitz* was more important than the safeguarding of any convoy, an understandable point of view but one which was to cause friction. Interference by London in decisions thus made by the senior officer on the scene of operations varied between irksome and dangerous, culminating in the disastrous PQ17 affair.

On March 20th and 21st, 1942, PQ13 and QP9 left Reykjavik and Murmansk respectively, their crossover point to be covered by a Home Fleet force centred round the carrier *Victorious*, the battleship *Duke of York* and battlecruiser *Renown*. This concentration of force was to counter the threat posed by the *Tirpitz*, the 'pocket battleship' *Admiral Scheer* and the heavy cruisers *Hipper* and *Prinz Eugen*. It was in the usual nature of the vagaries of war that QP9 should experience an almost totally uneventful passage whilst PQ13 was beset by problems.

The latter had a close escort of two A/S trawlers and three armed whale-catchers, reinforced by the cruiser *Trinidad* and the destroyers *Eclipse* and *Fury*. All went well until the 24th, when a storm of near-hurricane force blew-up. It persisted for four days with wind and sea of proportions that scattered the merchant ships far and wide. Then, as the blow moderated, the escort had the task of rounding them up to reform the convoy. *Trinidad* had by then been joined by her sister *Nigeria* from the distant covering force and was searching the area NW of North Cape. She was joined later by a rare appearance of three Russian destroyers, but evidence that the Germans were aware of their presence came in the sighting of enemy reconaissance aircraft. These were to be followed up effectively by Ju88s which picked off two straggling merchantmen.

With the storm-ravaged ships scattered from the Norwegian coast to Bear Island the enemy put six U-boats into the hunt and, even more ominously, the 8th Destroyer Flotilla, three 3,500-ton ships bearing five 5·9-inch guns and eight torpedo-tubes apiece. Sailing from Kirkenes, hard by the Finnish border, they headed west in a line of search along the convoy's estimated track. They found evidence abounding in the form of wreckage and even some survivors and then, in the small hours of the 29th, a straggler was sighted. She was sunk and also yielded information on the whereabouts of the remainder.

Acting on this intelligence, the three destroyers headed out into weather which was again deteriorating rapidly, with snow showers cutting visibility to virtually nil and raising an ugly sea that froze on the superstructures as they were lashed by spray. In these abominable conditions, both sides were surprised when the *Trinidad* and *Fury*, corkscrewing with a following sea at 20 knots, ran straight into the German line. Z26 was closest to the cruiser, which opened a rapid and accurate fire that soon reduced her to a sinking condition, but she was rescued by her two consorts, which in turn forced *Trinidad* to turn away by means of a combined torpedo attack. Determinedly the cruiser returned the compliment, rather unusually firing three of her own torpedoes. These were seen to miss and then almost immediately, the ship was shaken by a heavy explosion on the port side. It was clearly a torpedo hit and caused heavy damage, but fortunately the two undamaged enemy destroyers were too concerned with taking-off the survivors of their stricken compatriot to press home their advantage. With both injured adversaries in fairly close proximity an interesting situation developed, complicated by the destroyer *Eclipse* arriving with a group of the convoy in, fortunately, distant company.

Both British destroyers were determined to finish off the Z26, but were no match for her two larger companions and, when the fire of the latter's 5·9s became too hot, they fell back on the now near-immobile *Trinidad* for heavy support. *Eclipse*, in making a determined effort to put a torpedo into the enemy, stopped a couple of large shells, having to creep away into the murk as the Germans finally scuttled the destroyer themselves. *Fury*, meanwhile, was actively engaged in keeping down the submarine U585, which was attempting to frustrate the cruiser's efforts to get way on again. Fortunately both allied ships were successful and *Trinidad* reached Kola Inlet, near Murmansk on the following day.

Damage survey revealed the irony that the torpedo that had struck the ship had been one that she, herself, had fired, for pieces of the offending weapon were there as evidence. Not for the first time, a control system had malfunctioned in the extreme cold, so that it had apparently circled with jammed steering surfaces. It had been incredibly bad luck and a valuable ship was now laid up through lack of dockyard facilities. Pre-cut and shaped steelwork had to be sent from the UK as deck cargo on the cruiser *Edinburgh*, which formed part of the escort of the next northbound convoy, PQ14, which left early in April 1942. No less that 16 of this convoy's 24 ships were forced to return by heavy ice, but the remaining eight arrived safely on the 19th in spite of another sally by German destroyers, which fortunately missed them in the poor visibility.

Having stored and refuelled, *Edinburgh* left again on April 28th, accompanying the homeward-bound QP11 with the destroyers *Forester* and *Foresight*. A close escort of four destroyers and an A/S trawler were also provided and the heavy cover at the crossover point with PQ15 included also a strong contingent from the US Navy, whose war this now was.

QP11 was contacted by both enemy aircraft and U-boats within 24 hours of sailing and the following day, *Edinburgh*, out ahead of the convoy, was fortunate to evade torpedoes from U436, only to run later into a spread from U456. Of these, two hit, one amidships and one right aft, removing stern and steering gear but leaving all four propellers and shafts intact. Though saved by her protection, *Edinburgh* lost some power but, more seriously, could now steer only by the adjustment of engine revolutions, a method of little use in the heavy quartering seas. Her accompanying destroyers took her in tow for Kola, some 250 miles back, but in the conditions they proved to have inadequate power and gear for the task. An excellent seamanlike solution (often used by tugs) was adopted by *Edinburgh* towing *Foresight* and good progress was made for the better part of a day, until the destroyer had to cast-off to join her compatriot in a hunt for U456, which was still stalking her damaged prey. During the next day little distance was covered until the three ships were heartened by the arrival on May 1st of a quartette of ocean minesweepers and a Russian tug capable of handling the wayward cruiser.

About this time the two remaining German destroyers of the action against *Trinidad*, Z24 and Z25, now accompanied by the smaller 5-inch-armed *Hermann Schoemann*, made contact with the convoy and its now-depleted escort, headed by four destroyers whose own surface armament had been reduced in favour of extra A/S capacity. However, these succeeded in deterring the more powerful enemy in a grim game of peek-a-boo, using snow squalls and smoke to good effect until, after about four hours, the Germans lost heart and went to seek the

Dazzle-painting was little used in the Second World War, but the French cruiser *Gloire* was an exception. First opposing the Allies at Casablanca and Dakar, she later joined the Free French forces, serving with distinction.

Edinburgh, which offered an easier kill. They found her early on the morning of 2nd May, one of the sweepers giving a warning before engaging with her solitary 4-inch gun. Tows were slipped and the cruiser circled at her best speed of about eight knots, her still-intact main armament shooting accurately and rapidly to such good effect that the *Schoemann* was quickly disabled. *Forester*, attempting a torpedo attack, was stopped by three damaging 5·9 hits. Z24, probably trying to finish her off, fired torpedoes which just missed but went on toward the *Edinburgh* which, unable to take avoiding action, was again hit amidships, exactly opposite her earlier damage. Sagging and nearly severed, the cruiser kept her adversaries at bay, the faithful *Forester* closing in a last-ditch attempt at defence and being heavily damaged for her trouble, being forced to a halt. At this stage, all three of the larger British ships were dead in the water, but the enemy was once more preoccupied in taking off the crew of the sinking *Schoemann*, assisted by the U88. Fortunately, they then lost heart and withdrew, when they could have annihilated the British force. The presence of the large minesweepers gave them the impression in the poor visibility of a strong defence, but in the event, *Edinburgh*'s hour had come for, with massive damage she was unable to proceed further, was abandoned and despatched with *Forester*'s last torpedo.

Both damaged Allied destroyers returned to Kola for repair and were able to take part in the final act of this drama when, in company with two other destroyers, they sailed on 13th May with *Trinidad*. She was cobbled together with the plates brought by *Edinburgh*, and was able to sail at half speed for the US. However, all exits from the Barents Sea were well covered by the Luftwaffe from the cluster of airfields around North Cape and, though the squadron had been promised air cover by the Russians, this proved virtually non-existent when the enemy made contact the following morning. Having withstood a strike by a combination of torpedo-carrying He 111s of the 'Lion' Geschwader, KG26, and dive-bombing Ju 88s of KG30, the defenders were surprised by a low level attack of a lone Ju 88, one of whose bombs ruptured one of *Trinidad*'s temporary plates, while another started a serious fire below the bridge. Another torpedo attack was evaded shortly before the onset of darkness but the fire was spreading rapidly; though still capable of steaming and fighting, *Trinidad* was too far from help to stand a chance of ultimate survival. Night covered the sad task of abandonment and she was torpedoed by her own escort in the early hours of 15th May.

Both cruisers had been well handled and well fought, but the odds were stacked against them. Their loss in the north was to be keenly felt.

The shadowing cruiser – the *Bismarck* pursuit

At the end of 1940 the German High Command was stepping up the mercantile war against Britain. Actually spearheading the onslaught were six auxiliary cruisers, recently joined by the *Scheer* and *Hipper*, and further regular warships were completing repair of damage suffered during the Norwegian campaign of the previous April. Of even greater concern to the British Admiralty was the imminent completion of the battleships *Tirpitz* and *Bismarck*, which with a full load displacement of over 51,000 tons, carried an armament of eight 15-inch and twelve 5·9-inch guns on a hull protected by armour up to 360 mm thick, yet capable of over 30 knots. With a maximum endurance of some 8,000 nautical miles they represented a very considerable threat and the progress of the leadship, *Bismarck*, was monitored regularly. By early in 1941, she had shifted from her Hamburg builders to the relatively safe waters of the Baltic for working up, wearing the flag of the very able Admiral Lutjens, recently returned from commanding a raiding group that included the battlecruisers *Scharnhorst* and *Gneisenau*.

In spite of earlier false reports, *Bismarck* did not actually sail on her first foray until 18th May 1941, accompanied by the new 8-inch cruiser *Prinz Eugen* which, with a full load displacement of 19,800 tons was no mean threat herself. Under the code name Rheinubung, the operation commenced at Gotenhafen (now Gdynia), preceded by the stationing in the Atlantic of no less than 13 auxiliaries for the purpose of supply and weather reporting. Their sailing was, in fact, two weeks behind schedule as a result of *Prinz Eugen*'s detonation of a magnetic mine close aboard but, when they were reported passing through the Kattegat on the 20th, part of Admiral Tovey's Home Fleet immediately took up its planned dispositions.

The battlecruiser *Hood*, in company with the brand new battleship *Prince of Wales*, and six destroyers, left Scapa for Iceland to cover the German's breakout into the Atlantic through either the Denmark Strait or the Iceland-Faroes gap. Further reconnaissance reports noted the enemy's call at Korsfjord, near Bergen, to top up with fuel, and their subsequent departure the following day. On receiving this news Tovey sailed his remaining strength, the battleship *King George V*, the carrier *Victorious*, four light cruisers and six destroyers, to attempt an interception. Cruisers were already covering the two strategic gaps, *Norfolk* (soon joined by her sister, *Suffolk*) in the Denmark Strait, between Greenland and Iceland, and the 6-inch cruisers *Birmingham* and *Manchester* between Iceland and the Faroes. In addition, the light cruisers *Arethusa* and *Hermione* were in the area but operating on independent missions. At this stage the capricious northern weather turned foul and both sides found themselves bereft of aerial reconnaissance. Early on the 23rd the battlecruiser *Repulse* joined Tovey's force north of the Hebrides as it sped on a NW course to its station; simultaneously Holland, in the *Hood*, pressed on along the south side of Iceland. All reasonable dispositions were being satisfactorily made – but where was the enemy?

The final class of French 'super-destroyer', the Mogadors, were remarkably similar in concept to the Italian 'Capitani Romani', which represented the bottom end of the cruiser spectrum. Their value was never to be fully realised due to the French fleet's immolation at Toulon. Here *Mogador* is seen lying in shallow water alongside a Vauquelin class destroyer.

On this day, 23rd May, as on many a weary day before, *Norfolk* and *Suffolk* were cruising the Denmark Strait. On paper, this is a spacious waterway some 200 miles wide from Iceland's North Cape to the Greenland coast, but even in summer ice stretches from the latter to about the strait's median line in a flat, featureless sheet. Furthermore, the shelf running NW from the Icelandic capes had been mined by the British, leaving only a deep water corridor some 30 miles in width running along the ice edge, and it was along this route that the cruisers were running.

The day was calm with the cold air over the icepack crystal clear, but where it lay over the warmer water a dense fog had formed, the two regions clearly defined as if by a boundary wall. Both cruisers had radar; *Norfolk*'s was a very early set with a fixed antenna covering a sector straight ahead, whilst her sister had a trainable antenna, which however had a blind sector right aft, where it was blanketted by the superstructure.

At 19.00 *Suffolk* was heading SW along

the fog wall on a routine leg of her patrol, with her stern presented to the enemy's most likely bearing of approach. Alive to her radar deficiencies in this direction extra lookouts had been posted and it was these that sighted *Bismarck* and *Prinz Eugen* about eight miles astern. Rapidly increasing speed, the big 'County' heeled as she headed for the fog's comforting murk, sending a sighting report as she did so. *Bismarck* had made no discernable reaction and *Norfolk* was about fifteen miles distant in the gloom to the south. *Hood* and her group were a bare 200 miles beyond and things looked good for an interception if only the enemy's movements could be monitored.

Captain Ellis of the *Suffolk* let his fast-moving quarry pull well ahead before he emerged from the fog to keep them in visual contact from astern. Still the Germans bore on, apparently oblivious, until *Norfolk*, responding to her colleague's reports, came out of the murk to find *Bismarck* only 10,000 yards away in his radar's blind sector. As she spun on her rudder, *Norfolk* was lent wings by four 15-inch salvoes close enough to cause splinter damage, but her sighting report was received by Tovey, who turned on to a near-westerly course, aiming at an intercept along the enemy's projected course in the event of *Hood* not making contact. At this juncture, the C-in-C had every reason to feel confident.

The two shadowers, *Suffolk* and *Norfolk*, were now faced with problems for, although May in these waters is a time of near-perpetual daylight, they were moving into an area of deteriorating weather conditions. Visibility was becoming patchy, with intermittent showers of both rain and snow but, though their inclination was to move in closer, they were forced to remain at about 23,000 yards by respect for the battleship's well-calibrated main battery, any damage from which to themselves could cause loss of contact. Another consideration was that Lutjens might suddenly reverse course, in which case the cruisers would need to react

Whilst supporting the seaward flank of the German land forces withdrawal along the Baltic coast in October 1944, the cruisers *Prinz Eugen* and *Leipzig* came into collision off the Hela Peninsula. Both survived, though the latter had a machinery space flooded.

swiftly for, with a combined closing speed of over 60 knots, they could be caught and obliterated at close range. At 32 knots, the maximum speed of the Countys had only a knot or so superiority over the Germans, a slender enough margin.

In the northern twilight patches of warm and cold air produced strange mirage effects and at one stage, in spite of what their radar screen told them, the apprehensive watchers on *Suffolk*'s bridge were convinced that *Bismarck* had, indeed, made a 16-point turn. The cruiser followed suit, only to find that the alarm was unwarranted, but valuable ground had been lost. Later, in the half light of midnight, both sides moved into a large area of falling snow, which blanked out *Suffolk*'s radar completely. Fortunately the Germans did not realise this and maintained their course into clear weather, being sighted again during the early hours of the 24th. Whilst out of touch, the cruisers' flow of positional reports ceased and Holland, now very close, turned his squadron on to the enemy's base course to avoid being overtaken. At 02.47, however, transmissions were resumed and the heavy British ships went to action stations ready for what might be to come. By 05.00 near full daylight was filtering through a heavy overcast and the ships rolled to a beam swell.

Norfolk and *Suffolk*, spaced out on either of Lutjen's quarters, had done a model job and, once Holland's presence was appreciated, excitement mounted aboard at the results of their successful shepherding. They maintained range and bearing to be of use in spotting the fall of shot if required.

Unfortunately, the British admiral's handling of his ships was totally unimaginative as he manoeuvred them in concert using the old 'line-of-battle' thinking. His great flagship was efficient but over-age, and the *Prince of Wales* by contrast was so new as to have builder's personnel still aboard. Operating independently, they could have split *Bismarck*'s fire, which proved devastatingly accurate, and the

The German light cruiser *Nürnberg* lying alongside at Copenhagen in May 1945, when she was surrendered together with the heavy cruiser *Prinz Eugen*. Taken over by the Russian Navy in 1946, she was renamed *Admiral Marakov*.

Washington Treaty Cruisers

Kent class (Great Britain, 9,850 tons, 1927). Only British cruisers to be built to Treaty maxima, 6-inch guns being found to be more economical.

Brooklyn class (USA, 9,700 tons, 1937). Powerful main battery of fifteen 6-inch guns to counter Japanese Mogami class. Large hangar below quarterdeck.

Trento class (Italy, 10,500 tons, 1928). Well-armed, but protection sacrificed for speed. Aircraft on foredeck.

Tourville (France, 10,000 tons, 1928). Well-armed, but without protection in order to achieve trials speeds in excess of 36 knots. The experiment was too extreme and not repeated.

Mogami class (Japan, 11,200 tons, 1935). Five triple 6-inch turrets exchanged for five twin 8-inch. Compare with Brooklyn class.

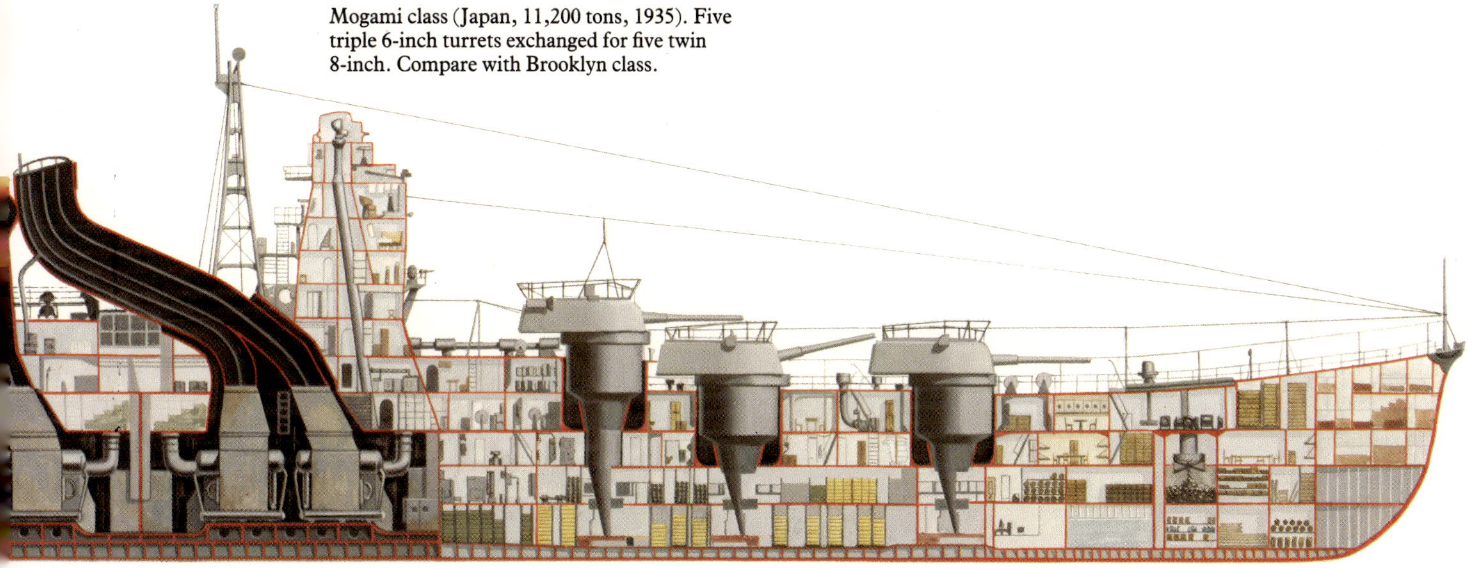

situation was not helped by *Hood* approaching end-on to close the range rapidly (which left her after guns unable to bear) and her mistakenly firing at *Prinz Eugen*, whose silhouette was remarkably similar to that of the *Bismarck*. Minutes before 06.00, following a fire on the upper deck, *Hood* blew up in one vast eruption, sinking in two halves, almost a carbon copy of the disaster that overtook Beatty's battle-cruisers at Jutland about a quarter-century earlier. *Prince of Wales* took heavy punishment herself but succeeded in hitting the enemy battleship before being forced to break off the action, largely because of the failure of many of her untried systems, including most of her main armament.

Rear-Admiral Wake-Walker found himself the senior British officer on the spot and kept the *Prince of Wales* in the area as he settled down to continue dogging Lutjen's progress until Tovey could make contact. *Bismarck*, damaged and trailing an oily slick, had had to abandon her mission and was faced with the task of breaking through to a friendly port in the teeth of a Royal Navy now bent on vengeance.

To make life more difficult for them, the German battleship suddenly reversed course later on in the day, and brought her shadowers under heavy fire and, whilst their attention was thus distracted, *Prinz Eugen* was detached to make an independent return passage. Tovey, yet some way distant, was sufficiently concerned about the situation to have *Victorious* launch an air strike with the extremely scratch force of aircraft that she had aboard. That they were able to make contact with *Bismarck* about midnight on the 24th/25th was surprising, and that they managed to score a torpedo hit was miraculous, though its effect was trifling.

Even worse was to follow, for at 03.06 on the 25th the cruisers lost contact when their

May 1941, and *Suffolk* and *Norfolk* keep tabs on the *Bismarck*. Here *Suffolk* recovers her Walrus. Both starboard 4-inch HA mountings can be seen, a 2-pounder 'pom-pom' in the right foreground, and the snouts of X-turret guns beyond the superstructure.

quarry changed course. For 31 hours *Bismarck* was 'lost' whilst the Home Fleet and Force H, up from Gibraltar, searched with diminishing hope of success. Then, at 10.30 on the 26th, a patrolling PBY re-established contact though with the depressing news that Lutjens was heading straight for Brest and was near enough home as to make interception unlikely. Somehow he had to be slowed and the only possible means of doing this was making use of the antiquated Swordfish of Force H's *Ark Royal*. During the afternoon, in appalling weather, they staggered from the wildly pitching flightdeck, but in the poor visibility they attacked the cruiser *Sheffield* in error. This ship was acting as link and escaped the onslaught by rapid manoeuvre and by the fact that some of the torpedoes exploded on contact with the water. Chastened, the aircraft returned to *Ark* to rearm and, by the time they sighted their true target, the light was fading. In spite of this, the appalling weather and *Bismarck*'s evasive steering and fire, the old aircraft atoned for their earlier failure by putting a torpedo into the giant's starboard quarter. With her steering gear wrecked and slowed by flooding, the great ship was to be tormented throughout the long night by a half-flotilla of destroyers under the redoubtable Vian. However, kept at a distance by *Bismarck*'s accurate, radar-laid gunnery, they scored no hits but they did keep the enemy's gun-crews closed-up all night until, in the dreary dawn of 27th May, they wearily saw the dim shapes of the battleships *King George V* and *Rodney* making visual contact.

Fire was opened at 08.47 and, two hours later, *Bismarck*, which had fought to the end, was no more. Her blazing hulk refused to sink from gunfire alone and it devolved upon the *Dorsetshire* of the County class, to despatch her with three clinically placed torpedoes, two to starboard, one to port. Also in at the kill was *Norfolk*, which had fully earned the right to a few valedictory salvoes; her running mate, *Suffolk*, had been forced to leave in order to refuel. Both had seen the job through thoroughly and had played a key role in what was to be the greatest maritime hunt in history.

German light cruisers *Köln* (nearer camera) and *Leipzig* bombard the Baltic island of Dagö, prior to its capture in October 1941.

The Second World War

Prinz Eugen (Germany, 13,900 tons, 1940). Largest German heavy cruiser design. Highly regarded but little-tried in action.

Dido class (Great Britain, 5,750 tons, 1939). First cruisers purpose-built with dual-purpose armaments. Rather unsatisfactory compromise.

Atlanta class (USA, 6,000 tons, 1941). Inspired by Dido class but superior in having all 5-inch armament geared to their primary role, A/A defence. Early units mounted sixteen 5-inch.

Cleveland class (USA, 10,000 tons, 1941). Largest group of cruisers ever built. Note symmetrical layout common to all later US cruisers.

Oyodo (Japan, 8,200 tons, 1942). Early hybrid design combining light cruiser armament with capacity for six large reconnaissance bombers.

Swiftsure (Great Britain, 8,000 tons, 1944). Derived from successful Crown Colony and Town classes. Later Tiger class was similar before conversion.

Des Moines class (USA, 17,000 tons, 1948). The ultimate gunned cruisers, their size largely attributable to their automatic armament. Completed too late to see action in the Second World War.

AFTER THE SECOND WORLD WAR

At the closing of hostilities in August 1945, the US navy found itself the world's leading naval power; a rather redundant giant awaiting a new role. This was to emerge gradually as Great Britain, exhausted by two major wars and years of depression, entered a new phase of her history. Having led a large part of the world to democratic self-sufficiency, her old confidence suddenly evaporated and a mood of self-recrimination took over. Old imperial ideas became unacceptable and the empire was dismantled at a rate which surprised not only the world but, in many cases the 'liberated' themselves. In shedding her world-wide responsibilities she cast off, too, the unwritten role of international policeman, which she had shouldered for so long. Her fleet, the instrument of the empire's foundation and its underpinning, likewise went into decline.

In 1945, however, this was still in the future and the British and US navies had been left without peers; so utterly had the fleets of their enemies been shattered that they were now largely without a function, for who was there to challenge them? So ships were disposed of at an alarming rate. By 1950, the Royal Navy had shed from the active list all pre-war cruisers with the exception of the Towns. Ten Crown Colony and their Swiftsure derivatives remained, with two more in the Royal Canadian Navy, which had expanded tremendously in taking its full part in the Battle of the Atlantic. Three more remained in a state of suspended animation, to be completed long after as the Tiger class; a fourth was scrapped and another, to have been the leadship for an enlarged Bellerophon class, was cancelled. Six Didos had survived the war, together with four of their 'improved' derivatives, two of which had been transferred to the Royal New Zealand Navy. Of the remaining County class, *Sussex* lingered in reserve until 1955 and *Shropshire*, loaned to Australia as a replacement for the *Canberra*, returned after twelve years, to be scrapped with her sister *Australia*. *Devonshire* lasted as a training ship until 1954, but last of these famous ships to go was *Cumberland* which, as a trials cruiser, tested the armaments that were to take the fleet into a new age.

The Americans shed fewer cruisers as the majority of their units were still nearly new, but many went into long reserve. All of the Omahas (less *Milwaukee*, serving in the Russian fleet) went in 1946, having spent the war in lower-hazard zones such as the US eastern seaboard. Of the 6-inch Brooklyns, two each went to the developing navies of Argentina, Brazil and Chile, the remaining pair going into reserve until 1960 when, in company with the surviving pre-war heavy cruisers, also in reserve, they were scrapped. Joining this clearance were the 5-inch gunned A/A cruisers of the Atlanta class, for which there was little peacetime use.

A formidable force still remained, with a core of the fourteen 8-inch Baltimores, 13,600-tonners derived from the prewar *Wichita* but whose twin funnelled profile was discontinued with the last three, the Oregon Cities. With their compact superstructure and single large stack, these were very similar to the trio of enormous Des Moines, the nameship of which was laid down shortly before the end of the war. While retaining the standardised nine 8-inch, twelve 5-inch armament they contrived to displace 17,000 tons through their machinery at 120,000 shp was still well below, say, a Trento of twenty years earlier. Their great tonnage was largely accounted for by their fully automatic main battery and vertical protection of up to 8-inches in thickness. Nine more were cancelled but those completed, in 1948–9, proved popular as flagships.

Of light cruisers, the 27 Clevelands of 1942–6 comprised the largest group ever built, mounting one less triple turret than the preceding Brooklyns and terminating in a single-stacked variant, the two Fargos. A

The British Crown Colony *Gambia*, with the Emperor of Ethiopia aboard, on one of the rare occasions when a jack is worn at sea. White Ensigns are aft and at main gaff and the Ethiopian standard at the foretop. Centre guns in the 6-inch turrets are set back to avoid interaction of projectiles in salvo firing.

Six-inch shell cases litter the deck of the Canadian cruiser *Uganda* (later HMCS *Quebec*) after a 1944 bombardment of a Japanese island airstrip south of Okinawa.

Gunnery at the end of the Second World War

Mk 34 Gun Director
Working in conjunction with sensors detecting a ship's own movement, the director provided data on the target. All this information was then processed by the gunnery computer, the guns being laid accordingly to the correct angle and elevation and fired simultaneously, with the director updating information as the ships manoeuvred. The optical rangefinder, so often failing due to smoke or bad visibility, was greatly assisted by the installation of radar above it.

1. Radar antenna
2. Radar antenna elevation gear
3. Stereoscopic optical rangefinder
4. Telescope
5. Periscope
6. Rangefinder stabiliser gear
7. Telescope
8. Director equipment
9. Revolving armoured barbette

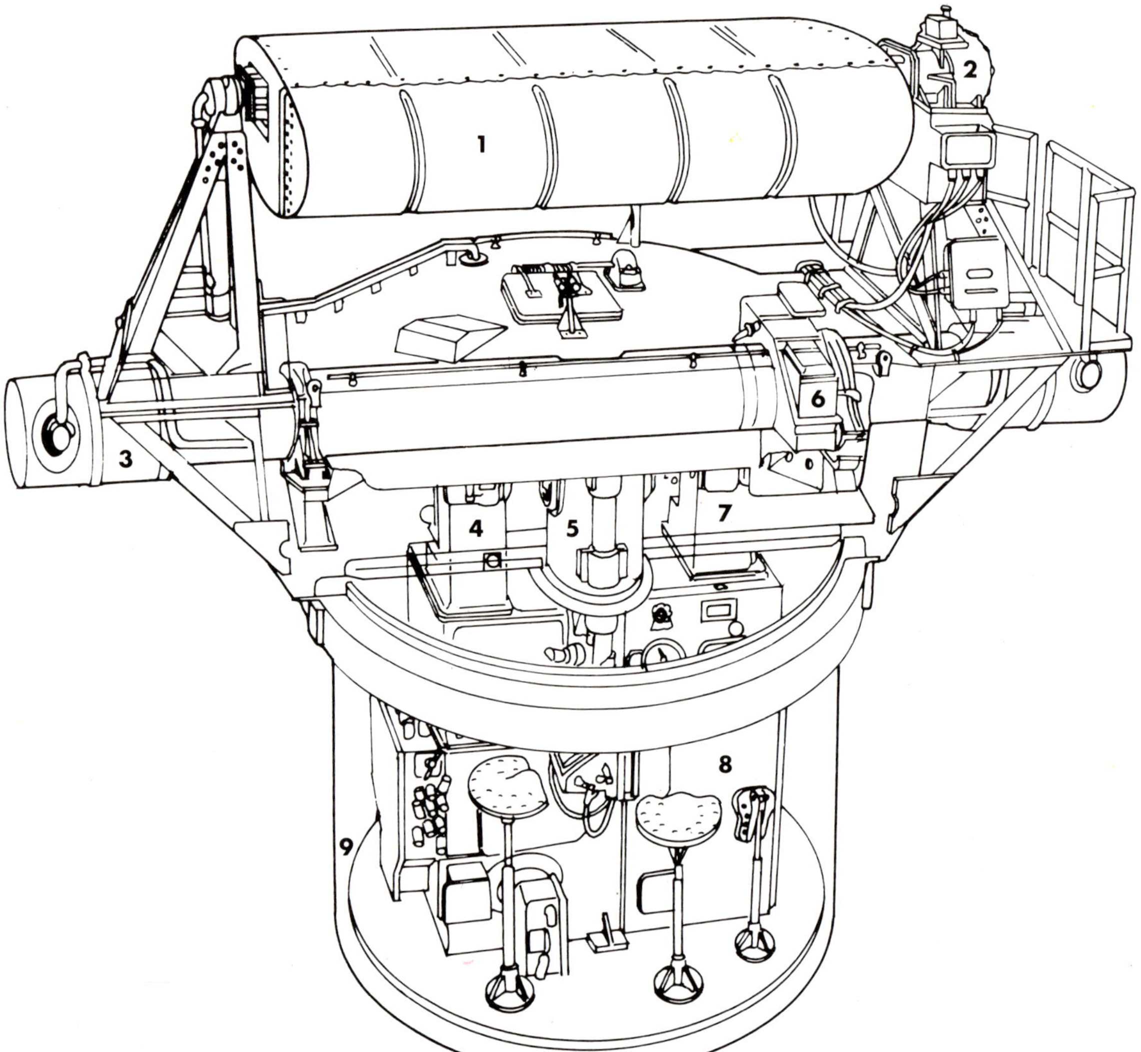

Opposite, top
Schematic diagram of training system used in US automatic 8-inch triple turrets.

1. Electrical 'gun train' order (indicating)
2. Sight deflection (electrical)
3. Line of sight
4. 'Turret train' to turret officer's indicator
5. Sight deflection by voice to sightsetter
6. Sight deflection
7. Rangefinder operator
8. Computer
9. Sight setter's indicator
10. Range scale
11. Trainer's periscope
12. Train indicator and transmitter
13. Handcranks
14. Sight setter
15. Parallax range
16. Trainer
17. Parallax corrector
18. 'Gun train' order to local control
19. 'Train' response
20. Electrical 'gun train' order (auto)
21. 'Train' receiver regulator
22. Training gear
23. 'Train' response
24. Motor
25. Clutch
26. Training gear
27. Training rack

Opposite, bottom
Schematic diagram of elevation system used in US automatic 8-inch triple turrets.

1. Electrical 'gun elevation' order (indicating)
2. Sight angle (electrical)
3. Pointer's periscope
4. Line of sight
5. Sight angle by voice to sight setter
6. Computer
7. Sight setter's indicator
8. Sight angle
9. Velocity loss
10. Gun elevation indicator
11. Elevation response
12. Rangefinder operator
13. Hand cranks
14. Sight setter
15. Pointer
16. Roller path tilt and erosion corrector
17. Elevating bar
18. Elevating screw
19. Electrical 'gun elevation' order (auto)
20. Sight angle
21. Gun elevation order
22. Elevation receiver regulator
23. Motor
24. Clutch
25. Elevating gear
26. Training rack
27. Turret train response

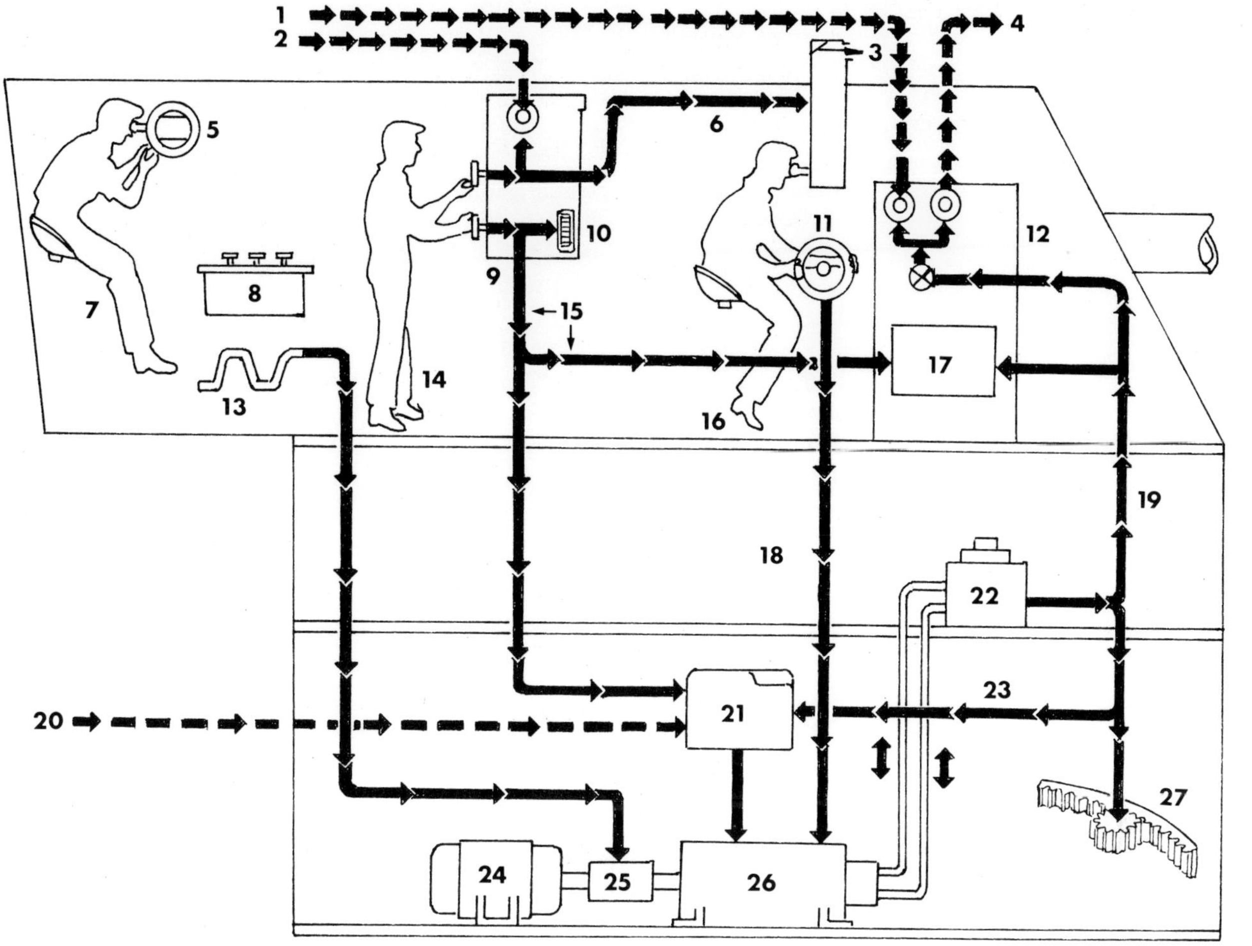
1
2
3
4
5
6
7
8
9
10
11
12
13
14
15
16
17
18
19
20
21
22
23
24
25
26
27

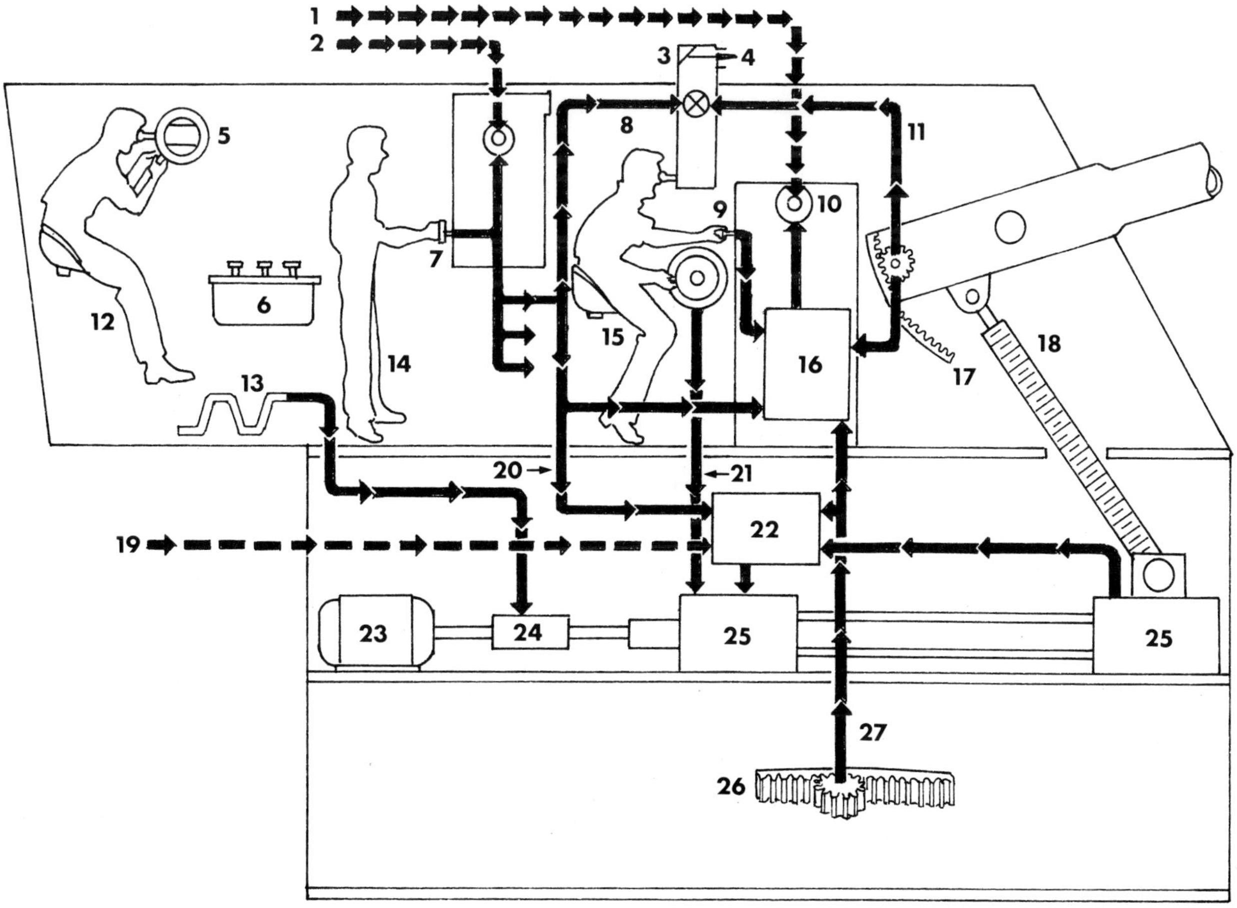
1
2
3
4
5
6
7
8
9
10
11
12
13
14
15
16
17
18
19
20
21
22
23
24
25
25
26
27

new, automatic 6-inch gun now became available, its bulk demanding twin gunhouses. As a twelve-gun battery was still required, the six-turret Worcester class was spawned, 680-feet in length and, at 14,700 tons, the largest 'light' cruisers ever. A secondary armament of twenty 3-inch guns was fitted, a legacy from the Kamikaze war where heavy projectiles and a high rate of fire were needed to destroy a diving aircraft. British practice had been, long since, to remove all aircraft from cruisers (retaining the crane for stores and boats) but, despite disastrous wartime fires the Americans retained up to four floatplanes in a hangar below the quarterdeck and the large crane on the fantail remained something of a trademark.

In spite of France's great losses in cruisers, none had actually been sunk in action at sea, so a true evaluation is difficult. Most had been scuttled at Toulon in November 1942 rather than be taken by the Germans, but a couple were destroyed actively fighting for Vichy France, the *Primauguet* and the *Lamotte-Picquet* at Casablanca and Saigon, respectively. Surviving the war were both Tourvilles and the *Suffren*, three la Galissonnières, *Duguay-Trouin* and both training cruisers. Of the three de Grasse class cruisers building in 1940, two were dismantled, but the nameship survived on the slipways at Lorient; later progressed in slow time, she was commissioned in 1956 – about 18 years after being laid down. With a change of emphasis toward A/A defence of the carriers that now formed the core of the fleet in place of battleships, her original 6-inch armament had been changed to sixteen 5-inch and twenty 57 mm weapons, presenting a uniquely bristling appearance. The names of her defunct sisters *Guichen* and *Chateaurenault*, lived on, carried by two ex-Italian Capitani Romani, ceded in 1948.

Italy concluded a separate armistice with the Allies in August 1943 and the greater part of her still-powerful fleet was then immobilised for the duration. Under the terms of the eventual Peace Treaty of 1947 the fleet was reduced both by scrapping and transfer. Besides the two light cruisers allotted to France, the *Duca d'Aosta* went to Russia and the *Eugenio di Savoia* to Greece, being re-named *Helle* and a fair exchange for the old cruiser of the same name sunk by submarine without warning on the declaration of war in 1940. A pair of ships that did not survive were the two 6,000 tonners

The largest conventional cruisers ever built, the three Des Moines class each have a standard displacement of over 17,000 tons. *Newport News* (CA 148), is seen here during a 1961 exercise.

building for Siam but appropriated for conversion to A/A cruisers. Renamed *Etna* and *Vesuvio*, they were launched in 1941–2 but were scuttled before completion.

Little remained of the Japanese fleet in 1945 except shells of once-proud ships whose fates were to be short, one-way trips to scuttling or scrapping. Where the Imperial Navy had fought itself into virtual oblivion in the face of insuperable odds the Kriegsmarine had maintained its 'fleet-in-being' approach to the end, much of it escaping until the war's final days when Allied air power roamed unopposed in the skies of Germany. Either scuttled or bomb shattered were both the remaining 'pocket battleships' *Scheer* and *Lutzow*, the heavy cruiser *Hipper* and her incomplete sister *Seydlitz*, (partially converted into an aircraft carrier), and the light cruisers *Emden* and *Köln*. *Leipzig*, heavily damaged by collision with *Prinz Eugen* late in 1944, was loaded with poison-gas ammunition and scuttled by the Allies. *Prinz Eugen* herself was surrendered, fully operational, at Copenhagen and was eventually expended by the Americans in A-bomb experiments in the Pacific.

Taken with the *Prinz Eugen* was the *Nurnberg*, to be ceded to Russia and becoming the *Admiral Makarov*. *Seydlitz* was also salvaged by the Russians from shallow water off Konigsberg but, though renamed *Poltava*, was too far gone to be of use. Her sister, *Lutzow*, (not to be confused with the 'pocket battleship' which took the name later) had been transferred to the Soviet navy in the palmy days of 1940. Renamed *Petropavlovsk*, her fate was later to be destroyed by German bombs at Leningrad.

After a dismally inept showing during the Second World War the Russian fleet was about to begin its expansion into the vacuum that followed the peace treaties. Powers that had lost their sovereignty during German occupation, found themselves in the grip of forces scarcely more benevolent, bent on the inculcation of a new creed. The West, that had poured hardware and technological know-how into the Soviet war-machine, now found itself threatened as its erstwhile ally rapidly switched to a course of consolidation and subversion. Though a near-self-sufficient land power, Russia had always maintained a sizeable fleet: she had destroyed its spirit in the purges of the officer corps in the thirties but now sought to increase its strength for the new ideological struggle in the West. The

Backed by the rugged grandeur of the Pacific coast, the Canadian cruiser *Quebec* makes a good 30 knots. Built as the Royal Navy's Crown Colony class *Uganda*, she was transferred in 1944. Note the cut-down foremast with its US-pattern radars and 'A' turret trained on an after bearing.

The Cruiser since the Second World War

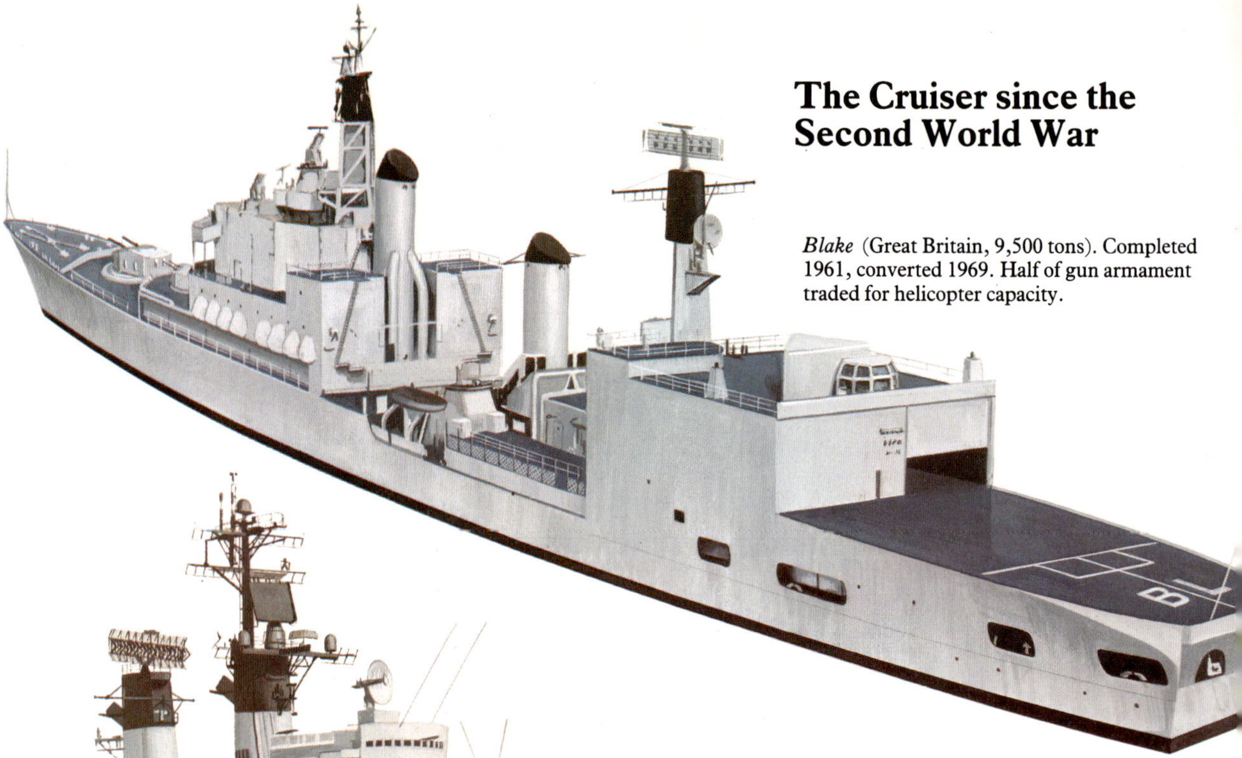

Blake (Great Britain, 9,500 tons). Completed 1961, converted 1969. Half of gun armament traded for helicopter capacity.

Albany (USA, 13,700 tons). Completed 1946, converted 1962. Total gun armament traded for SAM systems.

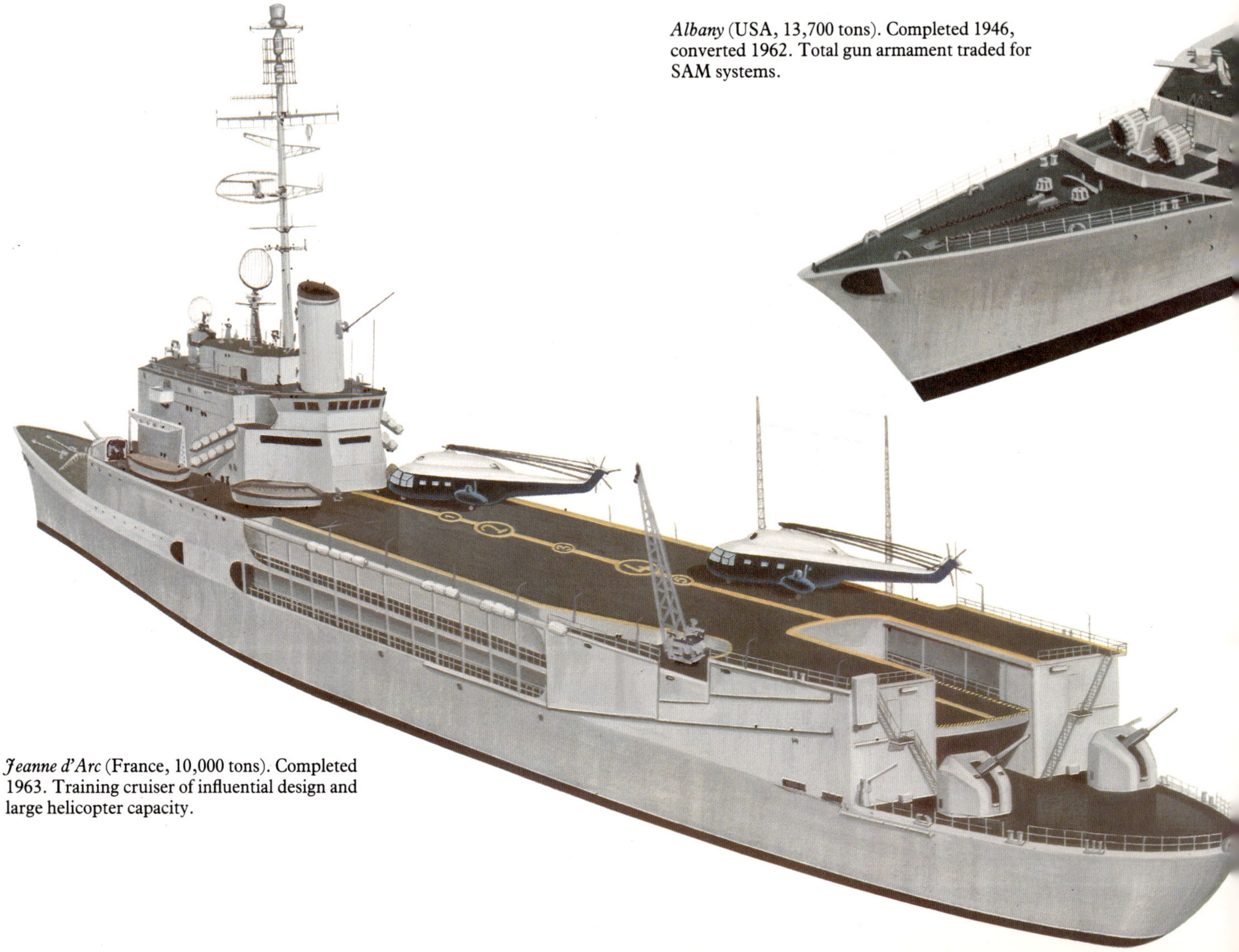

Jeanne d'Arc (France, 10,000 tons). Completed 1963. Training cruiser of influential design and large helicopter capacity.

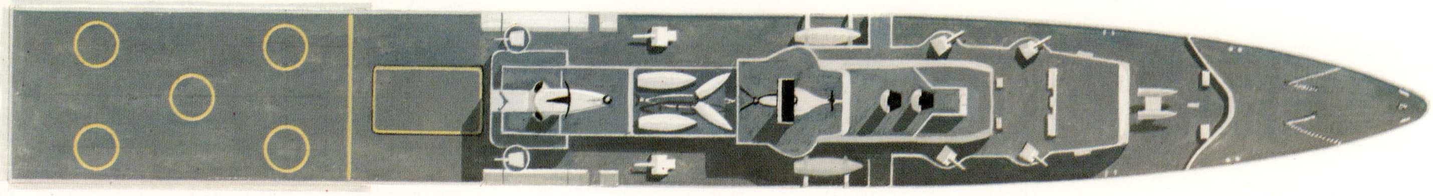

Vittorio Veneto (Italy, 7,500 tons). Completed 1969. Purpose-built A/S helicopter cruiser. Development of earlier *Andrea Doria* design.

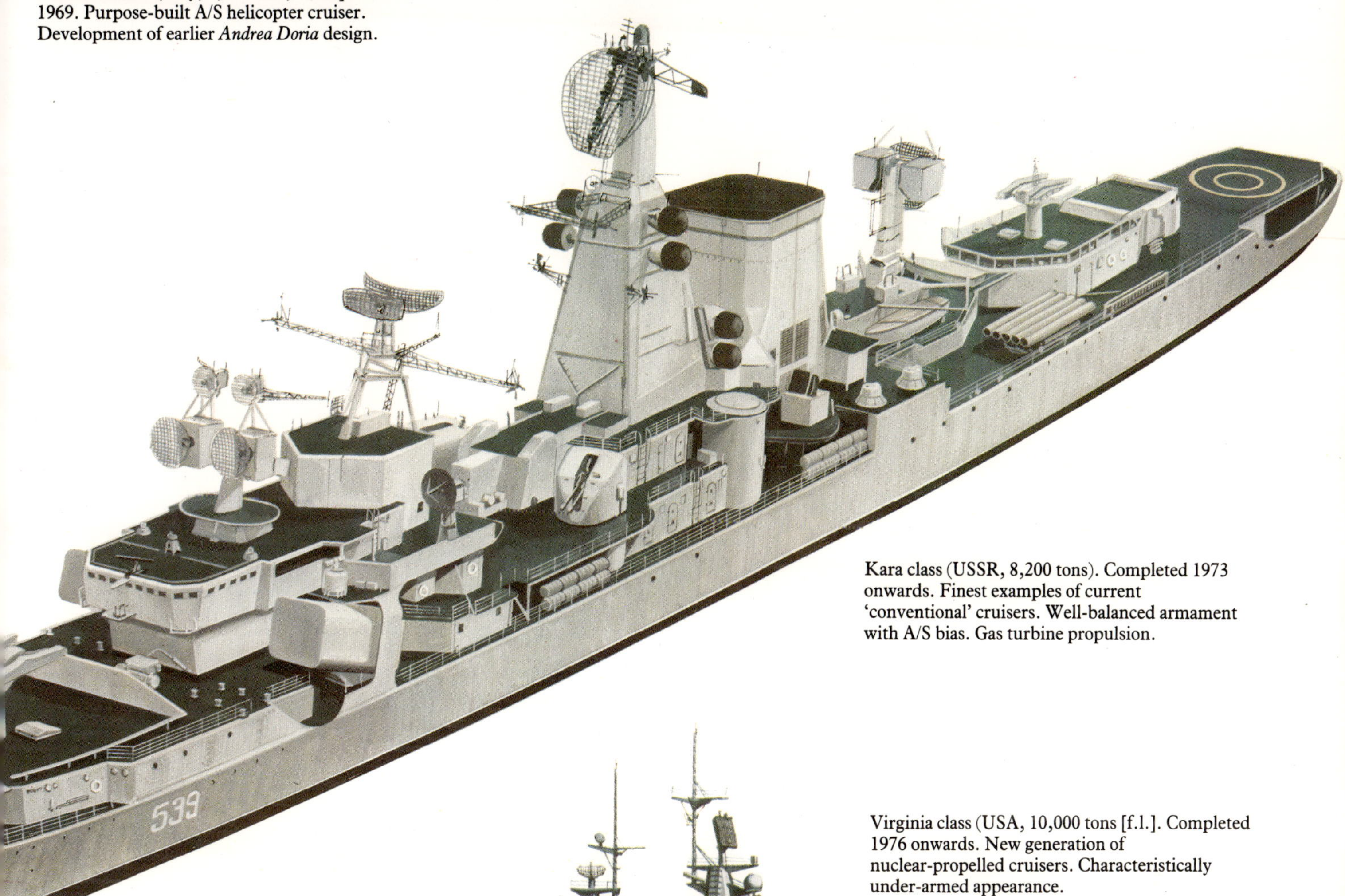

Kara class (USSR, 8,200 tons). Completed 1973 onwards. Finest examples of current 'conventional' cruisers. Well-balanced armament with A/S bias. Gas turbine propulsion.

Virginia class (USA, 10,000 tons [f.l.]. Completed 1976 onwards. New generation of nuclear-propelled cruisers. Characteristically under-armed appearance.

Kresta I class (USSR, 6,000 tons). Completed 1967–70. Anti-ship biased armament.

Kresta II class (USSR, 6,000 tons). Completed 1971–79. Development of Kresta I design with A/S bias. Both types steam turbine propelled.

This 1950 picture shows the Baltimore class heavy cruiser *Helena* (CA 75) engaged in shore bombardment during the Korean War. Note A/S escort ahead, seaboats swung out, and secondary 5-inch guns at high elevation. The usually conspicuous aircraft crane is folded flat on the deck.

process had to start almost from scratch as shipbuilding capacity had been severely reduced by war and there was lacking the ability even to operate the more advanced technological features of ships gained as prizes of war. Great reliance was placed on the newly-acquired eastern zone of Germany.

Stalin had little appreciation of the subtleties of sea power but, aware that the West had used it with devastating effect against the Axis powers, embarked on the creation of a 'balanced fleet'. Capital ships must wait, but cruisers, destroyers and submarines began rolling out on a series production basis in simple yet proven designs.

By the late 1940s the world's major powers had polarised into two major camps bound by NATO and the Warsaw Pact; the former consisted largely of sea powers with global interests and the latter of contiguous land powers. The NATO fleets were firmly founded on aircraft carriers, which had made such an impact in the Pacific, and any projection of force for political purposes was likely to be preceded by the establishment by them of a '*cordon sanitaire*'. Again, in wars throughout history it had been shown that the mercantile strength of the West could also be its Achilles' heel. These were the twin targets at which the new Soviet Navy was aimed.

Long-ranged air and surface-launched missiles looked to be a likely means of countering the carrier without the need for close approach, and research was directed towards suitable weapons and launchers. Meanwhile, Russian submarines went into series production as a temporary expedient, but a useful one also in a war against commerce. With the long-ranged missile dependent for guidance upon radar which cannot be 'bent' over the horizon, a third party is required for mid-course correction, a function which can be carried out by an aircraft or submarine, which creates a measure of inter-dependence. To assist in *Guerre de Course* the Russians produced the anachronistic Sverdlov class of cruiser, of which the name-ship was first seen in 1951. Strongly based on the pre-war Kirov design via later 11,500 ton Chapaev development, the Sverdlovs, in spite of their 15,500-tons, yet mounted only twelve 5·9s, probably due to a Soviet inability at that time to produce a better weapon. This impression was strengthened by the secondary directors being virtually identical to the German 'Wackeltöpfe' of the Second World War. The class, though formidable-enough ships, were being built at a time when the West was looking to the missile as a direct replacement for the big gun and of the planned 24 ships, only 18 were ever completed.

Opposite, top
Sweden's *Tre Kronor*'s distinctive layout is here shown to advantage. Of special interest are the triple 6-inch turret forward with twins aft, the 40 mm 'bowchaser' popular with Swedish ships, and the seaboat swung out.

Opposite, bottom
Laid down in 1939, the two Dutch De Ruyters were not completed until 1953. One, *De Zeven Provincien*, was later converted as shown, with a Terrier SAM system aft. In 1976–7 she was converted again to operate a flight of three Sea King helicopters and sold to the Peruvian Navy, becoming *Aguirre*.

C802

Cumberland, one of the early Kent group of British Counties, lasted until 1959 through being used as a trials ship. This 1956 picture shows her re-masted for a modern radar outfit, and her sole armament is a prototype 6-inch and a 3-inch 70 turret of the type built for the Tigers.

Opposite, top
Though originally termed 'destroyers', the British Counties equate to light cruisers, and *Norfolk* is one of four to exchange a 4.5-inch turret for four Exocet SSMs. Note the Seaslug medium-range SAM launcher right aft.

Opposite, bottom
The American *Chicago* (CG 11), a converted Baltimore class cruiser, tops up in the Pacific from the oiler *Passumpsic*. Talos are fore and aft, Terriers flank the bridge, and sharp eyes may even spot her two 5-inch guns.

In the Far East, there was to be little peace after the Second World War as new creeds sought to establish their sway in wake of the fallen shoguns. China fell to its revolution in the late 1940s and the new regime's surrogate armies swarmed over the 38th Parallel into South Korea to give the infant United Nations its stiffest test to date. Further west, a general atmosphere of unrest was heightened by early Egyptian attempts to render the Suez Canal inoperative by a policy of non-cooperation, a prelude to the debacle of 1956.

The Western powers still maintained their trading interests in China until the revolution and British interest quickened when the frigate *Amethyst* was trapped by Communist forces in what came to be known as the 'Yangtse Incident'. Her eventual solo escape overshadowed attempts to break up-river to her assistance, though in one such effort the rebuilt County, *London*, suffered a severe mauling, her 8-inch guns useless against a myriad of smaller weapons on the banks. Mahan's dictum that warships will rarely get the better of prepared shore positions was well underlined in the action.

In Korea, the cruiser was again largely relegated to shore bombardment support and as escort to the invaluable carrier which ranged the coasts, offering the only air support to a zone devoid of airstrips.

With production of conventional cruisers at a halt in Great Britain and the US, it fell to the smaller fleets to have the last word, together with the Russians. In Sweden, the two Gota Lejons were completed in 1947, mounting a fully automatic armament of a triple 6-inch forward and two twins aft, light enough to leave a large reserve of stability for powerful protection topsides and the large deck cargo of mines obligatory for most larger Swedish ships. Of nearly 10,000 tons apiece, the two Dutch de Ruyters were completed in 1953 after having been laid down pre-war. Four twin 6-inch mountings could elevate to 60 degrees in a token A/A role, though their rate of fire of only 15 rounds per minute would have been of doubtful effectiveness against the new breeds of jet-propelled aircraft entering service. As with the above-mentioned French *de Grasse* and her later sister *Colbert*, designers were showing concern about the threat from the air but guns, even rapid-firing and radar laid, were obviously becoming of less use as time went on. Such progress was being made with aircraft that it was obvious that soon only the surface-to-air-missile (SAM) would be capable of countering them and both East and West began to sink vast sums into research programmes in a deadly race that is still being run.

Secure with its carrier striking forces, the West had little requirement for large SSMs

for which there were few targets. Priority lay in a capacity to destroy the dual-role Russian aircraft, and a viable SAM was required to be deployed by specialist escorts placed in a wide defensive ring around a carrier and her close screen. This was a great technological challenge for, compared with a ship, an aircraft presents a small, fast moving target to system radars, which have to react rapidly, tracking and guiding a missile which, itself, must be fleet and agile. Stimulated by the threat from German and Japanese glider bombs, the Americans had been early in the field of SAM development and, as early as 1948, had the first usable Terrier system in service. The technology of the time meant that Terrier had to be a 'beam rider', following a radar illumination of the target by the firing ship. This reduced its electronic content but it was still 26½ feet in length and weighed over 3,000 lbs at launch, figures which, when applied to stowage and feed to the launcher, began to define the ship parameters. Even as sea-trials progressed in the old battleship *Mississippi*, the two heavy cruisers *Boston* (CA69)

The top hamper of the USS *Belknap* after fire resulting from a night collision with the 82,000-ton carrier *John F. Kennedy* in 1975. She is seen alongside in Sicily, prior to being towed to the USA for rebuilding.

and *Canberra* (CA70) were being rebuilt and were re-commissioning in 1955–6 as the world's first guided missile cruisers. Unusual in having two twin-arm launchers aft, together with a mass of new control antennas, their Terriers were, at that time, good only for use against subsonic aircraft at heights below 50,000 feet. It was a realistic weapon only until the Russians introduced the formidable combination of the Tu-16 (Badger) bomber armed with the AS-2 (Kipper) stand-off bomb. This aircraft had a range of 3,600 miles and could launch its 7,500 lb missile from 100 miles out, a threat that resulted in the second American SAM, Talos. Similar in weight to the AS-2, it was 33 feet in length but could travel 70 miles with sufficient payload for a nuclear warhead for airbursts. With experience gained in the first two conversions, the Americans rebuilt six Clevelands, three for Talos and three for Terrier but, with the restricted size of the light cruisers, putting only one system into each. They rejoined the fleet in 1959–60.

Completing their SAM 'family', mean-

The American Sixth Fleet cruiser *Little Rock* (CLG 4) at the re-opening of the Suez Canal in 1975. A Cleveland class cruiser converted to carry SAMs, her forebridge was extended, the super-imposed 6-inch turret having to make way for a smaller twin 5-inch.

while, the Americans brought the Tartar into service, only 15 feet in length and designed for engaging short-ranged targets at up to 10 miles. They first went to sea in the three Albany conversions of 1962–4. These incredible-looking ships were the first 'double-enders', having a Talos fore and aft and two Tartar launchers flanking the bridge, which had to be of great height to clear the blast. Funnels and masts were combined in unlovely 'macks' which seemed to soar upwards, bearing search antenna.

With these three ships, the conversion programme ceased, hopes for up-dating the large number of remaining gunned cruisers being dashed by the cost and difficulties attendant upon stowing between 150 and 200 large missiles on end (Coke bottle stowage) and of providing the means to feed them rapidly to their launchers inside narrow-gutted hulls designed for speed rather than capacity. This and the intricate subdivision incorporated to improve damage control militated against a whole generation of cruisers receiving a new lease of life.

Other factors were at this time complicating the future course of cruiser design. Following their successful application of nuclear power to submarine propulsion, the Americans bent themselves to the task of producing an all-nuclear surface force of carrier, cruiser and frigate by the early 1960s. The promise was one of nearly unlimited range at high speed, though how this was to be achieved without the replenishment of consumable stores received little publicity. The cruiser *Long Beach* became the world's first nuclear-propelled surface warship in September 1961, the carrier *Enterprise* and frigate *Bainbridge* following within a highly creditable 13 months.

Commissioned in 1961, the USS *Long Beach* (CGN 9) was the world's first nuclear-propelled cruiser. Originally intended to receive either Polaris or Regulus II, she was completed with two Terrier systems forward and a Talos aft.

Designed to counter the threat of Western carriers, the four Russian Kynda class cruisers carry two quadruple launchers for Shaddock SSMs, together with a Goa SAM forward. The *Varyag*, seen here in 1967, demonstrates the 'two of everything' approach of the time.

The Soviet Kynda class cruisers were the first with both SSM and SAM systems, allowing them to work independently. A quadruple SS-N-3 (Saddock) mounting is sited fore and aft, and a SA-N-1 (Goa) forward. A helicopter can land aft, but cannot be housed. Just visible below water is a bow sonar dome for use with the MBU-2500As on the forecastle. This is *Admiral Golovko*.

Just over a year previously, in July 1960, another event occurred which was to affect the future fate of the cruiser when the SSBN *George Washington* successfully fired the first A-1 Polaris/ICMB whilst submerged. This 1,200-mile weapon offered a new way of delivering the nation's nuclear deterrent, taking the place of the ageing and increasingly vulnerable aircraft of the Strategic Air Command. Initially, both *Long Beach* and the *Albany* conversions were seated to be for the deployment of Polaris but these plans were abandoned in favour of delivery by the near-undetectable SSBN. By doing so, the Americans stole a march on the Soviets, who were still at the stage of putting their 300-mile SS-N-4 (Sark) missiles into diesel-electric Zulu V class submarines, which needed to surface uncomfortably close to an enemy coast before launching. With both sides working furiously to improve their systems, however, improvements would obviously follow rapidly and a renewed interest in ASW was apparent in all camps.

Meanwhile, the pilot conversion of the USS *Gyatt* to take a Terrier system had shown that destroyers, too, were uneconomical to rebuild, and 1960 saw the commissioning of the first 3,370-ton (standard) Adams class, designed around a Tartar system and the prototype Terrier-armed *Coontz* at 4,700 tons. These were followed by the first of a new class of British County, weighing in at 5,400 tons to accommodate the ponderous Sea Slug. All three classes were termed 'destroyers' though their functions were not those of destroyers and neither was their size. Correct terminology should have been something like Light Cruiser (Missile) but their lack of medium-calibre guns made such a term unacceptable to those used to the conventionally-armed cruisers, of which many still remained.

This line of progress was also followed in the East, where the 130-mile SS-N-1 (Scrubber) had been rushed to sea in the creditably small 3,650-ton double-ended Krupny class ships. To counter the fighting power of their designed targets, the carriers of the West, they needed to be escorted by a SAM-armed ship and, for this purpose the Kanin variants were built, carrying the 17-mile SA-N-1 (Goa). Two-ship combinations not always being available, it made sense to combine both types of missile in one hull

Last of Britain's conventional cruisers, the three Tigers were close derivatives of the Crown Colonies. Though carrying a fully automatic 3- and 6-inch armament, they were obsolescent on completion, two soon being converted for helicopter operation and the third, *Lion* (seen here), being scrapped in 1975.

resulting, in 1962, in the 4,700-ton *Kynda*, with two quadruple launchers for the improved SS-N-3 (Shaddock) with a possible range of 250 miles (with mid-course correction), backed up by an SA-N-1 system. This double-ender was the first, purpose-built, universal cruiser of the missile age and provided the basis for further development.

Of the Western designs mentioned, the British County class had two further features that were to foreshadow the future. Firstly, the horizontal stowage and feed system for the Sea Slug demanded a hull with sufficient space topside to include a flight deck and hangar for a Wessex helicopter, an aircraft with range and payload great enough to be an A/S system in its own right. Secondly, half the ship's 60,000 shp were generated by a pair of gas turbines, compact, easily automated and capable of developing full power almost instantly from cold. Their inclusion meant that the ship could lie alongside and yet be at instant readiness for sea without the necessity of maintaining steam; whilst running on steam turbines at sea the gas turbines could also be instantly run up to give a speed boost to meet an emergency. However, though both these factors were greatly to influence future design, it was to be some time before other fleets followed suit. Innovation is not, of course, a British prerogative and both the Italians and French early recognised the potential of the helicopter sufficiently to design ships to exploit its full capabilities. Thus Italy's first postwar cruisers, laid down in 1958, were the handsome pair of 5,000-ton Andrea Dorias, with a twin Terrier launcher forward and with a deck and stowage aft for a flight of four Agusta-Bell 204As. Like the British Wasp, these are too small to carry both A/S sensors and weaponry, though the multi-aircraft approach overcomes this limitation and larger helicopters were planned to replace them. Significantly, too, the gun armament of the Dorias is eight single 76 mm weapons, the calibre progressing downward from the American 5-inch and the British 4·5. Described as 'helicopter cruisers' they continued a line of thinking that we have seen already in the pre-war Swedish *Gotland* and Japanese designs, and they have been paralleled by the French *Jeanne d'Arc*, a 10,000-tonner built to replace the earlier training cruiser of the same name. She can still accommodate a large

The US Leahy class ships, of which the *Turner* (CG 20) is an example, has space aft for 'Vertrep' operations but cannot service an aircraft. Note the after Standard ER launcher, its two Mk 76 control systems and the rather weak gun armament of four 3-inch in the waist.

Gutted and rebuilt as a missile cruiser, the USS *Albany* (CG 10) presents one of the oddest profiles at sea. Talos launchers with their paired directors are visible at either end, together with an ASROC mounting between the lofty 'macks'.

One American Leahy class ship was modified and completed as the nuclear-propelled *Bainbridge* (CGN 25). Armament is on a similar scale, with eight-cell ASROC launcher abaft the forward Standard ER. Note the rectangular antenna of the SPS 52 '3D' search system, and the frigates *Koessch* and *Badger* beyond.

complement of cadets but there the resemblance ends, for her after 200 feet is all flightdeck over a hangar that can stow up to eight Super Frelon helicopters that can be used for ASW or assault and even to engage surface targets with the AM 39 version of the Exocet missile. Versatility indeed. As she is not designed as a component of a task group, *Jeanne d'Arc* does not carry the essentially defensive SAMs of the Italians but supplements her four modest 100 mm guns with a splendid battery of MM38 Exocets in the SSM version.

Though now established as one of the World's most successful SSMs, the Exocet was initially produced in a hurry to fill a gap in the West's defences, a gap highlighted dramatically when the Israeli destroyer *Eilat* was suddenly destroyed in 1967 by missiles from two Egyptian FACs that had not even left their harbour basin. The weapon was the Russian-built SS-N-2 (Styx), a diminutive of the large SS-N-1 (Scrubber) and, at 15 feet overall, small enough to put into an FAC at a time when the West had no equivalent. To exploit their lead, the Russians series-produced Komar and Osa class boats, transferring them at will to a variety of states, some of dubious political stability. With a vast preponderance of carriers, the major fleets had neglected the eventual requirement of an SSM subsequent to the cancellation of the Regulus II, only to suddenly rediscover the need for them when over-age flight decks began to disappear without hope of a one-to-one replacement. Without air cover, even quite a large warship would thus have been at the mercy of the 20-mile Styx, having to rely totally on ECM for survival. Thus the Exocet had a guaranteed market, particularly as it was an excellent weapon, wave hugging and difficult to counter, yet requiring a minimum of electronics aboard the firing ship. Further, the helicopter had emerged as the best counter to the FAC, most of which were poorly-armed to counter it.

In the US, the carrier task group was still at the core of naval thinking and successive classes of escorts reflect this. Between 1962 and 1964, the nine-ship Leahy class was completed (the planned tenth unit was the nuclear-propelled *Bainbridge*); though of 6,600 tons and doubled-ended with two Terrier launchers, they otherwise had only an ASROC A/S launcher and 3-inch guns. As a result, they were classified as guided-missile destroyers (DLG) until 1975, when they were regraded as cruisers. With the follow-on Belknaps, a modified single launcher was fitted, capable of firing both SAMs and ASROC rounds. This left the after end free for the 5-inch gun to be reinstated and,

Versatile and highly accurate with new types of laser-guided ammunition, the gun is still a very cost-effective weapon. The new American lightweight, here on trial aboard the destroyer *Hull* (DD 945), can heft a 260-pound round over 31,000 yards, and will be retro-fitted to many larger ships.

more important, there was room for a pad and hangar for a Kaman SH-2 Seasprite helicopter, a great improvement but at the cost of complexity in the missile system, where a single fault could rob the ship of two weapons.

As the 'sixties progressed, Britain and France joined the US in putting their major deterrents into SSBNs. Almost one a month, armed with the 2,500-mile A3 Polaris, was coming from American yards together with nuclear-propelled attack submarines, aimed specifically at killing the Russian SSBNs. It was not surprising, therefore, that the Soviet fleet shifted its priorities to meet the ICBM threat from far out in the oceans, rather than the waning carrier threat closer in, within their aircraft range. No longer could an anti-submarine war be won by attrition; with the totally destructive power of the weapons they carried each SSBN needed to be neutralised, and immediately. Russian weapon mix thus moved from SSM/SAM to AS/SAM.

As the quartette of Kyndas joined their fleet in 1965 the Russians began a new class of 6,000 tonners, menacing-looking vessels known to NATO as the Kresta I. By increasing their length by some 44 feet a good weapon mix was incorporated – four SS-N-3 launchers, paired neatly under either bridge wing and twin SA-N-1 at either end. Significantly, the Russians termed them Large Anti-Submarine Ships, and though shipborne A/S hardware was limited to the ubiquitous multi-barrelled rocket launchers and torpedo tubes, these were backed for the first time by a helicopter with full facilities, providing not only A/S support but also capable of issuing mid-course corrections for the SS-N-3s.

While the Kresta I was a great step forward, the class was again terminated at four, making way for the improved Kresta II in 1968. Besides mounting the later SA-N-3 at either end and with better-designed helicopter facilities, the newcomers sported a new quadruple launcher on either side of the bridge. Western observers were persuaded by their size that a new type SSM was in use but later intelligence has shown it to be the SS-N-14, an A/S missile with a range of up to 25 miles, probably possessing an anti-ship capability in addition. Again the Soviet designation was that of a large A/S ship but this was ignored.

1968 was also the year in which Soviet aviation went to sea, when the *Moskva* passed through from the Black Sea. At 15,000 tons, she was described as an Anti-Submarine Cruiser and was a logical progression from the concept of the *Andrea Doria* and *Jeanne d'Arc*. Half a ship length is devoted to the flight deck, which flares out steeply from the fine waterline for the operation of no less than 18 Kamov Ka-25 (Hormone) helicopters. The A/S capacity of these is complemented by that of the ship herself which carries both VDS and hull-mounted sonars and, right forward, a twin-armed launcher for the FRAS-1, believed capable of putting a torpedo or nuclear depthcharge onto a submerged target up to 15 miles distant. Taken in combination with A/S rocket launchers and torpedo tubes she represents a considerable threat to a submarine, and is in addition, armed with two SA-N-3 systems and guns to deter those who would dispute her main business.

This progression of the cruiser into ASW continued in 1969 with the entry into service of the Italian *Vittorio Veneto* and the British *Blake*. The former is a 7,500-ton development of the smaller Dorias, having capacity for nine small helicopters and a dual Terrier/ASROC launcher. *Blake* was the first of the Tiger class conversions from a trio of improved Swiftsures that had lain

The secondary armament of a Russian Sverdlov class cruiser. Firing is a twin 37 mm mounting; beyond are two of the three portside twin 100 mm guns in large, fully stabilised gunhouses, with the secondary director on the right.

Opposite
The Sverdlov class cruiser *Aleksandr Suvorov* in the Philippine Sea during the ambitious world-wide exercise 'Okean'. Notice the small size of the main turrets and the long-based optical rangefinders; also the portside secondary director stabilising against roll.

In a rebuild completed in 1960, the Italian Condottieri *Garibaldi* was recast as shown, with a Terrier SAM system aft, two twin 135 mm turrets forward, and four single 76 mm guns down either side. Her earlier two funnels were trunked into a single casing.

incomplete for years before joining the fleet with two fully-automatic, twin 6-inch turrets and three twin 3-inch, 70 calibre mountings. With the conventional cruiser already disappearing rapidly from the Royal Navy list they were obsolescent in spite of their armament and, after a short career, *Blake* and *Tiger* were taken in hand for four-year conversions that enabled them to house and operate a useful flight of four large Sea King helicopters but the cost was astronomical.

The American cruiser developed along different lines. Having adequate A/S capacity already in such ships as the Iwo Jima class LPHs, they felt no need to build hybrids and proceeded along more conventional lines, though capitalising on their lead in nuclear propulsion. Two Californias were laid down in 1970 and completed in a creditable four years. Like most modern American warships, they have an underarmed appearance and attract unfair criticism from those who fail to take into account their capacity for future modification in a hull packed with volume-critical electronics. Also, their overall function is very different from that of their Soviet equivalents. The Russians are in the business of sea denial, the Americans, sea control. Even so the Californias' two Standard SAM systems, ASROC, A/S torpedo tubes and a brace of 5-inch guns does not seem much on a 9,560-ton displacement commanding a price tag of 200 million dollars, though their two pressurised water-cooled reactors can produce steam for 30 knots for an estimated endurance of 750,000 miles. In actual fact, they are weak in ASW and their follow-ons, the Virginias, have combined Standard/ASROC launchers, saving space for a quarterdeck pad with two helicopters stowed below. Two aircraft are now becoming common in escorts, guaranteeing the availability of at least one and simplifying stalk-and-kill tactics on submerged targets.

At a time when most fleets are moving toward smaller calibre guns, the US navy is evaluating a new, lightweight 8-inch weapon for planned retro-fitting to larger units. It can fire ten 260-pound rounds per minute out to 31,000 yards, compared with

The conversion of two Tiger class cruisers enabled them to operate a flight of four large Sea King helicopters apiece. The loss of after armament was partially offset by the Seacat SAMs flanking the after funnel. This is *Tiger* itself.

40

The American nuclear-propelled cruiser *Mississippi* appears grossly under-armed, though incorporating much space for future modification. The 5-inch 54 will eventually be replaced by a new 8-inch lightweight gun. The port anchor is stowed well aft to avoid fouling the large underwater sonar bulb.

V/STOL aircraft will certainly revolutionise aviation at sea, though opinions are divided as to how it will do so. The pioneering British Harrier has a maritime version, and the Americans are refining it as the AV-B. Here one hovers above the flight pad of the fleet auxiliary *Olwen*.

the standard 5-inch 54 which fires 70-pound projectiles to 26,000 yards, but at twice the rate. Battle experience in Vietnam showed the value of the gun in shore bombardment and experiments are continuing with guided ammunition; information is sparse but success could lead to a new lease of life for the gun as a cheap, versatile alternative to the missile.

Great promise is being shown by the newly-introduced Harpoon SSM which, like the Exocet, can easily be shipped on to virtually any hull without modification and, as the Virginias can easily take eight, they may be compared the better with their most recent Soviet equivalents the 9,000 ton Karas, developed from the Kresta IIs. Though gas turbine propulsion experience goes back to the Kashins of 1962 the Karas are the first cruisers to be so propelled, though a 12,500 ton nuclear-propelled design, coded Kirov, is under construction.

The Karas bristle with weaponry – two SA-N-3 launchers, two quadruple SS-N-14s, and two SA-N-4s, stowed retracted into silos. As only four 76 mm guns are fitted, it is likely that the A/S orientated SS-N-14 has also a measure of anti-ship capacity and the little SA-N-4 is a rapid-reaction point-defence system like Britain's Sea Wolf, capable of handling aircraft or incoming missiles alike. A close-in weapon system (CIWS) is also fitted, four Gatling-type guns grouped around the funnel, with multiple 23 mm barrels revolving around a common ammunition feed. The American equivalent is the Vulcan-Phalanx, with six 20 mm barrels firing fragmentation or depleted-uranium, high inertia rounds at the rate of 3,000 per minute; its target is tracked by an integral high definition radar with a built-in computer to predict the right deflection.

Developments in Japan are becoming interesting. After years of working to a limited 'self-defence force' image, Japanese ships are increasing in size and again showing originality of design. The *Haruna* and *Hiei*, completed in 1973–4, are similar in size and concept to the Italian Dorias but carry three Sea King helicopters, together with ASROC and a pair of 5-inch guns. Their two 5,200-ton derivatives, still building, will also carry three Sea Kings but will

The *Kertch* of the Russian Kara class, seen here in the Mediterranean in 1976. Quadruple launchers flanking the bridge house SS-N-14 missiles, mainly A/S weapons, backed up by A/S rockets forward, dual-purpose torpedo tubes and a helicopter.

have a Sea Sparrow point defence missile system in addition to the ASROC. It can be expected that developments will not end there and will certainly be worth watching as one of the world's richest nations, and one time contender for the crown of the Pacific, again acquires maritime muscle.

In the Royal Navy the demise of the gunned cruiser proceeded apace with obsolescence now acknowledged, coupled with the need for a smaller fleet. Successive defence cuts fell savagely, a major casualty being the 53,000 ton CVA-01, a proposed replacement for the carrier *Victorious*. In addition, it was decided to withdraw a permanent presence East of Suez, a decision with an all-too glib corollary that all flight decks could be phased out without planning replacements.

Once the carrier had ceased to be built, the need for specialised escorts lapsed also, and a logical line of cruiser development was cut short with the *Bristol*, the only Type 82 to be completed. Of 6,100 tons, she carries a launcher for the medium range Sea Dart, a missile predominantly A/A but with anti-ship capability. Unusually, she lacks a helicopter, her A/S potential being vested in an Ikara system which functions like its equivalent, the FRAS-1, Malfon and ASROC. She is a modern naval rarity with three funnels, a centre-line stack exhausting her steam turbines and an athwartships pair for gas turbines, the machinery being in a COSAG configuration, putting a maximum of 86,000 shp on two shafts. Hers was the last steam installation in the fleet, which has now turned completely to the gas turbine and the diesel. Four later Counties of approximately similar size, have exchanged their 'B' gunhouses for a battery of four MM38 Exocets.

The orthodox line of development of the cruiser in Great Britain took a new direction with the introduction of the V/STOL aircraft. Virtually synonymous with this term is the Harrier which, in spite of being acknowledged as an infant prodigy, had a stormy childhood which it barely survived. It first went to sea for trials on the carrier *Bulwark* in 1966 as the Kestrel, or Hawker P1127, and, though taken up later by an

Is it a cruiser? Though the Russian Kashins are termed 'destroyers', they are 'double-ended' with a Goa SAM system at either end. Some units have been modified to carry later Styx SSMs in addition, making them far more formidable than an American Leahy or British County. Detail of the gas-turbine propelled *Obraztsovy* is here shown to advantage.

The *Bristol* was the only Type 82 built because the Royal Navy's carriers, which they were designed to escort, were phased out. It carries an Ikara A/S system abaft the 4.5-inch gun, and a Sea Dart aft. Notice the distinctively paired after funnels.

With her superstructure blocking the forward end of the flight deck, the Russian helicopter cruiser *Moskva* is not capable of operating V/STOL aircraft with a rolling takeoff, and only two of the type were built. The starboard 57 mm guns are tracking the American aircraft from which the picture was taken.

Projecting a line of development pioneered by the French and Italians, the *Moskva* can operate up to 18 A/S helicopters, and contrasts with the more conventional Kara class cruiser beyond.

The *Kiev* is more truly an aircraft carrier than the Moskvas, though classed as a 'large A/S Cruiser'. With her angled deck she can operate helicopters or V/STOL aircraft, the jet blast of which can be seen right aft. The break of the bow wave betrays a below-water sonar bulb of heroic proportions.

The nuclear-powered guided missile cruiser USS *South Carolina* under way in the eastern Mediterranean.

enthusiastic US Marine Corps, nearly died in Britain from the attentions of the same determined political lobby that had killed the carrier. Fortunately, service opinion and an aggressive sales drive by its dedicated manufacturer overcame those who tried to argue that fixed wing aviation at sea was not possible after the phasing out of the aircraft carrier. As the latter term was no longer acceptable, an unknown genius coined the euphemism, 'Through-deck Cruiser', and the Invincible class CAH was born.

The Soviets took a similar line to the British with the much larger 50,000 ton Kievs because the design of the Moskvas had overlooked V/STOL and cut the flightdeck short with a mass of superstructure that denied their V/STOL aircraft, the Yak-36 (Forger), the short rolling take-off so necessary to carrying an adequate payload. Like the Invincibles, the Kievs have a starboard-side island with a through flightdeck above a large hangar; both are termed 'cruisers' (the latter 'anti-submarine cruisers') but, as a ship dedicated primarily to the operation of aircraft is an aircraft carrier, both must, by definition, be aircraft carriers and are beyond the scope of this study.

The Moskvas had shown, like other ships of similar layout, that a cruiser could effectively operate a flight of helicopters, but the inclusion of the V/STOL must change a ship radically. With improved perfomance versions they must inevitably get larger and heavier, affecting the course of a ship's development as surely as had the aircraft on an earlier generation of carriers. With their instant response irrespective of ship's heading, ability to intercept an enemy aircraft acting as a mid-course link, and to arrive over a submerged target rapidly to deposit sonobuoys for the slower A/S helicopters to follow up, the V/STOL will prove indispensible but will inevitably change her parent ship from a 'helicopter cruiser' to a true carrier in the process.

With classes such as the Karas and Virginias, the more orthodox type of cruiser still lives. The US navy recently cancelled what had been termed the 'Strike Cruiser' but have reconfigured the basic Virginia hull as the CGN-42 to accommodate its main feature, the Aegis system, which can monitor and assess all external threats and direct the resources of a whole task group to meet them in the most effective manner. It is apparent today that the majority of large escorts that can be considered 'cruisers' have roles geared towards either anti-ship, anti-submarine, anti-aircraft or early warning functions, paralleling neatly the tasks of the specialist frigates of the previous generation – appropriately, for it was with the frigate that the cruiser story began.

Overleaf
Like the Kievs, the Royal Navy's Invincibles are difficult to view as cruisers, though that is what they are officially. The nameship is here seen on contractor's sea trials off Ailsa Craig. Clearly visible forward is the Sea Dart SAM launcher and the interim 'ski-jump' to assist V/STOL aircraft into the air.

INDEX

Page numbers in Italics refer to illustrations

40